40.39

Psychology of Executive Retirement from Fear to Passion

Escape the Rat Race & Save Your Life

Doug Treen

iUniverse, Inc.
New York   Bloomington

Psychology of Executive Retirement from Fear to Passion
Escape the Rat Race & Save Your Life

iUniverse books may be ordered through booksellers or by contacting:

iUniverse
1663 Liberty Drive
Bloomington, IN 47403
www.iuniverse.com
1-800-Authors (1-800-288-4677)

ISBN: 978-0-595-49282-4 (pbk)
ISBN: 978-0-595-61041-9 (ebk)

Printed in the United States of America

iUniverse rev. date: 03/3/2009

In loving memory of my mom

Contents

Preface

Executives, managers, and professionals live a psychological paradox: their professional strength can become their personal weakness. The psychological and personal sacrifice needed to become a corporate leader works against the individual in retirement. Personal psychological needs are repressed in order to achieve the success criteria of corporate culture. The seductive nature of corporate rewards only encourages this self-sacrifice, which is by and large repressed. This can lead to a later personal crisis in retirement.

To address this paradox, this book aims to raise awareness by questioning the status quo of executive life in regard to preparing for retirement. My method is not empirical. However, I will analyze the key elements of a long, happy retirement: personal health, personal Life Planning, personal values and meaning, and spirituality, and show how the executive lifestyle fails as a foundation and preparation for this. These elements for a successful retirement and a long happy life after retirement are shown to be sadly missing in the competitive success criteria, collective culture, and workaholic lifestyle of the typical executive life. I will show that the executive life in a corporation fails to psychologically prepare the executive for a successful retirement. In addition, I aim to raise awareness of this reality to facilitate and to help coach the executive in better preparing for a fulfilling retirement. The success criteria for a long, successful retirement in many ways are the opposite of those for a successful executive career. Since I have observed that most executives are unaware of this issue, I will not use executive opinion or empirical data, but rather analyze the executive life to expose how its psychological weaknesses limit preparation for a successful retirement. I also offer insights to enable the executive to create a personal solution, but doing so will involve personal change. I will provide the psychological and emotional insights for change that will help the executive overcome any personal deficit and set the foundation for replacing career rewards with personally fulfilling projects and lifestyle. After years of corporate dedication and contribution, executives deserve the best retirement possible. I want you to have that best life, earned from years of commitment to the corporation. *The best is still to come after retirement!*

This work has been inspired by personal experiences from over twenty years working in diverse corporations as an HR executive as well as ten years as an organizational consultant. The many colorful professionals, managers, and executives whom I have grown to admire and respect have taught me a lot about their motivations, frustrations, fears, and joys. They have also helped me learn the complex burden and stresses of their diverse roles, commonly referred to as the *rat race*. Based on my experience advising and coaching executives in the pharmaceutical, financial, information technology, and automotive industries, I have projected their psychological and emotional readiness for retirement. This critique of executive life in the corporation is based on general conclusions about what it takes psychologically to be a successful executive, drawn from numerous corporations in the above industries. This opportunity to experience and understand firsthand the executive-corporation relationship and its human dynamics from the trenches has given me a deeper, more realistic sense and understanding of management psychology than the textbook variety.

This is a practical book for professionals, managers, and executives, and is not targeted toward an academic audience. Given the well-educated target group, the book tries to be fair to the complexity of the subject matter in order to create greater self-awareness as the foundation for self-help. It is a book validated by thirty years' experience of the executive life and current psychological, health, and management research. The book aims to create a hypothesis that applies to different executives in varying degrees but affects all executives to some degree. As a working hypothesis, I hope to create executive self-awareness through discussion and debate of the issues involved in executive addiction to the role, its rewards and their impacts, and the corresponding lack of psychological preparation for retirement. It is only through challenging the status quo of executive retirement can a new awareness lead to executive enlightenment, the basis for being proactive and prepared for retirement.

This book shows how preparing psychologically for retirement requires a total personal change from executive life. Given the huge differences between executives, this cannot be a traditionally directive, step-by-step self-help manual for retirement. Rather, it raises issues for awareness building to better empower the executive to create his or her personal version of self-actualization and happiness in retirement. The best way for you to actualize yourself in retirement will be different from what is best for others and cannot be put into a directive, universal formula you can follow like a job description. The paradox of attaining your own self-actualization outside of the job box of the corporation in retirement will involve your higher sense of personal freedom, spirit, and creativity not appreciated or nurtured by most corporations or through most job descriptions. As your mind, spirit, and potential are unique, so will be your retirement solution in finding your authentic self. I only aim to bring you to the brink of awareness of the issues so you can conquer them your own way, not by being reduced to another's prescriptive formula.

This is the fundamental challenge: corporate job and task methods will not permit you to find and use your full freedom, spirit, and creativity to reach your full potential. These objectives are mutually exclusive, or executive retirement would not be an issue. Although I will make you aware of the issues, I do not and cannot provide you with personal answers. Only if you discover your own path can your retirement solution fit you. For example, you cannot learn to drive or fly from a self-help manual. If you aspire to become an artist, you will never get there by number-painting other artists' works. Through awareness building, I will bring you to this understanding and attempt to guide you through the process, generally without limiting the process by simple, predefined steps that are not your own. I will, however, guide you by suggesting some general questions and challenges you need to answer in your own way. By doing this, I will set the stage for you to help yourself authentically at the high end of complexity. You will be the winner and not wonder why someone else's simple predefined solutions did not work.

My experiences include teaching social theory to adult undergraduate students and organizational behavior to MBA students. I studied both psychology and social science integrated in a PhD in social philosophy. As an executive coach and trainer, my passion to write this book has come from a desire to continue coaching executives in their transition from the corporation. After twenty years of working as an executive inside several corporations and ten years as a lecturer and organizational consultant, I am in many ways a product of the corporation. I too had to work through many of the "fear of retirement" issues discussed in this book to follow my own life plan and to devote more time with my young family before the normal retirement age. This book aims to coach professionals and executives to work through these issues of leaving the executive life. In this way, the book will be an extension of my practical coaching roles rather than an academic study.

The target audience for this book is the professional, manager, or executive Baby Boomer who is soon to retire or has already retired. Because the hallmark of the executive life is highly visible performance, high stress, and great psychic rewards, this book's message is also relevant for highly paid athletes, politicians, or entertainers who are preparing to retire from the limelight. This is an awareness-building book dealing with the nonfinancial, emotional, and psychological issues of retiring. Given the plethora of financial planning materials for retirement, this book instead aims to fill the gap and delusion left by thinking of retirement as primarily a financial planning issue.

It is important to point out that I will be referring to the diverse roles of professional, manager, or executive generically through the use of the simple term *executive*. Secondly, I recognize that each person represented in this classification is unique, with a widely varying personal history from childhood through retirement. Consequently, the ability to deal with the stress of retirement and the level of motivation before and after retirement will vary. Nevertheless, I will explore the full range of common psychological issues and challenges faced after retirement. Finally, these same issues can affect to some degree anyone who has been dedicated to their organization or profession and provided lengthy service in any role.

Retirement means leaving behind the profession that one has spent a lifetime becoming a master of by being educated and trained to be kept current. Extensive preparation, perseverance, and dedication throughout one's corporate life are usually richly rewarded. Executives rise to a significant level of power and authority in an organization given their technical, social, managerial, and leadership competencies. Leaving such a role is not easy. I will address the commonly shared psychological challenges of leaving a professional career to retire. As these challenges are latent, I will first identify them to create better awareness. Surviving the "executive retirement shock" first requires greater awareness of the unexpected emotional challenges that lie ahead. These personal change issues can trigger stress unexpectedly and cause health problems if not managed: the link between stress and diseases such as heart disease and cancer, for example, has become well known medically (e.g., in the works of Barry Sears, PhD, Gabor Mate, MD, and Norman Cousins).

Each executive will experience the stresses of change in his or her own way and to a greater or lesser level of intensity or severity. The executive's "fear of retirement" represents the premonition of emotional challenges ahead, but with a lack of clarity or definition of the personal impact. Because these issues are latent, they are more difficult if the individual has not identified them and does not start to deal with them until after retirement. It is for this reason the healthy executive needs to increase awareness of these issues as early in his or her career as possible. Few executives plan to deal with the emotional issues of retirement because they are not conscious of them. They perpetuate the myth that if they have a good financial plan, all the issues will take care of themselves. Nothing could be further from the truth!

As we will see, unmanaged psychological and emotional issues can undermine the retired executive's health and cut retirement short in spite of a fine-tuned financial plan. Financial planners are always reminding us of the risks of outliving our money without a solid financial plan. Although this concern is valid, I will challenge this conventional retirement-planning perspective as missing the larger picture. For example, I will present the converse position of "underliving" your money if the executive lacks a meaningful life plan.

Terminology Used in This Book:

Defective genes: Our genes are unfortunately all defective to some degree because we are not perfect. These are the roots of our mortality or the cause of our death by natural causes or of dying from old age. Some of us are born prone to diabetes, others to certain forms of cancer or heart disease. All of us are programmed to age and weaken until nature wins out.

Hyper-stress: This type of stress is rooted in an internal, unplanned awareness of the need to change. Ordinary stress has a specific external stressor for a cause such as heavy traffic or a specific conflict. A specific stressor can be dealt with, or you can remove yourself from it. Hyper-stress is triggered by an unexpected, undesirable personal change or loss, such as personal bankruptcy, death of one's spouse, or loss of one's job. It is both an external stressor and an anxiety producer, and it requires both coping with external factors as well as changing oneself.

Anxiety: This is more debilitating because the individual cannot identify the external cause or stressor. It is harder to remove or deal with the stressor since it is mainly internal and may require a personal adjustment.

Life Planning: This is the fundamental planning for one's life based on one's unique roots and experiences that create personal values, purpose, and meaning. This is different from the conventional use of the concept of retirement planning, which often is used synonymously with financial planning. Life Planning creates your primary foundation that must be in place prior to retirement and financial planning—but usually is not. It represents the opportunity for you to creatively differentiate yourself on your own values and purpose and to actualize your full potential for yourself and others.

Retirement shock: This is the experience of the sudden change from being a busy executive or professional to retirement without the preparatory value of a meaningful individual life plan. It represents the shock of the self-discovery that a good financial plan will not give one the "golden age" of retirement. The idea that a retirement golden age can be guaranteed by a solid financial plan is a myth: money is not enough, for happiness in retirement can only be achieved by putting one's life foundation, purpose, values, and meaning in place through fundamental Life Planning.

Traditional retirement: The stereotype of retirement from the past is that of being essentially passive. After a hard life of work, the idea is that one has now deserved to quit working, put one's feet up, and be a couch potato with the few years that one has left to live. This idea of retirement is challenged by the longer-living Boomer retirement generation, which will reinvent retirement as actively engaged and meaningful. The goal of this book is to help create the vision and planning for such a new, dynamic retirement.

Part One: Executive Roots

God frees our souls, not from service, not from duty, but into
service and into duty, and he who mistakes the purpose of his
freedom mistakes the character of his freedom.
—Phillip Brooks

Introduction: Boomer Executives

We are the Champions, my friends
And we'll keep on fighting
Till the end
We are the Champions
We are the Champions
No time for losers
'Cause we are the Champions of the World
—Freddie Mercury, Queen, 1977

Fear of Retirement

Fear of retirement? Sounds like an oxymoron when you think of how much busy professionals, managers, and executives dream about getting away from the rat race to a place in the sun: golfing, sailing, fishing, or sitting under a palm tree with a cool drink. Yet retirement represents the biggest single life change that professionals or executives will make, and so the fear is not so much a fear of giving up the stress of the so-called rat race but fear of change, of moving toward a great abyss representing the unknown future: whatever will I do if I am not working? Given the busy nature of most executives, this fear is usually pushed down into the subconscious as an issue to be dealt with later.

It is important to point out that not all executives fear retirement. Those who do not fear retirement typically have a life plan that has been emerging for years. They know what they want to do. They may have already begun spending more and more time with that plan. For example, they may have already bought a seasonal residence near family or in the Sunbelt where they can spend more time pursuing their favorite activities. As a former human resources department head, I found that these lucky executives look forward to retirement with a plan. As a consequence, their interest in the job has faded. These individuals have gotten to the point mentally where they don't care about another promotion and are happy to stay in their career niche. Their challenge is often to put enough effort into their job so that they are not perceived to have retired on the job, which may lead to a sudden, actual retirement earlier than planned for. The smart ones in this category know this, and although they are looking forward to retirement, they know enough not to talk too much about it at work but to focus on the job. On the other hand, those executives who fear retirement typically want to actualize themselves through more success on the job in the later stages of their career and have never developed a vision for themselves outside their professional careers. These executives who feared retirement found the issue of retirement difficult. This question of retirement usually put them on the defensive. This is the conundrum of the executive and why executives typically avoid retirement planning. If they put the retirement pieces of a serious plan in place, it may entice their attention and motivation away from the job. It may be safer to act like you are a dedicated executive for life and deal with the retirement issue later. It is hard to do both at once insofar as the executive's emotional requirements for absolute dedication to the job challenges. Many talented executives who lose their motivational edge given their newly minted retirement plan are invited to leave the company before they want to due to the corporation's insatiable hunger for growth and demand for competitive zeal among such executives. Executives are not stupid, and this is why they fail to deal well with retirement as a long-term plan. They are often inside of the corporate pressure cooker of executive performance. Serious retirement planning and high performance do not mix well. This is why it is a sensitive, defensive, and feared issue.

As an HR executive, I interviewed many later-stage executive and managerial candidates in the recruitment process as well as in career-planning interviews. It was always easier for them to have an earlier session with the head of human resources than with the boss. This is because it was politically and psychologically sensitive, and feeling the situation out with the head of HR could prevent embarrassment later. Admitting one was going to retire was perceived as limiting if one wanted a promotion, particularly if it would take training and serious time to learn the new role. Executives felt trapped in situations where new high-level roles came open in their area of expertise. Common questions were:

- "Should I apply?" This question was code for, does my boss, usually the CEO, want me in this role?
- "Will it look bad if I don't apply?" This question was code for, will the CEO think I am slowing down, losing interest, and getting ready for retirement?
- "What would you do?" This question was code for, please check it out and advise me as I don't want to let the boss down if he wants me. On the other hand, I don't want to embarrass myself by not getting the job.

Such questions opened the door for a career-planning discussion, but this would raise the retirement issue usually avoided by the executive above fifty-five for fear of losing his or her established power base. In fact, this new position being recruited for may be the executive's future replacement if his or her retirement plan were known. Given these executive politics of power and control, many executives simply choose to put up the front that they have no intention of retiring as they are committed for the longer term, and they apply to increase their responsibilities and power base. Executives love their work, but you can see that the early fear of retirement manifests itself as fear of losing one's power base, influence, and stature inside of the corporation and the industry.

As the topic of retirement often came up in such interviews and often put the unprepared executive on the defensive, I will provide you with more examples of typical, later-stage executive comments, paraphrased from such interviews below. In this context, please bear in mind that all HR executives know the age of every executive as reported on the HR information system from the forms filled in on the first day of employment. This is legally mandatory and must be accurate for tax and life and health insurance identification. Nevertheless, as I would never remind them of this fact, executives would often forget this and refer to their actual age as being well below the actual age.

- "I'm almost fifty-five; this is scary as it's the age for early retirement. This is not far from sixty and regular retirement at sixty-five … then it's all over!"
- "I'm sixty-two, but I still can do more than most forty-year-olds. I want this promotion. I deserve it. I plan to work well past age sixty-five. Besides, I'm fit—just ask my wife!"
- "My age is confidential given the new privacy act; besides, they outlawed mandatory retirement age."
- "I love working, I love the company, I love getting that paycheck. I can't imagine what I'd do if I couldn't work!"
- "If talked to my boss and he wants me back, he knows I'm good even though I'm over sixty-five. Besides, I feel fully recovered from my prostate cancer operation."
- "I plan to work as long as possible; besides, I have no retirement plan!"
- "I can't afford to retire. I lost everything in the stock market!"
- "I am now an empty nester; what would I ever do if I retired? No, I plan to work indefinitely!"
- "I'm not looking to retire. I'm looking for a promotion. I've always aspired for this position!"
- "Since I lost my wife, work is my life; I can't retire, it would kill me!"
- "I am committed. I've put my life into the business. They will have to carry me out in a pine box!"
- "Retirement is for wimps!"
- "I live for my paycheck!"
- "I may be sixty-three, but I've got ten more good years of work in me!"
- "As long as my health is good, I want to work; besides, I get bored when I'm not busy!"
- "My career as a professional is my life. I can't just walk away from it!"

What is the basis for these defensive attitudes toward retirement? It appears to be fear created by a corporate culture and executive politics that usually do not support thoughtful attention to retirement. The reality of human resources planning, which I have done for a large bank with over thirty thousand employees, is that the company must plan beyond the individual being in each role. Once an executive's retirement plans are known, several candidates are groomed rapidly for succession. There is the chance that the retiring executive may be put out to pasture or offered early retirement before being psychologically prepared. As such, if the executive openly plans for retirement, the company may pass him or her over for new opportunities or even think that the executive has lost interest in the job. Many executives avoid the retirement issue since they are afraid of the catch-22 consequences of embarking on the slippery slope of retirement. Further, given that retirement is one of life's biggest changes, adding to this executive dilemma, I offer the following possible explanations:

- Fear of a powerful executive losing control
- Fear of the undefined new lifestyle of retirement
- Fear of losing your professional role that you worked so hard to attain
- Fear of the economic consequences of losing your salary
- Fear of not being able to replace the satisfaction of work
- Fear of losing your status and rank
- Fear of the unknown, as there is no standard, identifiable role called retirement, and executives are used to working inside a highly defined role structure
- Fear of the ultimate accountability to yourself with no external, defined replacement such as your job description

Which attitudes, concerns, or fears do you think affect you as a later-stage professional? Can you identify with any of these defensive feelings? Keep reading, and I will help you work through such issues that may impact retirement fear.

By demystifying the emotional issues underpinning an executive's major life change into retirement, I hope to spark debate and controversy within the corporate world and executive ranks as a means of raising consciousness to benefit the retiring Baby Boomer by making it a more open issue for executives and corporations. It is often the executive who denies the relevance of emotional issues who succumbs to them. Fear begets the worst-case scenario because avoiding the psychological issues simply locks the mind and prevents overcoming the fear. This paradoxically leads to the insidious state that was feared. The unconscious, with its unaddressed fears and concerns, eventually takes control, to the executive's detriment. Resolving these issues through awareness, planning, and action can lead to enlightenment in retirement for a happier, healthier, and more meaningful longer life. By making Life Planning a vital life issue for the executive, I hope to help the executive be successful inside of the company and also make a smooth, proactive transition into a fulfilling retirement. I will provide the executive the basis for a Life Planning process that will help create a successful and fulfilling life in retirement.

Baby Boomers

The focus for this book is on well-educated Baby Boomer professionals, managers, and executives born between 1946 and 1966. This subgroup has swelled as part of the well-known population increase after the World War II. Given their numbers, the Boomer population has statistically dominated North American society. Gerontologist Ken Dychtwald (2006) says, "Beginning on January 1, 2006, every 8 seconds, another North American baby boomer will be turning 60; that's 11,000 per day and 4.5 million per year." By 2015, about 45 percent of the North American population will be age fifty or older. As we live longer, the issue of what we will do after our working years in retirement is a huge issue. How can an individual Boomer find meaning and add value in a long retirement? This is a vital question that Boomers need to answer, particularly those who are successful professionals or executives about to leave their roles.

Boomers are not about to go out easily. Boomers revolutionized society and as active players they are not about to quit and become passive spectators. They will remain engaged in life as players to the end! They will reinvent the retirement industry just as they have re-created everything they have moved through, changing every facet of society and culture. Marc Freedman, in his 1999 book, *Prime Time: How Baby Boomers Will Revolutionize Retirement & Transform America*, says that the Woodstock generation of Boomers will still be trying to change the world in their retirement years. They will not leave the mainstream and disappear but remain social activists, be volunteers, and pursue lifelong learning. To harness their energy for society's benefit, he calls on government and business to create flexible programs to capitalize on Boomers' love of activism, volunteerism, and learning. Traditional biases against age need to go.

Baby Boomers are historically unique. The post–World War II reallocation of funds into the domestic economy triggered prosperity, with a huge increase in the birth rate igniting an age of consumerism. Baby Boomers were born into good times and had the resources to pursue high levels of education. Compared to their Depression-era parents, Boomers had the economic basis to develop new skills and insights through education and travel. They discovered their freedom as individuals to change the world, and set off the cultural revolution of the 1960s. These "flower children" took a long time to grow up and rebelliously refused to succumb to their parents' post-Depression values based on economic survival. They insisted on a new, creative way: President Bill Clinton expressed his own form of counterculture by playing saxophone on the *Jay Leno Show*. Boomers eventually grew up and assumed family responsibilities. Former hippies emerged in the professional and managerial ranks, and with their high levels of education, revolutionized business through research and rapid innovation. The pharmaceutical industry had its most prolific period of new drugs. Many Boomer professionals helped create the computer era, including Steve Jobs and Bill Gates. Boomers also imported and created a new age era of spirituality that included mainstream yoga and meditation. They characterized themselves as being free-thinking, creative, and original, embracing cultural champions of the primacy of freedom and liberation. They followed creative artists and poets including Bob Dylan, Jack Kerouac, Allen Ginsberg, the Rolling Stones, and Jean-Paul Sartre, all of whom empowered the generation to recognize the primacy of their freedom to creatively express and optimize the value of individual existence.

Boomer Retirement Facts

A 2007 survey by Royal Bank of Canada's Financial Retirement and Affluent Client Strategy Group found that 53 percent of pre-retirees are concerned about having enough money in retirement, compared to only 36 percent of those actually in retirement. Paradoxically, money is more of a fear factor before retiring than after. Money is a greater fear factor when one is still employed and has more coming in than later on, when income declines in retirement. After retirement, more than half of the retirees reported that their main worry was their future health, but only 41 percent of the pre-retirees felt that their future health was their main concern; money was their main worry. In other words, planning for retirement in order to make sure you have enough money does not turn out to be the main concern of actual retirees: health becomes the number one concern.

Given this shift in concern after retirement from money to health, the focus of this book will be on the emotional and lifestyle aspects of health and longevity. Retirement represents the biggest change in the lives of Boomer executives as they move from the high-powered corporate professional or executive ranks into a well-adjusted, healthy, and happy retirement. This book provides new insights into the emotional side of executive retirement that may have health benefits.

The New Retirement Survey by Merrill Lynch (2005) of 2,348 U.S. adults, of which 1,061 were men between the ages of forty and fifty-eight, aimed to find out how Boomers plan to transform retirement. The survey concluded that Boomers do indeed plan to reinvent retirement. Eighty-three percent of participants planned to continue working in some way. Most importantly, only 37 percent of those who wanted to keep working thought that money was a very important part of the reason why. Sixty-seven percent wanted to work for mental stimulation. On average, those who intended to keep working planned to retire at about the age of sixty-four and then launch an entirely new job or career. This typifies the active Boomer who does not have the word retirement in his or her vocabulary. Although this was a general survey of Boomers, not focused specifically on executives, these findings support the need to focus on Life Planning to identify how to maximize mental stimulation after Boomers leaving the high psychic rewards of professional or executive jobs.

Another retirement survey of Boomers conducted by Bank of Montreal's Financial Group (2007) found that 50 percent of Boomers planned to stay employed past their traditional retirement age by running their own businesses. The key factors cited in order of frequency per individual cited were

- Wanting to become entrepreneurs, to "keep busy"
- "It's something I've always dreamed about"
- "I need the money"

Those planning to start their own businesses in retirement planned to work forty hours a week, while one in seven said they planned to work longer, and one in five said that they planned to work until they die.

One of the main reasons Boomers fear retirement is the loss of mental stimulation, challenge, and achievement they have received in their jobs. Secondly, Boomers have become disillusioned with the corporate world and want to express their latent entrepreneurial desire by throwing off their corporate fetters and doing their own thing, often by forming and running their own businesses. As a consequence, this book aims to help you, as a Boomer executive or professional nearing retirement, overcome the fear of retirement or fear of the loss of mental stimulation by helping you make a healthy transition from the collective corporate culture and become self-actualizing, whether as an entrepreneur, a volunteer, or a hobbyist.

By creating a new awareness and describing a Life Planning process, this book will facilitate such a change for the benefit of the executive retiree. This individual actualization is the process of fulfilling one's dreams and high expectations, which can never be fulfilled through the traditional, passive understanding of retirement. Boomers aspire to a long and healthy final stage, all the while robustly pursuing their dreams and new opportunities. Boomer parents had been raised during the Depression and worked hard to survive. They did not have the economic luxury experienced by their Boomer children, who had the education and money to demand more. The Boomers' drive to express themselves as unique individuals exceeds their needs for the security promised by the corporation. The final Boomer phase promises to be as iconoclastic and creative as the earlier ones. This book will help Boomers plan their lives for their denouement and the crowning glory of their "final act."

This book will help you, the Boomer professional or executive, conquer the fear of retirement. To begin, you'll learn about the corporate environment of which executives are products in order to understand why executives often want out once they have achieved financial security.

Becoming aware of what the corporation has typically done to the executive from a psychological point of view will help you avoid the "retirement trap." The corporation develops you to lead and perform, not how to leave and reestablish yourself. It has a vested interest in keeping you focused on your compelling role until the end. Conversely, you have a vested interest for your personal well-being to prepare yourself psychologically for retiring. Given that health is the top priority of Boomers in retirement, this book will create a method for you to optimize your personal health through an empowering personal change strategy. This method will be based on challenging you to optimize your mental stimulation, happiness, and health in your own personal way. By doing so, the book will challenge conventional thinking about not only retirement but about the corporation as your "cradle-to-grave" foundation for personal health, growth, and success. I wish to challenge conventional thinking that executive wellness is rooted in the corporation in order to spark debate about and awareness of your retirement issues for your benefit.

It is only by exploring where executives come from and how executives are created through the corporate socialization process can you fully understand what executives have become. The psychological challenges of executive retirement can only be understood if you discover the psychological makeup of corporate professionals and executives.

Content Overview

Chapter 1: Stone Age Genes to Metaphysics

Our genes are basically from the Stone Age. The executive has become the modern-day champion in the tradition of the archetypal ancient hunter, who created value through hunting and providing food that allowed the formation of the tribe and civilization. The anthropological roots of our ancient ancestors shed light on our own executive vulnerabilities and needs. Understanding these roots helps us overcome the limitations of corporate tribalism to become authentic individuals in retirement.

Chapter 2: Corporate Being

The psychological impact of the challenges and process of becoming an executive leads you to become anthropologically a "corporate being." As an executive, you must embrace, create, and lead the work, culture, and values of your corporation. This means that you must walk the talk and be the corporate being. Executive leadership results in you becoming the product of your collective corporation. As you become part of the corporate culture, you fear losing that culture; along with your role, that culture becomes the main pillar of your self-identity. This creates a psychological barrier and can increase your fear of retirement.

Chapter 3: The Retirement Trap of Corporate Being

This chapter explores how corporate life creates a collective resistance to an executive being able to break away and make a planned, smooth, and healthy transition to a meaningful retirement. Corporations have an interest in propagating the many myths of retirement addressed in this chapter.

Chapter 4: The Neurotic Executive

An unrealistic executive can easily become addicted to the corporate collective culture of work. As an addicted workaholic, the executive builds a fear of retiring to a life outside of the corporation. Because typical specialized work of the professional has taken over the executive's personal identity given substantial education and meaning, the executive needs to undergo a personal change process of self-discovery beyond the simple, traditional retirement-planning process.

Chapter 5: Sickness and Death: The Short Retirement

This chapter explores the health issues associated with the executive trap of retirement, given the dramatic change involved in the retirement process. The driver of sickness is hyper-stress, triggered by the emotional and psychological shock involved for the unprepared executive.

Chapter 6: Executive Stress in Retirement

Understanding the transition and stresses you face as a retiring executive is the key to coping and dealing with them. Doing so can lead to a healthy and productive retirement, and potentially increase your longevity by lowering the stress.

Chapter 7: Finding Oneself

Repositioning your executive self-identity allows you, as a former executive, to take charge and re-empower yourself. Finding your passion outside the corporation allows you to reconnect with yourself and gain the power of self-knowledge and personal meaning. This sounds simple but is very illusive to do. The chapter will discuss its challenges for the executive.

Chapter 8: Personal Change

Once one has rediscovered his life's meaning and purpose outside of the corporation, he or she has new assumptions to build a new plan of an active retirement. The passionate pursuit of new objectives keeps you focused outside of yourself, with new control of and satisfaction in your endeavors. But first, you need to undergo this life change process. The chapter will show the need for a former executive to use a new form of Life Planning that is not only different from corporate planning but contrary to it.

Chapter 9: Happiness and Health

Planning specific personal activities aligned with your new passion and sense of meaning helps to overcome executive barriers to happiness and health. This chapter discusses the limits of money in attaining happiness and health.

Chapter 10: The Meaning of Life

The final achievement of the Boomer is to attain a uniquely personal meaning. This chapter will discuss how you attain your authentic being—the personal transcendence and antithesis of the corporate being. The full circle is attained as you, the Boomer retiree, are reborn through self-actualization and the fulfillment of your highest needs and human potential.

Chapter 11: Transformational Life Planning

You can now see that the term *retirement* is a misnomer for the meaningful and healthy last stage of life. For a self-actualizing Boomer, the last stage is purposely active and can become the best stage of the Boomer's life: doing it my way. This guide and discussion will help the Boomer reinvent the meaning of retirement itself. Effective Life Planning is the best way to define, focus, and take charge of the rest of your life in a personally meaningful way.

Summary of Goals

The book aims to

- Raise the executive's awareness of the price of corporate success
- Challenge the conventional wisdom of the corporation as a vehicle for individual self-actualization
- Show that executive retirement fear is symptomatic of having become a corporate being
- Establish the primacy of the individual as free to find a new, unique, and healthy self-identity outside of the corporation
- Reinforce the Boomer by providing a liberating pathway to creatively reinvent retirement
- Describe how to create the condition of optimum health for the Boomer's last act: to go out with the same passion and joy of the Baby Boomer social revolution.
- Provide a Life Planning process for you to design your own fulfilling retirement.

Chapter 1: Stone Age Genes to Metaphysics

Ah, but a man's reach should exceed his grasp,
Or, what's a heaven for?
—Robert Browning

In the Stone Age, the economic hero was the hunter. Hundreds of thousands of years ago, civilization and culture began to form because, while some gathered what was available locally, hunters went out to hunt for, kill, and bring back food to support the development and survival of the tribal group. This early specialization of skills allowed for communities to settle and survive. Roles, rules, and culture began the economic organizational foundation for civilization.

The executive is the contemporary prototype hunter, creating wealth, jobs, and new opportunities for our families. The executive plays the key leadership role as a hero of the modern economy. As you will see, the executive roots still reflect the collectivism of the tribe. Executive language also reflects the hunter culture. When an executive makes a lot of money on a deal, that executive "makes a killing." The executive gets proportionately rewarded, and gets to eat what was killed or share in the spoils. The executive life is described as being a rat race with cutthroat competition. We make great advances in technique, like sales where we sell the "sizzle," but buyers demand to see the "meat." Linguistic metaphors express this deep, age-old genetic and cultural connection.

We have obviously evolved technologically from the Stone Age. However, although we have conquered cyberspace as well as outer space, unfortunately our genes are still basically Stone Age genes. Our genes are still defective, or we would never fall ill and die of old age. Our programming still has glitches. No matter how healthy a lifestyle we live, except for war and external calamities, defective genes are the ultimate cause of death. Properly administered pharmaceutical drugs often improve the quality of life by reducing symptoms of ailments and disease; however, they do little to prevent them. Biotechnology is beginning to focus on the genetic causes, but this work is in its infancy. We have too many moving parts to find the so-called fountain of youth. Our finitude at the moment appears infinite.

We remain connected to our Stone Age ancestors. Why do we still crave fat even though we know it will clog up our arteries and kill us? Our programming is still with us from the days before heat was transportable. Before central heating, fat had to be built into our bodies for survival, particularly in the winter. Why do we overeat and feast, particularly when celebrating with family and friends, renewing our communal bonds through celebrating our successes? This practice is probably rooted in the need to celebrate the hunter's kill. Since there was no refrigeration, if any food was left for long, other animals or an enemy might get it. Can you imagine a contemporary wedding with Lean Cuisine dinners and small dietary portions being perceived as a better celebration than the usual lavish portions? Even today we associate eating huge proportions as a sign of strength. In 2008, Nathan's Hot Dog Eating Contest was won by Joey Chestnut, who had to win it in an eat off against Taku "Tsunami" Kobayashi after being tied when both wolfed down fifty-nine hot dogs in ten minutes. This was not a one-time event but the ninety-third contest. According to legend, it was started on July 4, 1916, after four immigrants settled an argument about who was most patriotic by having a hot dog eating contest at Nathan's Famous Stand on Coney Island. James Mullen won by eating thirteen hot dogs in ten minutes. Obviously, after ninety-three years, we have grossly "improved" (Wikipedia, "Nathan's Hot Dog Eating Contest," retrieved, August 2008). Why do fathers like to pass out cigars to celebrate the birth of a baby or to celebrate a milestone such as a lucrative business deal or a championship? Yes, we do continue to smoke, even though it also kills. Perhaps it comes from the genetic-based, ancestral memory of the many pleasurable tribal celebrations and feasts around the open fire.

Luckily, although we still "get stoned," we are not completely Stone Age. Anthropologist Richard Klein explains (Bronwyn Barnett, 2003) that we modified one gene about 50,000 years ago. When civilization formed, cultures and language also developed together. The FOXP-2 gene became modified as cognition developed our ability to abstract from the physical reality and form ideas represented by words. This transformed gene plays the role of allowing human beings to develop language and to think abstractly. This change further allowed humans to differentiate from animals, to develop civilizations with laws, and to develop science based on research and our collective memories, which soon became recorded data.

Nevertheless, our Stone Age genes are alive and well in the best of us. The contemporary executive continues to have the Stone Age instincts of the hunter. We executives continue to be driven to create new value and to amass as much corporate wealth and shareholder value as possible. Our career opportunities and personal rewards flourish the more our corporation grows. This drive for growth is based on the same primitive fear felt by the hunter, which was essentially the fear of scarcity and concern for survival. Beings that failed to develop a strong, genetically driven fear of annihilation, or the drive to survive, became victims of extinction. Darwin's concept of survival of the fittest is still alive today in our "dog-eat-dog" corporate world, where everyone aspires to be the "top dog." You can see in the Fortune 500 list the survivors of ten years ago by and large have been gobbled up by more innovative or efficient corporations. Mergers and acquisitions have also allowed for predatory change, even though "poison pills" have slowed the swallowing-up process. We are making rapid progress as corporations build our gross domestic product (GDP), and our lifestyles are what our parents could only dream about. Given our state of economic development, competition is the main lifeblood of the corporation and the key means of strengthening the economy. The rat race is here to stay.

Executives are the leaders of this huge achievement, yet they must pay the primitive price of being in the cutthroat world of competition. Anthropologically, business language and slang reveals its primitive roots and reality. You can predict those executives who get the corporate vote of confidence and are promoted: they are the ones who have the street smarts. Shrewd investors know the rule of finding investor value: they buy when there's "blood on the street" or when there's lots of red ink. Executives learn to love the "cut and thrust" and the thrill of surviving to get the rewards of the corporate world. Failing to produce means the executive will get fired or terminated. Yet this fear-based world of the executive hunter has its own vulnerability.

Executive Vulnerabilities to Corporate Tribalism

> We have seen the enemy and it is ourselves.
> —Old Adage

In the competitive jungle, executive competitiveness is based on the fear of failure. This primal fear of annihilation comes from our survival instinct. Overcoming this fear through stockpiling profits to increase shareholder value and personal success is the best way for an executive to survive. The "up or out" reality puts tremendous pressure on each executive to become more and more competitive. Jack Welch, former CEO of General Electric, used to fire the bottom 10–15 percent of producers every year. For those few executives who think about and plan for retirement, this fear of scarcity carries over to the executive fear of retirement in the need to amass as big a nest egg as possible, and retirement planning becomes reduced to financial planning by this obsession with scarcity. Most fail to plan for the rest of their lives because this internalized belief of scarcity is dealt with by continuing to focus on working and making money as the essence of life. Although amassing the big nest egg is an executive survival motivator, the concurrent contradictory need to look prosperous through spending and consumerism often takes over the more the executive earns and undermines the goal of financial security. This cements the dependency of the executive on the corporation: more money is always needed to satisfy ego needs, helping to trigger the fear of retirement as many fail to attain the level of financial security believed to be necessary.

Executive competitiveness is reinforced by corporate tribalism. Given our Stone Age genes, we still compete and create economic wealth through tribalism. The corporation is the modern tribal unit, whose driving force exceeds the importance of the individual, including the executive at any level. Huge salaries placate and seduce the executive into feeling success and achievement, but within the corporation. The collective foundation of corporate values and culture forms the corporate tribe, which socializes the individual to differentiate himself or herself against the competition. Yet tribalism is only effective in satisfying lower-level needs.

Tribalism is present in other areas of society as well. In sports, tribalism helps satisfy our social needs as we use tribal membership to increase the passion and joy of victory over rival teams. Tribal-based hooliganism is well known in European football as well as in sports contests between countries that have had past conflicts and rivalries. Professional sports make billions based on this principle. We have a natural affinity to lose ourselves at tailgate parties, to cheer on our favorite teams at great expense, while wearing their official sweaters and painting our faces as warriors. We—and our favorite teams—are the hunters, and many teams typically adopt the ferociousness of their animal-based names to continue the bond to the savage reality of the hunter. We need to form our personal identity through a competitive based self-differentiation.

Tribalism is a huge societal issue and the basis for modern-day wars, whether religious, cultural, economic, or national. The key psychological mechanism underlying the force and success of tribalism is the coercive force of the collective on the individual. The executive is a product of the corporate tribe. However, this executive must rebuild himself or herself when leaving the corporation for retirement. Fear of retirement is fear on the part of the executive of becoming orphaned from the corporate tribe.

Male and Female Executives

The issues of executive fear of retirement and Life Planning are similar for male and female executives. Female executives are now catching up to their male counterparts when it comes to heart disease, cancer, and other stress-related or stress-affected diseases, as they adopt the same workaholic lifestyles that include a lack of exercise, frequent travel, and too many business lunches and dinners. Female executive stress may be greater in many cases given the fact that female executives often play a greater family-oriented, child-rearing role than male executives. Given the well-accepted link between stress and disease, Debra L. Nelson and James Quick (1985) developed strategies for professional women to lower their escalating levels of stress.

Nevertheless, female executives seem to have an edge over their male counterparts when it comes to the retirement issue. They are less prone to the fear and challenges of retirement, given their greater natural affinity to the family. Through child rearing and taking on a greater role of family care from an emotional point of view, they tend to take on multitasking and the balancing of work and family more so than male executives. This leads to creating a self-identity of the female executive less influenced and controlled by the corporate tribal culture. Women tend to have more important relationships outside the corporation than do men. This may hinder their corporate upward mobility, but it has its advantages. Given their "dual citizenship," women are more psychologically prepared to leave the corporation and adapt to retirement without the corporate culture. Even single women tend to play a stronger role in elder care of aging parents. I have known numerous female professionals who have taken a lengthy leave of absence to take care of a sick or dying parent, but not one male executive comes to mind. Male executives can learn from their female counterparts.

Fear and Love

> I am an old man and have known a great many troubles,
> but most of them have never happened.
> —Mark Twain

The two primal and most powerful emotions are fear and love. Can you think of any feelings more powerful and more pure, opposite, and mutually exclusive? All others stem from these and tend to be mixed emotions. Fear is the negative basis for hate, resentment, hostility, and anger. Love is the positive basis for emotions related to happiness, caring, development, and success. Both of these polar emotions are very powerful motivators, yet it is a product of corporate tribalism that most companies motivate their executives, who in turn motivate their employees, out of fear: fear of failure, fear of job loss, fear of demotion, or fear of not getting a salary raise or bonus, for example. Of course, there are "love rallies" to bond teams around the corporate missions, but few executives take the love to heart. Rather they feel the fear of not meeting the new targets more than the love they get for past performance. "What have you done for me lately" is the fear-based norm of competitive organizations. Fear is the mind's natural response to danger as the mind tries to quickly cope. A well-defined and negotiated performance plan can lower this fear and consequently job stress. *Fear is stress!*

From a health perspective, fear-induced stress is our enemy. Stress can be of benefit in the sense that it sends warning signals to us. If we act on these messages and negotiate realistic performance goals, then we can benefit from stress. However, the fear of retirement is more difficult to overcome because it is not defined and quite vague. It is the unknown aspect of retirement that we fear. General or less-specific fears, such as fear of the unknown or fear of change, do not go away since they have a longer time horizon. These less-specific fears have no obvious object to act against and so they become chronic, more debilitating, and more stressful. They lead to anxiety, which can lead to health problems.

As a later-stage professional or executive, you can first identify and understand this fear of retirement as a meaningful signal, and then analyze it by breaking it down in a way relevant to you. By doing so, you will escape the potential emotional ravages of this fear of retirement and create a framework for acting on your fear proactively. This will allow you, the executive, to move from fearing retirement to loving retirement. To help you do so, I will refer to Abraham Maslow's well-known Hierarchy of Needs (1954), which is a useful tool for our message. As Maslow's model suggests, it is important for you to move beyond satisfying the survival or physical needs identified in Maslow's first levels of need to focus on social and self-esteem needs and, most importantly, to embrace your freedom to attain and fulfill your highest need for self-actualization. Only through self-actualizing can you reach your full creative potential, unlikely ever to be attained inside of a job box on your organizational chart. You have nothing to lose and everything in the rest and best part of your life to gain.

The corporation as the modern tribe is used by the executive to fulfill the lower-level economic needs for income and physical survival along with some social and self-esteem needs. Yet this tribal basis for the executive self is also the cause of the executive fear of leaving the safety and meaning of the corporate tribe for retirement. The corporation fails the executive self by not supporting preparation for the emotional side of retirement. The rest of this book will show you how to escape this psychological dilemma.

Procrastination

Executives usually fail to overcome the fear of retirement while they are still working in their professional roles for a number of reasons. One of the reasons they don't act on the fear is that they are always too busy to prioritize Life Planning. Fear in this case manifests itself as avoidance in dealing with a major personal change. Executives mostly do not admit to the fear itself but procrastinate over preparing psychologically for it. Besides, given their high level of confidence, they deceive themselves into believing that they can do anything.

However, Life Planning is of a different order compared to typical executive planning tasks. The executive treadmill is driven by the squeaky door of immediacy: the horrendous daily onslaught of e-mails, voice mails, meetings, and the in-box of mail, not to mention the constant interruptions and re-prioritizations. They have difficulty achieving the different mind-set required to focus on something personal like Life Planning, which can be tough to think about, given its deceptive complexity. We prefer to cover up the anxiety with continued hard work and through denial that the fear is real. We prefer to focus on making more and more money and transferring the responsibility to a financial planner who one day will tell us when we are ready to retire. Secondly, we prefer to believe the corporate myths of retirement—more about those later.

This all helps to allow the executive to avoid the psychological dynamics and issues of retirement. Avoidance of the psychological side of retirement, which includes Life Planning, deepens the fear, and greater shock and trauma result later.

Another form of avoidance leads many executives to refuse to retire at the normal retirement age. This "die in the saddle" strategy can help you avoid such issues, but only if you are the owner and are in control. Most executives who decide to forgo retirement in large corporations cause resentment among younger employees waiting for promotions. The executive who will not retire will have to work even harder to keep the job given the high salary and extra energy needed to maintain political control at a time when energy wanes and evidence of one's mortality is seen as former colleagues die off. This may stimulate the thoughts of slowing up and of doing a few pleasurable things that there never was enough time to do when working.

Metaphysics and Meaning

Executives have the capacity to transcend this primal box of fear-based motivation and behavior. From our primal roots as the hunter, we have the ability to think outside the box and to find the full potential of our individual beings and spirits. Rising beyond the fear of annihilation and beyond our esteem needs for social recognition and personal differentiation from the collective executive crowd requires the will to use our higher metaphysical potential to search for our individual meaning.

This is essentially a quest to overcome the fear of retirement. It can only be accomplished by getting in touch with our higher-level needs beyond the tribalism of our corporate upbringing. Discovering our needs beyond physical survival allows us to freely choose our identities beyond the corporation. Shedding the physical shell of our corporate self-identities opens up a whole new psychological world of creativity as we move toward self-actualization. If we don't reclaim ourselves in retirement, then when will we? In a way, planning for retirement is our last chance. This is a self-discovery journey for the executive. It is not meant for weak and timid souls who want to retire passively to the rocking chair, but for the Boomer who truly wants to "rock" to retirement, doing it as creative and talented individuals. By rebranding and reclaiming oneself, by discovering our true love and passions in work and leisure, we have the opportunity to embark on the best voyage of all as we go forward into our last act.

Executive Questions

- Have you ever felt the fear of not having enough money to pay the bills?
- Have you ever felt the fear of failure in your career?
- Have you ever felt the fear of not pleasing your parents, your family, or even friends in your career success and reputation?
- Have you ever felt the fear of not keeping up with your peer group or neighbors in their latest cars, houses, or images of success?
- Have you ever feared for the economic security of your job or your professional income?
- How have your fears played a role in your success?

- Have you psychologically conformed to the rules of the corporation in order to gain job security or ongoing professional income?

If you have answered *no* to the above questions, ask yourself whether you might be repressing any fears. Might you need to repress your fears because of your executive perception that fear is a sign of weakness, or are you truly fearless? If you find that you are repressing your fears, ask yourself if what you fear is fear itself.

How have such fears held you inside of the corporate or professional collectivity and prevented you from breaking out and being your own person?

What would it take to conquer these fears, spend less and save more, become financially independent of the corporation?

Begin to create fresh images of yourself outside of the corporate or professional role you play, accountable to no one but yourself and your own values.

Begin to create inspiring images of yourself doing those things that you really love. How does this feel?

Part Two: The Making of the Executive

Chapter 2: Corporate Being

And ah for a man to arise in me,
That the man I am may cease to be!
—Alfred Tennyson

No employee embodies the being of their corporation more than the executive. Creating and implementing a corporation's values and purpose are core leadership functions. Executives come to personify the unique DNA or blueprint of their organization the more they lead it and represent it with increased accountability. A *corporate being* is the corporate values and culture of the company, internalized and brought to life by the executive who must lead by walking the talk of that culture in the context of each executive's job accountabilities. As this corporate being is borrowed from the company but given life by the executive who embraced it, it represents a learned role from the collective corporate tribe. This borrowed collective role is the executive but is not his or her authentic being or inner self.

Do you remember your first big promotion into management? This gratitude and excitement of finally arriving in management was personally inspiring. It rubbed off on your personal life, as you wanted family and friends to see the new you. You started to talk like a newly minted product manager, which you were. You also may have gotten a few groans from old friends who really didn't care much for the new corporate being that was emerging in their old friend. Yet this is only the beginning for the development and emergence of an executive's corporate being, which we shall see is the biggest retirement barrier for the executive.

The corporation is not a person. It is a legal entity and its balance sheet with fixed and liquid assets. And yet it is the people who bring the corporation to life and create the financial results. People buy into this abstract structure as shareholders and employees. Executives unify and lead the people by instilling a common set of values and purpose. The price of leadership is to become what one leads. Without total commitment, credibility cracks will appear in the executive and limit the executive's overall effectiveness, advancement, and rewards. An executive leader must be what he or she wants to create to be able to create it. You need to not just learn but embody those values of your corporation by being a role model. Successful executives end up personifying their company.

William H. Whyte, Jr., in his classic book, *The Organization Man* (1956), showed that the personas of American rugged individualism and the hard-working, competitive innovator had been replaced by corporate socialization and bureaucratic pressures to conform to the corporate values and culture in exchange for economic rewards and security. Corporate collectivism was replacing an earlier stage of entrepreneurial risk taking. The organization men took the vows of the corporation and gave up personal entrepreneurial potential. They embraced the corporation in exchange for lifelong rewards and security. Whether the corporation was capable of delivering on this implicit promise was usually not questioned in the formative stage of an executive's career, given the stronger and more immediate need for security. The larger the corporation, the greater the sense of security and ongoing legacy; however, this sense of security is deceptive given our current age of mergers and acquisitions, energy price shock and drop, stock market fluctuations and of course derivatives like 'asset' backed securities which turn out to be a financial mirage all magnified through globalization.

Professional compliance with the culture and values of the corporation is vital both to the corporation's and to the manager's success. This is the main reason corporations choose to recruit future management out of college as opposed to searching the market: the objective is to form the core values and even adult personalities of aspiring executives through early acculturation. Conforming to these corporate values will imprint these executives in ways that will make them less effective in different competitive cultures. This creates a human resources competitive advantage by increasing loyalty and integrating the workforce for better execution. Those who do not conform, for whatever reason, have a limited career path and are seen to be less effective. They become candidates for termination, which increases the pressure to conform. M. L. Burton and R. A. Wedemeyer in their book, *In Transition,* based on their Harvard Business School career seminars for those out of jobs, found that career difficulties stem from conflicts between the job and an individual's personal values. Having the smarts and technical skills becomes less important than being able to fit in with and accept a specific corporate culture.

At the other end of the career path are the successful executives who have resolved such conflicts in favor of the organization for what they believe to be their career benefit. Such executives may pay a later price for this success. Psychiatrist M. Scott Peck, who has counseled many successful executives, puts the dilemma this way in his book, *The Road Less Travelled*: "The road that a great executive must travel between the preservation and the loss of his or her identity and integrity is extraordinarily narrow, and very, very few really make the trip successfully. It is an enormous challenge" (p. 62).

My goal is to help you learn about and become prepared to deal with the challenge Peck describes as you consider leaving the corporation in retirement. Doing so will help you avoid becoming a victim of the identity challenge of retirement. First, however, it is important to understand this "corporate being," with all its dilemmas and pitfalls to better understand the escape route out.

The impact of the corporate being or corporate culture and identity on the self is variable. The degree of the impact depends first on the tabula rasa factor, or degree of having largely unformed behaviors and ideas, which is high in new college recruits with little work experience. These fresh recruits are open to being shaped by the corporate culture. This younger, unshaped recruit usually has a need to develop an adult identity, which later may emerge into the identity of an executive with greater power and authority. The affinity for allowing the corporate identity to be internalized and become personal depends on the degree to which the original self-identity has been developed before joining the firm. Often aspiring executives form their adult identities based on going through the process of learning the company and end up assuming an executive role identity. Those who come to the corporation with highly formed adult personalities and self-identities are more immune from the influence of the corporate values, and are less likely to define their self-identity as their corporate role.

The second factor in the degree of the impact of the corporate being on the individual's psyche is the size of the organization. Generally, the larger and more hierarchical a corporation is, the greater structural and process complexity. Large organizations are usually mature with generally well-developed structures and processes that have been successful historically. This makes them less flexible or likely to be open to change because they have hardened into a rigidity usually referred to as a bureaucracy. This creates an autocratic culture, where the individual has little control or influence and is less able to have any impact with his or her own personal ideas or initiatives. To succeed, the individual must follow the rules and fit in through consistency and dependability. This backward-looking rigidity of the larger, more bureaucratic companies is usually the basis for their downfall because they often fail to change and keep up with industry innovation.

On the other end of the scale, the smaller, more entrepreneurial companies depend on individuals' ideas and initiatives. They are also less well formed and are still creating their processes and structures in order to become more consistent and able to execute their new product strategy or service at a higher volume and speed. This formative organization needs individual inputs to survive. For this reason, the individual in a smaller, more entrepreneurial culture is less a product of the corporate culture than an individual who helps to shape the culture. This is why many individuals with well-formed identities and the need to be in a highly participatory and less-structured environment become less a product of the corporate being, and are less defined by the monolithic corporate culture. In a more entrepreneurial company, an individual can meld his or her own ideas, values, and purpose more easily into the managerial role of shaping the company. This is why many people prefer working in a more entrepreneurial, smaller company.

The downside, however, is that these entrepreneurial companies are far less secure: they may be dependent on a single new product or service. Even so, the corporate being is absorbed by the executive even if it is to a lesser degree. Here, the executive willingly trades having less security for a greater degree of personal freedom. Since freedom is a higher-level need than security, the person who is more entrepreneurial operates with a greater foundation of personal security and has a greater tolerance for risk.

To illustrate this difference I draw upon my experience with MBA students that I have lectured, campus recruitment I conducted as the head of human resources as well as former executive MBA classmates. Although the following is a stereotype, it is also based on my experience in having worked in a large bank with over thirty thousand employees as well as smaller, less-structured firms where I could see the very different success criteria and cultures.

The security-oriented individuals who often join larger organizations such as banks, insurance companies, government institutions, or hospitals often base their decisions on their perception that the organization will provide them with the chance for a successful career. Such organizations tended to be paternalistic and provided great security and support. When asked why they are studying for an MBA, they say that the degree will help their careers by differentiating them from those who lack the degree, and may lead to greater advancement. These individuals have a lot of pride in belonging to their particular organization. A particular organization that comes to mind was a global bank. Such MBA students further speak of the approvals that they have received to take some time off to do special MBA projects. They are proud of the fact that their companies are helping pay for their MBAs. They are very driven by the marks in order to impress their organization. They associate high marks with better job performance and a better image, which will lead them to faster promotions. These people are happy and feel in the sweet spot: they have large companies supporting them and providing the basis for their future careers. During campus recruitment, large companies experience great interest from such students, mainly because of the corporate image and the perception of gaining a greater career opportunity, not to mention more money. These security-oriented people are driven extrinsically by the traditional avenues for career success.

On the other hand, entrepreneurial types do not follow the traditional track toward career success. They have a certain sense of self-reliance and feel secure enough to take risks, and often they don't even see their actions as risk taking. These individuals are usually driven intrinsically by their own ideas. They may have an interrupted educational portfolio as they do diverse things and figure out what they want to do with their lives. They are more interested in what they can do in a certain function than they are about the company image. They are more likely to get excited by a certain role opportunity in a small company than by a general career path in a large one. If you ask these individuals why they are following an MBA program, often you will hear that they want to learn something they think they could use—like how to do a business plan, how to launch an initial stock offering, or how to read a financial statement. These individuals are not motivated by obtaining the MBA degree but by the idea of learning things that they can apply for their own purposes. They often do not show up for certain classes since they have a passion for their own personal projects. These people usually don't care about the marks except for the value that they can get out of a course. They define what they want out of the class and often do projects their own way regardless if the professor likes it or not. Many entrepreneurs drop out as they find the classroom education to be sterile and a waste of time when they could be doing their own thing. Come to think of it, weren't Bill Gates, Michael Dell, and Steve Jobs college dropouts?

Executive Lifestyle

Corporate executives in many ways give their lives to the company. The self-motivated drive to succeed in the corporation has been nurtured through years of university and professional training and preparation. This drive, coupled with the internal pressure to create individual results, leads to long hours and hard work in order to differentiate oneself for recognition, rewards, and promotions. Globalization requires ongoing travel and separation from family and friends. The need for corporate teamwork and collaboration creates close affiliation within the company. Colleagues often become the surrogate for friends and sometimes even for family.

Nevertheless, such sacrifices are highly rewarded with huge salaries and bonuses. Global travel is offset by the luxuries of business class, the best restaurants, and upscale hotels. Some executives prefer the luxuries of travel to the domestic realities of being at home. Communications are structured and supported with laptops, Blackberries, cell phones, and personal executive assistants providing global executive support.

The hard work and executive sacrifices begin to link success to money. It's all about the money! As executives learn that the reality of success from the corporation's point of view is to create shareholder value and to raise dividends, they begin to see their own success connected to the growth of the company, their departments, and their personal bank accounts. The executive's sense of meaning and self-worth becomes aligned with the corporation, which is not a person but an economic mechanism where quantitative value overcomes qualitative value. The success scorecard for executives in the corporation becomes the money, which is easy to measure. Given an executive's uncertainties regarding personally defined value, the executive may ask, is this all worthwhile? Nevertheless, the money usually becomes vicarious evidence or easy superficial proof that it is all worth it. The money becomes proof of personal success and "value." This connection between money and self-worth reinforces the corporate career cycle of working harder to move up the corporate ladder as far as possible. The hierarchy becomes more compelling the higher you go. It seems to show that *self-worth equals net worth*, as power and salary rise proportionately as you move up the hierarchy.

Executives in this career cycle of corporate motivation rarely will be satisfied with a certain level of career success without feeling the disillusionment of career plateauing and limits of personal value. Their managers will rarely tell them that their career has reached a plateau because they don't know for sure. Anything can happen in the volatile and political corporate environment. The corporate being, or culture, of extrinsic motivation based on satisfying economic needs is the treadmill or rat race. This cycle of dependency on corporate success can be addictive.

The executive can find it more and more difficult to not indirectly sacrifice his or her personal life if it intrudes on the success-driven corporate life. This sacrifice often becomes the unintended consequence of success. However, how can you ensure that you do not fall into the workaholic trap? Does it really matter if your new work-life balance does not fit the corporate culture? How can you work smart and get more done without the long hours that keep you away from your family, friends, fitness club, creative hobbies, and other interests? What's more important, your life or career?

Executive Self-Identity

Insidiously over time, the executive's increasing corporate or community identity becomes his or her professional self-identity and even personal self-identity. The more the executive embraces the corporate culture and enjoys its rewards, the more the person becomes the company man or woman. This in itself is rewarded by the corporation through social, superior, and peer recognition, not to mention increasing seniority and pension rewards. The executive comes to feel like a company icon or anchor, which feels deceptively secure, comfortable, and satisfying. This very sense of security and satisfaction reinforces the executive ego. The sense of success is furthered through unrealistic external social support. Society adores celebrities, strong executives, and people with power; this adoration neurotically reinforces the identification of personal success with economic success.

As the executive takes on this corporate being unconsciously, the reality of what the executive has become often surfaces or becomes apparent consciously only upon the shock of a job loss. Burton and Wedemeyer's (1991) Harvard career seminars point out the trauma of job loss experienced by a manager not as an external event but as a very personal inner loss. It is a loss of the executive's personal identity. One reaction of a vice president expresses this personal nature of his job loss: "I felt devaluated, frightened, abandoned, angry, devastated. The well-meaning consolation, 'It's only a job!' produced a bitter response: 'No, it's my life. It's me!'" (p. xii).

John Kinch's (1963) psychological experiments on changes in self-concepts found three key factors that shape self-identity.

The first factor was the more often a person sees others as responding to him or her in a particular way, the more that person begins to think of himself or herself as being that person. For example, if others see you as having a lot of power and influence, the more you will start to think of yourself as powerful. Having power often is relative to the perception of others seeing you as powerful. This is why executives need organizational charts as proof to others of their power, even if those charts fail to reflect reality.

The second factor was the more important you think the contact with another person is, the more impact that contact has on defining your self-identity. In other words, if a subordinate thinks your ideas are great, that will have less impact on your sense of self than if the praise came from your boss or someone else held in high esteem.

The third factor was the person's self-concept is most influenced by earlier evaluative feedback on a particular trait, especially the most recent feedback received. For example, even if you had received years of good feedback on your marketing skills, you may panic because of new adverse feedback from a new boss.

These three factors are relevant to the executive's self-concept being shaped as a corporate being. The executive gets regular reactions from other executives and employees given the interactive nature of day-to-day enterprise. Executive communication and leadership are necessary at all levels to assure the changing corporate situation and data are understood for that level or function and results are met. Given the frequency of employee feedback and the fact of reporting upward in the hierarchy, the executive comes to assume control, power, and authority.

Given the strategic nature of the executive interactions, the more likely these interactions will involve top management and will be seen as important to the executive. In this way, the executive comes to take his or her own leadership seriously insofar as top management also is influenced and impacted by the role.

Finally, the executive's rise through the levels of the organization leads the executive to explain his or her success by taking full personal credit and assume the reasons for this success were related to strong personal qualities. The specific qualities will usually be those praised by the boss who promoted the individual. Given the politics of executive power and influence, individuals will typically take personal credit for success but blame failure on external factors or reasons beyond their control. In this way, corporate success tends to breed executive self-concepts that exult in and exude confidence.

Since the self-concept is conditioned directly through corporate interactions, the executive's self-identity becomes a product of the corporate or professional culture. The executive becomes the organizational man or woman, the corporate champion or leader. The executive pays a psychological price for this corporate-produced self-identity insofar as it is not left behind at work. The executive often cannot separate the self from the work like an hourly wage worker who lives for getting out of the plant. The intensity and personal challenges of the role as well as the highly developed skill required to perform it do not allow the executive's self-identity to escape from the corporate culture. The high level of reward also positively reinforces this bond and glues together a co-dependency with the corporation. This self-identity produced from being married to the corporate role forms the basis for fear of retirement insofar as it is the fear not so much of leaving the job but the fear of losing one's self-concept and personality. The challenge is that when executives or professionals so strongly identify with the corporation, the corporate roles they play can take over and become who they are. There is more at stake here than just a job, a role, or a self-identity; there is a life at stake!

As an executive or professional preparing to retire, you may want to explore the following self-reflective questions and activities:

- Who are you? Take a piece of paper and define yourself. Write out the top adjectives that you identify with and are proud of. How many of these are job or professional characteristics? How will these professional or executive qualities ever retire? How can you transform these strengths into new qualities and person in retirement?
- Create a working action plan to refresh these strengths for your future as a new, bold, retired executive.
- What changes will you be happy with? What if you were an executive "quarterback"? Will you be able to live with being an armchair quarterback, or will the lack of executive recognition or applause kill you? How can you become a "color commentator" instead of an armchair quarterback in your retirement role?
- Don't forget you are used to high psychic rewards in your professional role. How can you transfer this psychologically and practically into a new role that fits you and a retirement lifestyle?
- What will you be happy with in retirement?

Desensitization through Technology

As the executive internalizes a corporate being, there is a desensitizing of the personal being. Part of this desensitization is the functional dependency on and often addiction to technology. Executives leverage their skills to attain greater success through the time-saving uses of technology. We tend to work more and more remotely from our colleagues, staff, and customers. As we communicate with the office more and more on the weekend or on vacations with our laptops or Blackberries, we become more remote with our families even as we communicate remotely with our colleagues.

This is the paradox of technology: we can spend more time at home communicating globally, but in reality the technology intrudes into our personal quiet time and the quality time we need with our families. Technology becomes addictive as we crave the high of being globally connected and need to keep up with the corporate global theater as we play our roles. Technology as a servant becomes our master. As executives move up and assume greater accountability and span of control, they have less time to manage by walking around, less time to look people in the eye and absorb their body language or human reactions. There is no time to detail the emotional side of a message, and so our e-mails are pure data. As the saying goes, the more data, the less knowledge. We lose touch with the reality underlying situations and people. This explains why we sometimes completely misunderstand e-mails. I can remember turning off the Blackberry at 5:00 PM and setting it to go on automatically at 7:00 AM. Nevertheless, I can also remember the rush and excitement of hearing the many buzzes as it turned on. As I rushed out of the house in the morning, I found it irresistible to at least look to see who had sent me the e-mails, and usually I started reading them at stoplights in busy traffic. I confess that I was not always able to stop reading them while I was actually driving. In my experience, I was no different from all of the other executives I knew. One executive actually preprogrammed set messages like these: "I'll get back to you later; I'm driving"; "Call me"; "I agree." By simply pushing the right button, he could insert the e-mail response and then push Send while driving. This is an example of losing touch with the human reality that we are putting other drivers' and pedestrians' lives in danger by the compulsive acts personifying a corporate being.

As head of human resources, I found that most of the emotional content was missing from e-mails for two reasons. First, no one wants to have e-mails about sensitive issues left in writing or on the server.

Second, if emotional content is included in an e-mail, it usually oversimplifies the situation and can be misunderstood by others when copied to the wrong people. E-mail histories are routinely copied, and before you know it, your simple, negative response can be copied in the histories of numerous other e-mails all over the corporate globe. Third, emotional content integrity depends on the interactive context and the body language of each other, which is absent in e-mails. I found it was much better and much more accurate to call the other person or speak in person before drawing any conclusions from an e-mail. One sales executive put this well: "I learned the hard way, never write an e-mail after drinking a bottle of wine!" We are desensitized from the limitations of technology given its ease and allure.

This desensitizing through technology and its overabundance of data lead us to lose touch with our own inner beings as we move to greater and greater dependency on the collectivity of our corporate being. As an executive, have you ever been in a meeting when your Blackberry buzzed in a message? We had a policy set by the CEO that during executive meetings, there should be no reading or responding to e-mails. Nevertheless, executives would "discretely" read e-mails under the boardroom table. No matter how important the meeting or presentation, the sensuous buzz was usually personally compelling and irresistible. In certain interactive situations, this was actually rude. In one presentation that I attended at an executive meeting, I actually witnessed the presenter read his Blackberry during his own presentation. No wonder this device has the nickname of the "Crackberry." Reading it under the table to meet the need to stay in touch instantly with the global corporate data flow is the corporate being's desensitization to the human importance of immediate, live human interactions. Personal awareness arises from the construction of meaning through human and interpersonal interactions; pure data desensitizes. The executive having internalized a corporate being becomes less aware of the inner personal being as technology amplifies the growth and consolidation of the executive's values.

The more we let technology separate us from live interactions with people and nature, the more we dull our sensitivity to and our understanding of them. Our own self-understanding is dependent on sensitive, intimate, and realistic interactions with others. Corporate data communications actually encourage executives to lose touch with their own inner personal being. Our new mastery over data through technology comes at a human price, the loss of sensitivity not only to others but to our own beings. We lose the sense of the human meaning of others in the sea of data, and in the process lose our own sense of being. We replace these losses through our corporate beings as technology becomes our tool and a "de-centered" center. I have heard executives say that they felt like aliens without their Blackberry or laptop. Personally, over a year after not having one, I admit I still occasionally feel my hip where my Blackberry used to hang, as if it was an appendage of my body. By losing touch with our personal beings and the possibilities of having unique, personal meanings and the freedom to be individuals, we assume the collective personality of the company's corporate clone.

As we gain greater control or mastery over global data and our span of control grows, we assume greater power and global control over certain corporate functions. This illusion of power and control, dependent on technology, leads to the corporate being's personality tendency of executive hubris, where the corporate being's ego threatens to become as big as the great outdoors.

Consider these questions for reflection:

- As an executive, are you becoming desensitized by the technology of your job and corporate being?
- Do you feel lost without your laptop, cell phone, or Blackberry?
- If you have a Blackberry or cell that buzzes during a meeting or discussion, do you shift your thoughts to the message?
- Have you ever seen others in a meeting periodically look under the table at their Blackberries or leave the meeting to

answer a cell phone while you were presenting ideas to the group? If so, how did that make you feel?

- Have you ever seen an executive sitting on the beach with his or her family on vacation but concentrating on a Blackberry or laptop?
- Have you ever sacrificed time with your kids to respond to your e-mails and felt that your kids' activities seemed trivial and that you had a more important and serious mission to attend to?
- Does receiving an e-mail on your Blackberry late at night make you feel needed and special?

If you answered yes to any of the above, you have experienced your corporate being in action. Since the corporate being is not human but rather processes and structures, rules and culture, it has no feelings or sensitivity. The more you internalize your company's corporate being, the more you will tend to lose touch with the emotional side of yourself and others. An addiction to a corporate being and its technology can lead to negative consequences. Read on to learn what those negative consequences are and how to prevent them.

Executive Hubris (or I Am the Power in My Role)

Have you ever felt hubris in a corporation? As a social scientist, I certainly have. This is one of the reasons I no longer work as an executive inside a corporation. What are the situations or signs of executive hubris? To begin, ask yourself the following questions:

- In your company, do you experience a behavior change when the boss walks into a meeting?
- How do you feel when your boss walks into your office unexpectedly?
- Do you feel more guarded and have a higher stress level in the presence of more senior managers or executives?
- When you mentally disagree with your boss or anyone more senior at a meeting, how do you express it? Do you say nothing, nod your agreement, and endure the stressful

dissonance? Do you ask a neutral question that you hope others will respond to in order to get your disagreement expressed? Or do you have the courage to openly and accurately express your thoughts? For example, the boss may have declared our product is the "best dog food on the market." Do you neutrally ask, "How can we increase the sales?" Or do you bravely get to the meat of the matter and say, "Quite frankly, the real problem is dogs don't like our dog food!"

- When a serious issue is raised, do managers tend to say nothing until they find out where the boss stands on the issue, even after that boss flags the issue and asks for others' views?
- Do you feel rising tension and stress when you find you must be honest and say what you think? Do you feel even more tension and stress after you openly disagree with the prevailing view of your boss and the more senior people?
- When you are the most senior person in a meeting, are you surprised how few ideas your staff seem to have and that you always must do the talking?
- Does your boss tell the team that he wants your ideas and thoughts but is openly defensive when anyone disagrees with him?
- How much is the hierarchy defined from a status point of view?
- Does each level of executive get a larger office space, and is office space clearly defined as a perk?
- Are the furniture, decorations, and fixtures at a visibly more expensive level the more senior the manager?
- Does the facilities department have an approved policy guide for what each level of management gets in terms of office space, furniture, and fixtures?
- Is there a policy that affects the executive's administrative assistant's office space and furniture? Is the assistant's office a smaller version of the executive's?
- Do the mahogany-lined walls, marble halls, and hardwood offices with thick carpets of senior management feel like

museum space, so quiet that you feel you should keep your voice down? If so, this usually is meant to intimidate visitors so that they act deferentially as they enter the hallowed halls of corporate power and wisdom. It is also a reminder to the executives who reside there who they really are—corporate beings!

- Are there crusty old pictures of retired founders, board chairs, and executives lining the walls?
- Does the car plan clearly define what each level of management can get, ensuring that top management drive the best cars?
- Does management qualify for a superior dental, disability, and health benefit plan as well as a better pension plan when they reach a certain level in the hierarchy?

If you have answered yes to most of the above, then you are living in the workplace with the culture of a strong corporate being. Here, status and one's corporate role are more important and more meaningful than individual ideas, experience, and suggestions. This is a highly political environment that does not encourage openness or creativity. Ideas must be vetted politically before risking expressing them. To do otherwise could be a CLM, or career-limiting move! This causes the individual to become alienated from his or her own thoughts, feelings, and sense of originality as he or she adapts by conforming to the rules of the company's corporate being or culture.

The above is the foundation for creating the stratification and executive hierarchy that reward executives through visible signs of their excellent work and success achieved within the criteria of the corporate culture. Providing executives with a tangible sign of their ascending power and rising importance is seen to be vital by most corporations as a way to motivate their executives. Many executives seem to need physical reminders of how powerful they are. This kind of everyday physical reminder of executive status and power encourages executives to really believe they are destined to be great and powerful.

Just like props and costumes in a play help create audience belief and credibility in the characters, so executive props are needed to create and support employee belief in the superior power of the executive. The extent to which a culture creates its own hubris through hierarchical differentiation varies according to the organization. As a former human resources executive, I have always tried to create the opposite environment of a flat, team-based culture. This is the challenge of most HR professionals as they try to add needed value as a counterbalance to the hierarchy. They add value in improving organizational effectiveness by repairing the problems created by the power structure and hierarchy. This intermediary role is one of the most stressful in the company as HR professionals strive to create optimal bottom-up communication and participation in their company through people systems. This valuable role connects and strives to overcome the natural conflict and human friction between the top and bottom of the hierarchy and between egos at the higher levels of power. HR professionals know that the real power is with the people who do the work. Many executives would like to blow up HR as a waste of money. Paradoxically it is that very ignorance of the value it creates protects those very executive egos from self-destruction.

- Are you prone to the hubris of the corporate being?
- Would you be happy and fit a flat, team-oriented culture?
- What motivates you more, the challenge of a new job or the status of the new role? In an interview, would you tend to ask: What's the salary? Could I see the office? Where does the CEO sit? What type of car plan is there? What kind of bonus could I normally expect? How many reports would I have? How much would my budget be?

The more you answered yes, the more you would be prone to develop hubris in a company.

The higher the executive climbs the corporate ladder, the more power is attained. Power is control over people, resources, and the strategic direction. This control delineates the executive from the rest of the organization, which reinforces the rising career as an ascent of the self toward greater success. More and more, the executive's self is supported by others in the organization. Social recognition of the individual executive through others not only cements the self-concept but satisfies the executive's social and self-esteem needs. As the Kinch experiments demonstrated, we internalize the other's recognition and behavior toward us as proof of our self-concept. When subordinates see executives as powerful, executives see their personas as naturally powerful, often not realizing until that this power is mainly situational, and lost in retirement, creating a later retirement shock. Others will be more prepared if they take their fear of retirement seriously and not bury it in the self-deception of hubris.

Executive hubris is a function of the executive internalizing the power and social control over others inside of the corporation, a sign of one's own being as increasing success. The increasing rewards and social recognition through ostensible respect and deference lead the executive to internalize this increasing power and control as a natural part of the self. Yet deference shown toward the executive can be groveling out of fear and not always out of respect. Few executives can differentiate this difference and reward those employees who positively reinforce the corporate culture of fear, given their degree of hubris, as they come to see the deference as natural given their level.

Each executive will differ on how such power and success will affect him or her based on previous ego formations and need for self-affirmation. Many executives have a well-established sense of self from earlier experiences outside the corporate life and are less susceptible to the internalization of the corporate role and its success. Their egos are normal, even though they have extraordinary power. On the other hand, the root causes of an excess of hubris often come from an original feeling of inadequacy or inferiority developed earlier in life. Such feelings are often perversely satisfied through the power found in the executive's role. The newfound power becomes addictive: the ego becomes self-satisfied as the original feelings of inferiority seem to have been conquered through personal "excellence." However, this is a superficial solution and will fall apart in retirement as the cloak of the role is taken away.

On the other hand, those who developed a positive sense of self-esteem earlier in life based on other roles and accomplishments are less prone to use the crutch of the power of the corporate being. Leaders who have not fallen victim to the ravages of hubris are usually very approachable and very supportive of their subordinates. Their power is usually based on their competence and personal relationships, and not on their positional power. A fierce loyalty to these kinds of leaders develops out of respect, not on the fear of their power. These bosses usually freely delegate power and share it in order to get the best results. Paradoxically, the more power that these bosses give away, the more is returned. By empowering their subordinates, these balanced and talented leaders often become much more powerful given the support of those who protect their leadership as if it was their own personal possession.

I was fortunate to have worked for a few CEOs who had such qualities, and this was probably the reason I stayed longer than I expected to when I joined the company. From a human resources perspective, shared power was always more exciting, not to mention more organizationally dynamic and entrepreneurial. Shared power is more the norm in a bottom-up culture, as compared to having the power reside with the senior individual, who covets it like a possession, which is more likely to occur in a hierarchical organization. Given their empowerment of others, CEOs I worked with felt the power as a huge responsibility, even though it was tempting to take it personally as a natural extension of what each had become as a person. They knew it was important to separate the self from the power and accept the power as a burden. These leaders who saw power as an opportunity to empower others were already secure. They were much more ready psychologically to retire. They did not take their power personally but shared it readily; similarly, they were ready to give it away as one must do in retirement. Paradoxically, by sharing and giving power away by empowering others, such leaders seemed to have even more power as they attracted stronger subordinates and got better results.

What is important is that the greater the executive's need for the self-affirmation of the corporate role, the greater the hardening of the emotional arteries. The greater the executive hubris, the greater the self's dependency on the role, which heightens the fear of retirement. Since hubris is based on an externally defined sense of the self as recognized by others, once the executive develops hubris as the real self, the hubris acts as a defensive mechanism to mentally reject any information that challenges the ego. Like an artificial self based on temporary power, hubris becomes a crutch that the executive fears losing, especially in retirement. Growth for this executive would require authentic learning by thinking through the corporate system of interdependencies, which would help dispel this self-concept of power that really depends on others' fears.

Ultimately, hubris based on fear of subordinates, or fear of loss of power over others, is fear of oneself as the executive suppresses healthy possibilities for the self other than the executive ego. The executive with hubris fears solitude and meditation, which is really fear or avoidance of real self issues or of the self trying to become authentic. Losing touch with one's inner being is common when the executive begins to absorb the power of the corporate being. Nevertheless, the self addicted to the corporate being will receive messages of anxiety sent from the unconscious and experienced in dreams or when alone. An inability or unwillingness to deal with feelings of anxiety feeds into the need to never be alone and to consume time alone with work. The workaholic is soon formed as part of the ego addicted to power. Many executives suffering from hubris choose to avoid such signals of anxiety, thinking they have enough job problems to deal with, let alone having to figure out what's going on inside of them; better to just keep busy as the anxiety only seems to surface when not working. This works until anxiety gets too severe, in which case the fear of confronting the unconscious self may lead the executive to a psychiatrist or psychologist to help create personal order and meaning by better understanding the unconscious signals or unresolved personal issues from the past. This schism between the corporate being and the authentic individual is the reason why many individuals leave the corporate role for something that better fits their authentic selves. Fear of facing this issue is the same as fear of retiring. The driving force of embracing the corporate being is the need for the security. Paradoxically, the ultimate psychological security for the executive is not by embracing the corporate being but in finding his or her authentic self!

In general, the more the executive internalizes the power of the corporate being as his or her ego, the more the hubris, but this comes at a psychological price of ignoring one's authentic self.

Sycophants (I am your support because you have greater power)

Hubris is a cultural system arising from the hierarchy. Each corporation has its own character dependent on the lead of the CEO. Corporate beings are served by sycophants, who form the underbelly of executive hubris. The alter ego of executive hubris cannot exist without the constant reinforcement of "yes people." The presence and number of sycophants in any organization is equal to the degree of hubris within the corporate culture. Human resources consultants often note that flattering the boss is an effective career strategy for getting ahead. The idea that flattery will get you everywhere is somewhat true, given the rigidity of the ego of the hubris boss. Flattery usually takes a very subtle form, like not telling the king he has no clothes. It normally exists as complicit support for the boss's hubris. It is not visible but implicit. The supportive sycophant may not even be fully aware of being one, and may experience this behavior as simply giving support and not rocking the boat. Sycophancy usually begins when you support your boss by not saying anything in opposition even if you do not really agree with the scheme. Over time, this support without question becomes institutionalized as the normal boss-subordinate relationship. In return, you will tend to get support from your boss when a promotion opportunity occurs. This represents the most difficult balance for talented executives who are subordinate to the hubris boss: how to grow and be yourself and still get the support of such a boss in a promotion situation. Many subordinates who get promoted out from under such bosses often surprise everyone with their own originality and differentiation from their former boss. On the other hand, it is common to hear those who failed to get promotions or who left a company report that they did not get the job because they spoke their minds freely or said that the person who got the job was a "yes man." If there is an entry point to becoming a corporate being, it is the behavioral decision to become a sycophant to some degree and support the culture of the hubris of the corporate being.

Colorful slang terms are routinely used in corporations to indicate the omnipresence of sycophants. Not only are derogatory terms for sycophants readily used in every company I have worked in as an executive and as a management consultant, but they are so common that they have become part of everyday language. In reality, the corporate being based on the hubris-sycophant principle is created by reverence for the corporate system. The executive who fears personal economic loss embraces this system. Subordinates also embrace such a system because of fear that not being a sycophant would be a career-limiting move. Paying homage to the corporate executives helps a person move up in the hierarchy and leads to hubris when the executive moves up. This helps to form the corporate culture and the individual corporate being.

Behaving as a sycophant also affects the self insofar as there is sacrifice of psychological integrity for later career gains. Naturally, in terms of the boss-subordinate relationship, the greater the boss's hubris, the greater the need for the subordinate to be able to be a sycophant. Sycophants, however, usually develop hubris later in their careers when they are promoted. Both behaviors are symbiotic, the psychological flip sides of each other. They represent the main behavioral glue of the hierarchy, and so their prevalence is a function of the degree of hierarchical stratification in a specific corporate culture. The presence of and rewards for sycophant behavior within the corporate culture means that when the sycophant becomes an executive, he or she will continue the behavior pattern. In essence, executive hubris creates and reinforces sycophant behavior in the same corporate game: one gives and one receives as part of the same cultural rules of mutual support. Because these cultural rules are those of a collective culture, authentic individuals become an endangered species. Truth becomes uncomfortable as hubris avoids it by demanding the flattery deserved by level of power. This distortion comes not just from the subordinate sycophants but from the executive. We will further explore this distortion and how to overcome this trap later in the context of executive retirement in chapters 7 and 8.

Each corporation needs the phenomenon of *sycophant-hubris mutual support system* to some degree to reinforce a hierarchy, but some rely on it more than others. Smaller companies are often less vulnerable to this system because they are more directly dependent on the market. Since they are leaner, with fewer bureaucratic levels, they interact more directly with customers for their survival. Executives in smaller firms get less bound up in internal bureaucratic power structures. The power lies more where it should be, with the customer. Survival often means pleasing the customer, so the primacy of power is external to the company, not internal on the executive floor. Executives in emergent companies cannot afford to take their power as personally, given that their survival is understood as based on the next contract or on finding new customers.

Powerlessness and Addiction to Corporate Power

Many executives allow the corporate culture to fulfill their personal purpose and meaning as they rise in the hierarchy. Career success becomes fused with personal success. When this happens, the executive is accepting an economic definition for his or her life's meaning when, in fact, being successful in the corporation can fulfill only one's lower-level needs.

Embracing the corporate culture as corporate beings is a self-fulfilling prophesy. The individual grows and is continually rewarded by an organization that fundamentally has an economic mission. In this way, the executive learns the ultimate meaning as basically economic. The corporate being shortchanges the individual's potential to find a higher individual purpose through the individual's spirit, innovation, creativity, or innovative entrepreneurship. Becoming the corporate being by merging the corporate values into the psyche sacrifices personal freedom to fully be one's self. The executive will pay for this sacrifice later.

Paradoxically, the executive does not consciously experience any loss of freedom; in fact the executive feels the opposite: totally empowered. Assuming the corporate responsibility, authority, and power is exhilarating but addictive. In reality, the individual feels an unconscious powerlessness because he or she is highly dependent on the collectivity of the external corporate being for one's sense of personal power. Corporate power becomes more important to meet the growing need of the individual to deal with the underlying, repressed powerlessness of the individual or self. This cycle of dependency deepens into hubris, which is experienced by the consciousness as normal, increasing success. In essence, the individual becomes highly dependent on the corporate being as an addiction to power. And yet the corporate being and its power is still a foreign substance to the human freedom of the executive.

Anne Wilson Schaef (1987) defines an addiction as "any process over which we are powerless. It takes control of us, causing us to do and think things that are inconsistent with our personal values and leading us to become progressively more compulsive and obsessive" (p. 18). The corporate being learns greater and greater power and assumes it as hubris. The executive becomes more and more dependent and addicted to it as it is deeply needed to cover up what is in reality the personal powerlessness of a self, sacrificed to the collective mission of the corporate being.

Yet the collective mind of the corporation is built to last, so the corporation in all its complexities can survive change and become globally successful as an ongoing institution. As a monolithic economic "state," it transcends any individual, so it can create ongoing economic value for society for its survival. Ultimately, it is not about the freedom or fulfillment of the individual executives' higher-level needs. James C. Collins and Jerry I. Porras (1994) show the key to the longevity of the corporation is the executive learning, embracing, leading, and becoming the macroculture of the collective mind of the corporate being. They argue that what is important for the company is not a charismatic, visionary leader but rather becoming a visionary company. "The key point is that a visionary company is an organization—an institution. All individual leaders, no matter how charismatic or visionary, eventually die. ... Yet visionary companies prosper over the long periods of time, through multiple product life cycles and multiple generations of active leaders" (pp.1–2). Executives then must learn and embrace the corporate values so that by personifying them, they can pass the torch on to the next generation. The executives become messengers for the corporation. By personifying the corporation they make the company last. Insidiously, while paradoxically serving the corporation to last, executives fail to prepare themselves to last in retirement.

Success of the corporate monolith occurs through the individual assuming the leadership. In contrast, this book focuses on the neglected personal dimension where the executive is sacrificed on the altar of success. The goal is to show executives how to escape this corporate trap of collectivism and hubris, how to reclaim psychological control and become your own person outside of the corporate being. The shock of the loss of one's corporate being can be traumatic. My goal is to redeem the psychologically beleaguered executive who has sacrificed so much to the corporate being, the price of "success." Instead of being another discarded executive who served the corporation and died off upon retiring from it, I will champion such forgotten heroes and create a pathway of renewal, health, and longevity for the retiring Boomer executive in part 4 of this book.

The False Self of Corporate Being

Most executives will deny that their corporate being is a false self because it feels so normal, and because they are happy and totally pumped up with enthusiasm and a sense of purpose. To rise to a senior level, every executive must go beyond simple, technical knowledge and step up, be the part, show enthusiasm, sell yourself, be committed, believe in your product, get into the spirit enthusiastically, differentiate yourself inside the corporation, show more commitment than others, get more and better results for the company—and more. You will never make it to the senior level if you do not embrace the corporate being by getting into the party!

All executives have a corporate being; in fact, they lead by helping to create this corporate being. Most human resources departments usually provide early employee-orientation programs to show and differentiate the culture of the company from the competition and why the company is the best company in the market, even though, for example, it may have been number three in the industry for years, but will be number one, soon. They have their "game face" on, just like a football team charging on the field to beat their competitors and win in their marketplace. Executives are the key players. The "party" is different for each company and corporate culture, but all companies reward and celebrate not only results but the anticipated glories in order to pump up executives to create such results. It is fun, but it requires total commitment and resolve to compete to get to the senior level called the executive. For example, you will routinely travel executive class, be personally rewarded with travel points, and feel it was all worthwhile. You will have only good food and wine between stops and enough leg room to sleep to prepare for the meeting, and you know that the sycophants at the other end have been killing themselves anticipating how to please you and want to impress you with the local best restaurants and comforts. It feels good to be an executive!

This is typical within company success and culture. If you don't like this corporate party, then leave and get out and set up your own party. If you are going to attract good people and grow, you will need to create a vision and a story of how the concept can lead to unprecedented success. This is the start of a new party as newcomers get addicted to the story of success and how rich they can become if they perform and be like you, the founder. The question of how the executive can be a false self is a legitimate one because it seems counterintuitive to think that this role, which is so rewarding and challenging, could not be the real "me." It may be so for others but not me, is a common thought. The answer to this is that the role of the corporate being fails to represent the full potential of the executive as a human being. To become addicted to the executive power and rewards distorts the individual's personal reality. Allowing this role to seduce you as a person, to confuse this temporary role—no matter how powerful or exhilarating—with reality, and to let it replace your reality and potential is a personal tragedy that will play itself out in retirement when the reality of the corporate being shows its empty truth as temporary and borrowed from the collective corporation.

All executives take on the false self of the corporate being by definition of being an executive leader. However, even though all executives have a corporate being, it always differs by degree. Usually the greater the hubris, the more this corporate being, and the more its power and personal significance have been internalized as being one's real self. This false self is hard to avoid because it feels so good, and the addiction to it is a matter of degree. Many great executives see through it and come out of it well by focusing on it as a segmented role, not as their real being or person.

Those executives who see the gap between their own potential and the corporate being usually get out early and set up their own small companies based on how they can offer value to other companies. In my own case, this gap often drove me back into my management-consulting practice. In general, if the executive does not do a mental time-out to differentiate himself or herself from the corporate party and make a personal career decision, he or she is embracing the false self of the corporate being.

The real issue of the false self is that many executives repress their real potential as human beings out of the economic fear of job loss and having to leave the comfort of being an executive. A typical example of becoming lost in the euphoria of the corporate being and losing touch with one's real self is the workaholic, who loses touch with his family. This occurs gradually: the executive returns home from business trips, he or she is engaged with e-mails and fails to rejoice in the return to family life. The executive gradually gets more and more remote, and the family becomes less relevant psychologically. The executive gets more instant gratification with his or her corporate being and power, which has perversely taken over. The corporate party is more exhilarating than the routine obligations of family life. The spouse often expresses unhappiness with the increasing distance between them, but this is brushed off as irrelevant, given the ascent to success and ego recognition at the office. Often this capturing of the ego through power can lead to an affair with the executive's assistant who may idolize the executive. At home, this executive gets no respect; in fact, only criticism is experienced for not spending enough time with the family. Too many Little League games have been missed, too many critical family events missed, the executive was in China arranging an outsourcing deal when his or her son hit his first home run and in Mexico checking out a new plant site when this executive's daughter got a standing ovation at the school play! However, when the executive returns home, he or she can't get the respect or reverence received at the office. The executive may be more enamored with a sycophant at the office with whom there is a romantic affair. Even though this affair is with an attractive support staff member twenty years younger, it seems to feel right given the executive's sense of power and stature. This executive begins to think that the family is irrelevant and mundane and feels that he or she has moved beyond their demanding "self-centered" needs and deserves better. The executive I am thinking about once told me, "I get no respect at home, but, boy, do they ever love my money!" However, the office affair soon self-destructs and the executive gets fired, given poor performance at the company. How can this happen and be so common? The false self of the corporate being needs to keep going until hitting a dead end. In the state of the false self, the person is adrift, and with no authentic foundation the sky is the limit, and you have lost yourself in the party of the corporate being's exuberance. The excesses from this false being come from the joy based on the hubris of success and the resulting feeling of being immortal as the "built to last" corporate being that the executive has internalized and become. Later, after this corporate being recovers from the workaholic addiction and gets in touch with his real feelings by purging his corporate being, this executive may beg for forgiveness from his or her family and start to work on bringing the family back together, realizing that this is more personally valuable than the big money and power of the corporate being. This is an example of the false self, which could quickly redeem itself through the renewal and reconnection with a forgiving and loving family.

There are many more examples of corporate beings having lost themselves legally, and who are now in prison because they spent company funds as if they were their own, pre-dated stock options to maximize their payout, or manipulated stock prices and personal stock sales through holding back and manipulating announcements. What is common in these examples is the inability of the executive to differentiate himself or herself from the power and rights of the corporate being. These individuals, by and large, were very talented people lost in a false self or the exuberance of the corporate being. This is a tragedy caused by losing touch with one's real self and becoming addicted to the workaholic, false corporate being. The point is not to marginalize those who have fallen over the edge, but rather to champion *all executives* who have the potential to become their full selves, including all those who need counseling. Although these individuals may have lost their way because they have not based their growth sufficiently on their authentic selves and real values, they can recover as easy as any individual who wishes to pay the price of reconnecting to what is important. All corporate beings risk going over the line no matter what their talents or level. Part 4 of this book will provide ideas for the individual no matter what their excesses. We aim to redeem all false beings to ground them in the knowledge of their authentic being and real potential!

Surrogate Power versus Personal Power

Certainly, the role of corporate being satisfies security and economic needs, but it cannot satisfy self-actualization needs. The culture collectively determines one's role. The degree of disconnection between one's own self and the required corporate role is psychologically based on the degree that corporate power is taken as personal power. An executive's power is borrowed from the role and the company. As the person is rented for their skills and behaviors to lead and create commercial results, the power given to the person is role power not personal power. *As bestowed by the organization it is surrogate power, not authentic personal power.*

When I think of an example of surrogate power a simple childhood memory comes to mind. I used to have an army of toy tin soldiers. You know the blue, red, and white classic patriots with the funny hats. The one I always put at the front was beating a drum. On about my seventh birthday I asked for and received a white and red drum with wooden sticks. It even had a cotton woven string for putting it around my neck. It allowed me to transform myself into a great general and to imagine that I was leading a powerful army into battle to save the nation as I walked around the house chanting and banging on my drum, the louder and fiercer as my army went into battle. This mesmerized state of joy and power came to a tearful end when the drum was taken away from me given how irritating I became with it, not to mention the sibling rivalry over its control. I was crushed. I lost my drum, my army, and my dream of saving the country with all the glory! I lost my power because I lost my drum which was the real source of the power in my mind. In essence surrogate power is borrowed as it resides externally in a position, mechanism, or other source of power. As all I could do was cry and beg I had virtually no personal power.

Obviously, surrogate and personal power overlap. It is rare that someone has high surrogate power and almost no personal power; for example, a despised despot may have very high surrogate power until overthrown. Conversely, an example of someone with very high personal power and very low surrogate power would be Jesus, who was killed by the authorities for his beliefs. Barack Obama had a balance. He won the election based on his personal power rooted in his populist ability to communicate and represent the feelings of diverse others hoping for change and economic renewal. Obviously, winning the presidency vaulted his surrogate power to very high levels.

What is your balance between surrogate and personal power? If you believe that your personal power is greater than your surrogate corporate power, would you risk your security, your job, or even your life for your values, principles, or beliefs? Do you have the personal power to make a smooth transition into retirement? Do you fear the loss of your professional surrogate power in retirement? I will show you how to develop personal power in the wake of losing your professional surrogate power later in the book.

Personal power is based on your own personal authentic values, principles, and beliefs based on and resolved through reflection of your lifetime struggles and experiences. Surrogate power is not personal but job-based like a new sheriff receiving a badge. The badge is a visible reminder of a certain power. You don't need a badge to declare your personal power. In what makes you unique and real in spirit, personality, convictions, and values. The problem is surrogate power of the role is to some degree confused with personal power, and when removed it can result in a personal crisis or shock. There is always a degree of this because an executive cannot lead in the corporation without to some degree internalize the corporate values and positional power as one's own. Those individuals who refuse to compromise their personal values to embrace the values and power of the job will fail to move up and be removed. Refusing the acquiescence of the sycophant is usually perceived as a form of insubordination. Those refusing to submit to the power structure are seen to be a poor fit for positions of greater power and even the position that they are currently in.

Fear of retirement is often a result of having sacrificed the development of personal power for greater surrogate power. Having become addicted to the power of the corporate being by adhering to its collective norms, it is more difficult to individually develop personal power. The development of personal power is usually sacrificed by the sycophant in the collective passage to surrogate power. Hubris usually signifies this lack of personal power but a significant dependency on surrogate power.

Consequently, this dependency on surrogate power becomes a fear of retiring from the corporate collective due to a lack of personal power which differentiates the individual from the collective.

As a personal example, I recall that one of my exits from the head of HR role was in a multinational automotive company where I was motivated by the fact that I did not want to work for my recently appointed boss, not the person who hired me. Assessing my multi-career option of returning to my consulting practice, I resisted his new exercise of power by simply telling him that although I cared about the success of the company, I disagreed with the new strategy; I preferred a radical back to basics CQI (continuous quality improvement strategy). He thought I was nuts because he thought that that was a low level union function because it was mentioned in the contract, but relying on unions for quality improvements and cost reductions made no sense to me. However, most critically his newfound ultimate power as CEO was insulted. While all the other executives were paying homage to "his supreme expansionary vision as a new savior," I had the gall to tell the king he had no clothes. Besides, this gave him a good reason to terminate our relationship because he was already threatened by the fact I was friends with the chairman of the board who originally brought me into the company, and this gave him a good excuse. So we both won. I knew I would die a slow death suffocating as a sycophant, or I could breathe the fresh air of my own free thinking with the satisfaction of saying what I thought. If I may say so, history showed that the CQI cost reduction did become a critical success factor in the automotive industry.

In retirement the corporate role will be stripped away, and the individual will eventually stand alone. The badge is gone, the organization chart and business card exhibiting your level of power is simply gone. The corporate false self may have come to seem like the real you, which is like a brief role in a Broadway play with a supporting cast and applause. Who will you be after you get too old to play the lead actress or actor? Your authentic self will survive age and the test of time. Even though your corporate being is embraced and experienced as the real you, it is only a temporary, commercial transactional role, which can never reflect your full potential. I will guide you on the passage from the commercial, rented role of the corporate being, which made you the money, to the possibilities of your unique, authentic being, which will allow you to feel the real joy of self-actualization and the expression of what makes you unique. *Personal power is real authentic power as it is based on your character, values, and talent, not your job. It cannot be taken away from you and is the basis of actualizing your full potential.*

Chapter 3: The Retirement Trap of Corporate Being

Man cannot be sometimes slave and sometimes free;
he is wholly forever free or he is not free at all.
—Jean-Paul Sartre

Executive Profiles with No Life Plan

Executives, leaders, managers, and even professional athletes and high-profile celebrities and politicians receive high levels of psychic rewards, social recognition, and adulation. They do not want to lose those rewards. The thought of retirement is pushed out of their minds by the fear of losing this stimulating sense of success and exhilarating lifestyle. The following are brief, paraphrased examples of executives with whom I had career discussions with in the capacity of executive vice president, human resources, which represented the company. These executives all were approaching the age of sixty-five and had no life plans. The fact that most had sound financial plans seemed to satisfy them as being fully prepared for the future.

Executive A is an automotive industry executive almost sixty-five years old. He is in good shape financially and could afford to retire with a somewhat less-expensive lifestyle. When asked about his plans once he reached sixty-five, he said, "'I have too much energy to retire. Besides, what the heck would I do? I'd be wasted." This particular executive had raised the issue of mandatory retirement at the executive committee and was successful in eventually getting the policy of mandatory retirement at sixty-five rescinded. He also raised the issue that he had no successor, even though he had had many opportunities to hire one but typically chose more junior candidates who would have a greater dependency on him. He had no hobbies other than staying at his seasonal cottage. He loved to travel but could do this best in his global role; he often took his wife as a companion and tacked on a few vacation days for sightseeing. He also stated that if he was ever forced to retire, he would find something similar and alluded to the many calls he got from headhunters looking to fill similar roles with competitors. Given industry recognition and his dominant role, he believed that he was indispensable to the company; he wanted to and should be entitled to work indefinitely. In fact, he felt that the company was lucky to have him, given his many achievements. In this sense, he would call the shots and write his own ticket. He ended up being asked to leave the company at age sixty-five even though the mandatory retirement policy at age sixty-five had been changed. The CEO wanted to restructure his area. This executive had built the old system and had resisted changes to his department. He further represented a big salary. This individual ended up setting up a consulting practice working for competitors, but had some legal issues over confidentiality and competitive trade secrets.

Comments: This individual loved his work but had little perspective of life. He avoided discussing his age and had represented his age not chronologically but based on how young he felt. He talked as if he was still early in his career and had not made a mental adjustment to the realities of a later stage. Careers do come to an end, as does life itself. Does he want work to be his final legacy? I would suggest he probably did, but only by default of never having thought about it. He had refused to discuss the "R" word and pushed back on any idea of retirement. He seemed to see retirement as a personal weakness and wanted to avoid it at all costs because, in his own mind, he was "strong." In my opinion, this individual was right to keep on working because he was simply ill prepared to not work and would suffer huge stress based on the loss of his reason for living without somewhere to go and work every day. He also saw the zest of life as consumption and did not want to cut back since he saw this as a sign of failure. He saw retirement as a budget cut.

Executive B is a chief investment officer (CIO) for a large financial retail company. His company was suddenly bought out. Since he was about sixty-five, he was given a severance package by the new owner. He did not take this easily, for he believed that he was the best performer with a stellar track record, given the choice between him and another person who had come from the acquiring firm. He said and I paraphrase,

I lost my job through pure politics. I have forgotten more about investments than the new guy knows. He is just the new CEO's guy. However, after sitting at home for a year I was not just bored but extremely bored. I couldn't stop thinking about a start-up. If no one would hire me, the hell with it, I had to start my own investment company and make it different. I started designing a new investment risk adjusted customized timing strategy based on the retiring Boomer needs for cash flow, balanced with both blue chip dividends as well as bond ladders. So far so good, I am undercutting the fees of the mutual fund industry and working with financial advisors. Even if I don't make as much money as I did, this is really not about the money, it's all about satisfaction.

This highly motivated executive is doing well after a few years and shows no sign of wanting to slow down.

Comments: This person was very proud of his skills. He had the right to be, given his accomplishments and the past recognition he had received. He saw his career as a great competition to get to the top, and to be out of the great game felt like losing. He just could not plan to replace what he loved to do. Retirement represented in his mind an end to what he loved to do and had felt so much pride in doing. In his mind whenever the "R" word came up, it was an empty proposition because he had no idea how he could combine his talents with a retirement lifestyle. His self-esteem was based on his financial skills. Given that he had never considered Life Planning, he had no plan but to work full time. It was survival for him, all or nothing. He seemed to see his career as immortalizing his life, and so his career success became his life's value. As such, he was probably better off working to avoid dying of boredom at home. Nevertheless, he certainly needs to learn from his empty experience at home and to start to develop some hobbies or other interests and consider how he could continue his passion for investing with a more diversified retirement lifestyle. Life Planning also needs to be done so he can put his career into perspective.

Executive C is a former vice president of manufacturing in the pharmaceutical industry. He had been "retired" for over a year, even though he was in his early sixties, because of a plant shutdown. This was caused by the high cost of goods as the global company decided to move much of its manufacturing to lower-cost India. At the time of his departure, he had decided that he would retire given the fact that the industry in general had a lack of such jobs in the area. The company held a retirement lunch in the cafeteria for employees in his plant and an executive spousal dinner. About six months later, he called me in my role as a head of HR to see how everything was going and perhaps set up a lunch together. He talked in glowing terms about his retirement. "Life couldn't be better. We just finished a Caribbean cruise, but we are already planning on going on a golf junket with some friends." He wanted to know what was happening in the company and the industry, and asked me to keep my eye open if anything comes up that I think he could do. He declared surprisingly that title and salary level were not critical. In fact he said that at the time he retired, he didn't think of it, but given that most of the manufacturing management jobs are moving offshore, he said that he might be interested in taking on a foreign assignment or project. Being an empty-nester made this possible for his wife and him. Besides, he enjoyed travelling and he missed work. He said what he missed the most was the pressure of feeling overloaded with deadlines. Now he felt that without the pressure, the wind was out of his sails. In fact, without the external job pressure of the daily plant problems and meetings, he was not motivated. He felt it was a shame that his skills were being wasted. "I know there are always problems in manufacturing, and I know how to fix them. Please let them know I am available to help anytime or place."

Comments: This individual had no life plan, but he at least had some hobbies that he loved. He also had friends, a valuable asset for health in retirement. He said he missed the daily problem solving and pressure. Because I knew him, I interpreted this as missing his team, since he was very people oriented and loved to meet constantly. His idea of doing projects was a good one. However, if such projects did not come through, he needed to reframe his career aptitudes through Life Planning, which could allow him to use his talents working on complex volunteer projects since he had a good people leadership and logistic skills. This could give him the satisfaction and the esteem that he missed from work.

Executive D is a former CEO of a financial savings and loan. He was sixty-seven years old. He had repeatedly refused to hire an official successor and always seemed to find fault with any possible successor candidates, leading them to quit. He had said several times when the issue came up, "This is not the right time to retire. We need to fix the computer system." If it wasn't this reason, it was something else, like, "I'll do it later," "I have no time to retire," "I have my eye open for the right person to succeed me." He finally agreed that he should hire a successor but repeatedly stated that he couldn't find anyone suitable. Most viable successors were not interested, given that he was a one-man show and quite autocratic. He survived doing this for years because he was an excellent business executive in very lean conditions and always grew the business. He saw himself as the best CEO in the industry. However, he worked too hard—about seventy hours per week—with limited staff support. The board was concerned that at his age and work situation that he would have a heart attack and that they needed to hire more senior support. The board finally solved the succession problem by merging with a larger financial institution. The CEO was quite unhappy with this as he did not get the new CEO role of the merged companies. He felt that the other CEO was a lightweight who ran a fat shop with excessive layers of management. He decided to fix it all by running for the merged board but unfortunately lost his bid. He had no hobbies or interests other than business. He eventually found an arrangement of working for equity and no cash as an advisor to small start-up companies. He ended up on the board of a small start-up company trying to export services to China. Unfortunately, given his hands-on style, he became the acting CEO and ran into conflict with the owner. He eventually left the board role after the owner hired another CEO. In his midseventies, Executive D moved out East to be with his family; he now devotes his time to managing his retirement portfolio and, yes, looking for the perfect business he could start up, which he could run and make a big profit. Although he is very well-off financially, he still has an ultimate dream of making his fortune.

Comments: This individual had never stopped to "smell the roses." As a financial executive, he was a workaholic, motivated by money to such an extent that he seemed to equate his life value with his net worth. He never even spent much of it. Whenever I talked to him after he retired, he was always working on a new business idea. It was admirable that he acted on his passion for small business in retirement. However, it always seemed unfortunate that he was not able to expand his horizons in retirement. Stepping back and doing some Life Planning might have helped him identify some of the emotional issues in his life that led him to be such a workaholic. He may have enriched his life through using his business talents to help others and seeing his life more qualitatively and not just quantitatively: there is more to life than "how much."

Fear as Resistance

The fear of retirement is embedded within the executive's internalized corporate being, which is needed to protect the corporation's need to survive and perpetuate itself. As corporate beings, we avoid the most critical part of planning for retirement because we feel comfortable and secure. A corporate being naturally resists giving up itself. Unconsciously, we recognize that giving up our corporate roles and identities will be a painful loss, requiring us to rebuild ourselves. Fear of retirement is built into our corporate beings as a psychological resistance to giving up the corporate roles we have worked so hard to attain and have become.

We are conditioned to look at retirement through the eyes of our corporate being and our belief in the corporate myths of retirement. This is reinforced by media ads depicting the perfect retirement full of leisure and consumption. Because earning money is the goal of the corporate being, so saving money is the principal preparation for retirement. This is why retirement planning is essentially financial planning in most executives' minds, denying the need to change. The idyllic vision of retirement is usually based on the joyful escape from the stresses of a heavy workload, like lying on a beach with a margarita or golfing by the ocean. The bigger the dream, the bigger the nest egg required to fund the so-called ideal but illusive retirement, which keeps the executive on the treadmill longer in order to save more. The retirement trap of the corporate being is that one can never seem to have enough money saved to live the perfect retirement lifestyle and so the executive must keep working to save. Having become accustomed as an executive corporate being to the best hotels, restaurants, vacation spots where corporate meetings were held, all paid for by the company, the bar has grown beyond the long-term affordability of most executives to sustain in retirement. In other words, the more money anyone has, the better the retirement one is "guaranteed." Because real Life Planning is resisted, it all boils down to, when can I afford to live my idyllic vision? This represents the retirement trap of failing to undergo serious Life Planning and lifestyle preparation before determining the financial requirements to fund that personal plan. *Fear of retirement is fear of facing the personal changes required by giving up our beloved corporate being.*

Hierarchy of Needs

Maslow's well-recognized Hierarchy of Needs is a useful framework to help explain the corporate barriers to executive change, self-development, awareness building, and intellectual and spiritual growth. I plan to refer to this hierarchy for communication reasons. This is not intended to be a formal academic interpretation of Maslow but rather an informal reference in the context of executive retirement. We start fulfilling our lower level biological and physical needs and then move to ensuring our safety needs are met, followed by the need to satisfy our social or belonging needs at the level of the collective family, social, and work groups. If these are met, we can satisfy our esteem needs for achievement and status. Finally, we can fulfill our unique potential and meaning through self-actualization. In general, you can only move to satisfying higher needs upon meeting needs at the lower levels. However, these categories are neither insular nor are they mutually exclusive. For example, although we first experience love as belonging in the collectives of the family, social memberships, and workplace, behind healthy self-esteem at the next level is self-love or self-respect, which is necessary for the individual to be motivated to give love and value back to others, in self-actualization.

The lower-level needs of physical and economic survival and safety are well met by the corporate being. We also meet our social, belonging, and early-stage love needs and esteem needs as we flourish as leaders and receive significant rewards, making us recognized as successful. However, needs such as love are incompletely met by the sycophant's glowing recognition of the corporate being. We cannot reach the highest level of need satisfaction as corporate beings. The highest need for self-actualization deals with our uniquely personal need to express our total being creatively, artistically, or intellectually, and to become spiritually connected to the world and beyond, giving personal significance to our life. Human beings have the intrinsic need to know how their lives made a difference or created value for others. This is a different order of value than the corporate being making greater profit. *We cannot reach this highest level of self-actualization as corporate beings.* The corporate being is a collective being with norms and controls set up to meet commercial organizational needs. The corporate being as a collectively designed process, structure, and culture gives us a slot or job, but this is an arbitrary design for organizational interdependence and fails to be a foundation for personal meaning and fulfillment. The individual must mentally break away from the corporate tribe to attain his or her own personal foundation for meaning and values.

Freedom and Meaning

The ultimate proof and testament of our freedom is our ability *to choose who we are*, what we will re-make of what our parents, the corporate being, and others made us become, who we will ultimately be, and who we choose to be ultimately accountable to—our boss, our self, our highest values, or the Almighty.

Corporate leaders fail to attain self-actualization as long as they are psychologically corporate beings. Corporate beings can only help us attain the lower-level needs, our economic needs, our social needs for recognition, and our esteem needs through the achievement of the exercise of power and authority. As long as we are executive leaders, we are walking the corporate talk of the collectivist culture of the corporation. Love needs satisfied by the adulation of the sycophant are still lower-level needs compared to the authentic love through self-actualization. Even jobs that are seen to be creative—advertising, PR, and communications—do not satisfy the personal need for the freedom to define ourselves creatively, because they all operate within the client or customer paradigm of the corporate being brand. Otherwise, the work will be seen as out of touch and fail to reflect the corporate flavor and character. The collective culture of the corporate being is one of constraints, including past history, shareholders, stakeholders, other executives, employees, union agreements, society as a regulatory body, and competitive pressures. Such a complex array of contradictory forces requires compromises, continual adjustments, and ongoing changes. The executive as a corporate being can only be a steward and servant to the process without having control over the company because each executive is essentially interdependent on each other part of the company. True originality and freedom of the individual are impossible in the complexity and groupthink required by the corporate conformity. The culture and rules require collective adherence to execute a complex strategy. Each other department depends on each executive to adhere to the plan. However, plans make huge assumptions of the economy and market which require ongoing changes. Collective action is vital to deliver the corporate results. Individualists are deviant mavericks who slow things up and usually put a "stick in the spokes of the collectivity."

Given the changes within any dynamic corporate system, the executive has limited span of authority and control over the ultimate outcome and can only offer limited influence along the way. This lack of control is why so many talented executives leave larger corporations for smaller ones or even to start their own entrepreneurial enterprises. They choose to take more control over their corporate being and merge it more with their own values and define themselves freely. Many entrepreneurs find meaning outside of the security of the corporate being by creating a more personal corporate being that better fits their own values and style even if it involves living on the edge of greater risk. Stepping into a personally defined entrepreneurial role reduces the personal dependency on the collectivity and complexity but increases the risk. This declaration of independence of the entrepreneur better helps prepare for executive retirement because there is no collectivity in retirement, only the individual choices. This loss of the collective comfort is scary, as freedom is a huge responsibility.

Personally, this dilemma always led me to escape the corporate claustrophobic boredom and straightjacket of the corporate being's job box for the fresh-air freedom of my own consulting practice. Although I was attracted to such roles given the challenges of leading and developing change and growth, inevitably the collective inertia of a growing company and narrowing and more specialized job description would lead to stagnation and boredom. Those two companies where I stayed the longest was due to the fact that their talented CEOs empowered me to feel that I was running my own business.

Collective Cultures and the Corporate Cult

I surmise that this gap between the collective culture of the corporate being and the individual's need for freedom and original thinking is one of the reasons that job satisfaction is shockingly low. The Conference Board Job Satisfaction Survey (2007) found less than 50 percent of Americans are satisfied with their jobs, which was down from 61 percent twenty years ago. Even older employees, ages fifty-five to sixty-four and those older than sixty-five did not do much better. Those in higher income brackets starting at $50,000 and up were only 52 percent satisfied. Less than 36 percent of employees expressed contentment with their workload, work-life balance, communication channels, and potential for growth. The corporate being fails to deliver its promise to the individual when many start to realize that there must be something better.

The collective nature of organizational cultures train employees and rewards them to conform to the processes. The employees must align their behaviors to the values and methods of the corporation to be rewarded. Management is responsible for this socialization, training, and aligning process to instill in employees the values of that company, to continually create and implement the corporate being for any company. Ken Blanchard and Michael O'Connor (1997) lay out the ideal corporate game plan goals that socialize and help condition executives as corporate beings.

- Clarifying mission and values
- Communicating to all employees
- Aligning values with daily practices
- Working on individuals, teams, and organizational sub-practices to conform their behavior to those values

Corporate beings are basically the same in most companies but have different flavors to suit the style differences of the owners and management team. If you read the mission statements and value statements of many companies, they have a remarkably generic quality about them. The bottom line of the corporation is the same: to grow profit and shareholder value through meeting and exceeding customer needs. In this way, we need to understand that the mission and values are simply the language of the philosophy of the corporate being or spirit. Even though corporations want to differentiate themselves, they all speak the same language with different flavors. Corporate beings are basically clones of each other. The corporate language forms the linguistic structure and socio-anthropological rules of the collective culture. As the individual becomes socialized into the culture by learning and speaking the language, there is an important tribal differentiation from the competition. This differentiation is usually based on why their competitors for a number of reasons are inferior, undeserving, barely ethical, etc. Even if the competitor is larger and has been more successful, it helps create a tribal differentiation for why "we" will fight the competitors and win. This also helps to create identification with the "superior" corporate tribe as a cultural barrier to prevent defection to the competition. Such indoctrination also subdues the employees from thinking that they could ever do better outside the company on their own. As such it also works as a barrier for the individual to freely differentiate himself or herself from that corporate culture.

Communicating and instilling conformity must be done in an inspirational manner. The new individual employee experiences the joy of belonging from the compliance that leads to personal career success and reward gratification. Belonging to a winning team is an important social and esteem need for any employee. Success means ongoing security and economic rewards. Belonging to something great is an exhilarating experience, which can even transform the average corporate culture into being a cult with its own unique flavor: Google, Apple, or Southwest Airlines are only some examples. The cult requires an even higher level of devotion to the company values. The old IBM had a stereotype corporate being. Only clean-shaven men or polished women with white shirts, blue suits, and ties fit in. The "super-clean" tribe members were informally promised lifelong employment to compete with the Japanese. This was considered *the place to be,* but belonging required a psychological price of rigid tribal uniformity. The high levels of devotion and conformity needed to attain the monolithic image of the corporate stereotype were thought to lead to great personal success and esteem. The standardization of the IBM corporate cult certainly would not allow executives to freely choose their styles or be different through self-actualization. Not surprising, the institutionalization and rigidification of such an elitist culture helped blind IBM executives to the external forces of competitive change that forced a later cultural revolution to save the company.

Nevertheless the more the needs fulfilled in a corporation, the greater the dependency the executive develops on that corporate culture. Paradoxically, without facing one's need for self-actualization to develop individual differentiation, the executive more and more relies on the corporate culture to do this, which it cannot. The result on the executive is the onset of boredom. The executive has difficulty understanding this mental malaise because it is the unconsciousness trying to send signals to the conscious: "I am different!" "I could do better!" "My job is not really me, it's only my skills!" These reminders of private and personal growth needs of the individual represent the classic plateauing of the executive career and the eventual crisis represented by a career change or retirement.

However, the individual often does not know what the issue is, let alone what to do about it. The corporate being that the executive has embraced is very difficult to reject or move beyond for fear of lowering one's performance, losing out of the next promotion or salary increase, or losing of one's job without a clear plan to replace it. The corporate being holds the executive in the rut through habit, comfort, and fear of change.

Corporate Being and Personal Despair

The executive's success has been based on fulfilling the corporate needs, instilling corporate values, creating shareholder value, increasing net earnings, and growing dividends, among others. This is done by expanding sales and by increasing the consumption of products and services. This corporate purpose driving growth is a "grow or die" competitive mentality. The underlying assumption of the corporation is the more customer consumption of our products and services the better. The raison d'être of the corporate being is to create and grow more and more consumption or use of its services to grow that company into an industrial powerhouse. The underlying value that the individual executive adopts as a corporate being is a belief in consumerism: "I must have this product." "I am a better person if I consume this product or service." This is easily extended into "I am a better person the more I consume." The corporate being in essence is an empty shell which looks good but has no soul. The corporate being is bankrupt emotionally and spiritually at the human level as a substitute for the personal meaning of self-actualization. If we allow our lives to be reduced to the superficiality of consumerism, we take on the emptiness of the corporate being, whose ultimate goal is to produce maximum profits through burgeoning sales. This is not to suggest that there is anything wrong with the corporate being doing its important job of creating and growing profits. The corporate being is not a person and is just unfolding itself as a set of cultural and administrative rules and processes. What I am suggesting is that this is our own fault. If we let this culture of consumption replace our own individuality, it will later become a barrier to tap into intrinsic needs to actualize ourselves. By being compliant to the conforming culture of the corporation and its advertising, we not only bankrupt our savings accounts but fail to actualize the promise of the ads.

Allowing ourselves to become a corporate being ultimately leads to despair, for it implies that the meaning of life is consumerism. "The more I consume, the better person I am"; "The better the model I buy, the better person I am." These are advertising messages that sell. Step back and watch ads from an objective perspective, and analyze each ad you see by asking yourself, what need does this appeal to? Would having this really satisfy this need in my case? These ads work because they are driven by the greed to fast -track to attain instant dignity and respect. *Satisfying ego needs is the ultimate goal of the corporate being but fails to go beyond this level and is a trap preventing the satisfaction of our highest needs.* Since the more we consume, the better our lives are, the corporate being and its hubris hates to see another person consuming more. Fear of being a lesser person than one's neighbor or colleague helps to cement the executive to the corporate job. Envy is the cousin of greed. The fear of not having enough is central to the fear of retirement, keeping us within the corporate world. We must keep working so we can afford higher levels of consumerism to assure our "dignity and value" in the eyes of others. This despair, wallowing in fear, is symptomatic of having not overcome the corporate being through self-actualization. We get locked into the self-defeating, vicious circle of consumption to prove our worth, but this paradoxically reinforces the fear of retirement: we cannot afford to retire with the cycle of personal debt and the lack of retirement savings.

The best example of the corporate being taking over an executive's life is *Citizen Kane*, the 1941 classic film. This hyperbole of executive hubris is a parody of media tycoon William Randolph Hearst, showing the limits of power and money, which fail him in being elected governor and making his second wife, Susan, an opera star. Most tragically, power and money fail to buy and win the respect and love of those in his life. Kane became a hollow tragic figure, living in his mansion while vainly and desperately trying to find happiness through material possessions and conspicuous consumption. In the end, he dies in despair and fails to reach the moral stature of the inspiring moral character of the American Dream.

The sooner the individual manager or executive becomes aware of this need for self-actualization or authenticity, the earlier he or she can embark on the voyage of self-discovery and growth. However, as the hierarchy of needs is indeed a hierarchy, this is unlikely until the lower-level needs are satisfied. However, the retirement trap of the corporate being is that the socio-psychological industrial complex is so compelling. It will not let the individual go freely, given the endless conditioning and ego rewards of consumerism. The executive corporate being gyrates between greed and fear. The executive comes to believe that there will never be enough money or consumer potential to keep up with the neighbors or to sustain the image of success provided by corporate rewards. Paradoxically, this high level of consumption locks the executive into dependency on the lower-level needs for financial security. This dependency on ego consumption creates unsatisfied security needs and holds back the individual from fulfilling higher needs for self-actualization based on freedom, or in this case financial freedom. Once the executive has defined his or her image by the high level of consumerism of the corporate being, the fear of losing that image by reducing the level of conspicuous consumption follows close behind. This is why the perceived need for retirement planning is allowed to be financial planning, driven by the fear of running out of money. The longer one stays in the corporation in a job one dislikes out of fear, the harder it will be to undergo the self-discovery of one's real talents and needs, which could lead to an entrepreneurial role based on what one loves to do. Doing what you love will be more satisfying than achieving the retirement myth of buying what you dream will create that ultimate fulfillment. It can also lead to your spiritual revival. The vital link beyond the corporate being and consumerism is to feel the pain and futility of the trap of getting no satisfaction emotionally and spiritually from consumerism. The pain of the limits of consumerism covered with debt leads one to look to finding healing, health, and happiness through a more spiritual path. Pain is the body's message to heal ourselves to be more complete holistically by using our own mind and spirit to express and allow our talent to shine. We will discuss ways of attaining our higher level needs in part 4.

The only escape is to begin to create a new vision for yourself outside the corporation before leaving it. The risk of this is the retirement trap where if you appear to be losing the zeal and interest in your job, you may be retired before you are prepared. Nevertheless, finding yourself outside of the corporate being can reap tremendous rewards. It can unleash the passion for a hobby, which can lead to finding a link to some entrepreneurial small business or artistic endeavor as a designer or musician.

Discovering oneself outside of the corporate being is necessary to avoid the ultimate retirement trap. The corporation has unlimited resources with its communication systems, budgets, social support, and others. The executive need only send an e-mail to marshal resources. Unfortunately, these support resources reporting to the executive are all gone after retirement. The executive cannot solve the issues of internal self-identity through the usual external resources, assignments, or meetings. After retirement, the collective problem-solving process is gone. Not only must the executive solve problems on his or her own, but solve the biggest one of all: who am I outside of my corporate role? Those executives who think they will never need to do this are likely so bonded to their corporate identities that they fail to realize that their corporate being will not retire with them. It will only be a memory and as dead as history. Filling the vacuum left by the corporate being can only be done by the executive as an individual. Although the collective corporate process may have appeared to solve all previous problems, including self-identity, having to deal with these issues alone is a shock and threat to the executive's identity as a leader. The reality is that the corporate being and its structure, way of life, rewards, social satisfactions, and daily pride will be gone the day you retire, and will never provide further value but a memory. Listening to your gold watch tick and remembering the good old days is a death sentence for the proactive corporate leader used to making things happen and collectively controlling outcomes.

Those executives who feel supremely satisfied on the job, given their high level of psychic, social, and material rewards, and think that this will continue forever are deluded through hubris. Even if you own the company, either the shareholders or family will eventually ask you to slow down or you will sell the company. Being an executive is only a temporary, learned role. It is not who you are. It is not your life. The company is only renting your behavior to conform to the requirements of customers and shareholders. As you internalize the corporation's values and behavioral norms, you become the corporate being. The shock of the retirement trap is this: you can't take the corporate being with you because it is dependent on you being in the corporation.

Fear of Change

Fear is the signal of the need to change. It is usually bound up with what we have avoided and resisted in our minds and pushed out of our thoughts into our subconscious. Deep down, we know the corporate adventure will eventually end, but what we will do resides as the "angst" that we will solve out later. The mental search for a quick-fix solution is the beginning to our search for our real self outside of our corporate being. If corporate life was our authentic being, then what would our retirement be? Recognizing that we need to invent and create a new life is the beginning of growth. Perhaps we have stayed in corporate life too long and should have found something more personally meaningful, but now all we can do is keep working as it is all we know.

As we become more aware of this personal need to find ourselves outside of our corporate being, we are beginning to see value outside of the corporate life. This glimmer of a new vision is the beginning of a new self-awareness of our potential as a noncorporate being. This often quickly mushrooms into the reality that we begin to feel better and better about ourselves, and given our new awareness, we begin to hate our corporate beings as well as our jobs.

So why don't we just change and get out of the rat race of workaholism and consumerism that keeps us in the corporate being we hate and holds us back from reaching our full potential in self-actualization? The answer is the vicious cycle created by the corporate being of consumerism, which helps us fulfill our ego or esteem needs but only superficially. The true fulfillment of our esteem needs would be to consume fewer things we don't really need and invest for financial independence. Only then can we move up to truly satisfying our esteem needs, because we know we can make the change out of the childlike dependency on the corporate being that is really not our real, authentic selves. Only if we can do this and truly develop self-esteem authentically, and not merely appear as if we have high self-esteem through consumerism, can we then move up and work on self-actualizing ourselves. This is what an active retirement is all about. Only by developing true self-esteem through earning our financial freedom from frivolous and unnecessary consumption will we be able to be financially free to authentically take on the emotional issues and ultimate challenge of self-actualization. Frivolous consumption keeps us trapped in the emotional slavery of the corporate being's earning power as we work in a job treadmill that fails our authentic needs to buy things that we do not need. Such objects can define ourselves superficially and clutter our lives through the toil of maintenance, cost of insurance, and loss of depreciation. The value of finding ourselves and our real values and desired lifestyle allows us to consume wisely around those things that fit the life and real values. Buying those things that fit our own authentic needs will be a lot less than buying all of the things to look good in the image of the ego of the corporate being. Financial freedom is freeing yourself of expenditures that do not fit your life plan but only the ego and image of the corporate being. This is why financial planning fails retirement without Life Planning. Your financial planner may arbitrarily tell you that you will be ready to retire when your retirement fund yields 80 percent of your preretirement cash flow. The reality is that this is like budgeting for an eight-day vacation based on last year's cost of a ten-day vacation before you decide where and for how long you want to go. Once you really know what will help you get what you want in retirement, you may need less money than you think, particularly if your life in retirement involves part-time work based on hobbies you love.

For the executive, change is constant. One could surmise that executives are change masters leading the corporate change process. This may be true but only inside the corporate role. However, being a change leader inside the corporation often requires little change personally. An orchestra conductor directing a change in tempo or the beginning of each new stanza only leads others. Personal change is a lot harder and of a different order of complexity. It is relatively easy to tell others they should change and why. We normally do not think we need to change. If it becomes obvious that we must change, we may experience being frozen with fear as we see the need outside of ourselves, not internally.

We also do not understand exactly how to change. We usually need direction, but as executives, we are the leaders. Fear of retirement is really the fear of losing our self-identity, our power base, our skills and competence that we have spent a lifetime developing. We are afraid of losing it all. Retirement is our first premonition of death: our job and our role are more easily replaceable than we think, and our corporate being dies. This is a difficult thought for most executives because they have been used to or addicted to control. Many executives fear retirement like death, but it is only the death of their mundane corporate being, which is not really their inner self.

The fact is that retirement is the death of the executive, but only of her or his corporate self or being. There is life beyond the end of the corporate existence, but the executive needs to find and create it.

The first step beyond fear is having the courage and imagination to visualize new, meaningful actions beyond the comfort zone of the corporation. Having been a socio-psychological product of the corporate life, the retiring executive needs a new, creative approach to think expansively to search for a new personal meaning. The pain of being in this vacuum helps to galvanize our belief in the need to change and can help propel the process to avoid the inevitable executive retirement trap.

It is important to become aware of yourself and to gain new insights about your situation well before planning to retire. The following questions can start this process:

- What life experiences do you cherish the most?
- What things are you willing to fight for and go to the wall for?
- What are your most important values outside the corporation?
- What activities are you the most enthusiastic about when you are not at work?
- What makes you unique?
- How does the real you differ from the corporate being? Why?

It is important to take these initial steps before you retire, while you are still on the job. This is just as important as saving for your retirement. Becoming psychologically prepared will help you better understand the activities and lifestyle, and where you want to do them, vital to you for your retirement. This will allow you to better understand your cash flow retirement needs. Instead of using a financial planning rule of thumb of saving to afford 75–80 percent of your last year's earnings, you will be able to gauge finances more decisively and precisely based on your new, productive, and meaningful lifestyle.

You also need to consider that in retirement, unlike on vacation, you will be able to cut back on expenses. If you will be an empty-nester, you may not need the big house, SUV, and new wardrobe. You need to downsize away from objects that encumber your new creative lifestyle.

As you continue to undergo the depersonalization process of your corporate being in favor of a personalization process of your own self as a unique human being, your commitment to the job may suffer. The greater the perceived gap between your corporate being and your emergent personal life vision, the sooner you may decide to retire from that job. However, retirement from your job does not necessarily mean playing golf or pursuing a hobby all day. It can just as well mean using your talents to go into your own business on a part-time or full-time basis, depending on your needs and enthusiasm.

The most important thing is to start doing personal Life Planning so you can escape the job plateauing, which becomes meaningless if you are hanging in there just for the money. If you need transitional money to start your new, more meaningful life, then there is nothing wrong with expressing your new awakening or divergence from the corporate being regardless of the consequences. Being openly honest is the first step in differentiating your real self from your past conformity to the corporate collectivity. The point is that time is too short to deny yourself and continue to repress your real self and needs. This unhealthy repression will come back to haunt you in the form of stress. Bottled-up stress can shorten your life! Better to face it sooner than later and stand up for real self—no one else will, no one else can! Part 4 will lead you through the greater detail of Life Planning.

A couple of final self-awareness questions:

- What do you want to retire from?
- What do you want to retire to?

Chapter 4: The Neurotic Executive

To be or not to be, that is the question.
—William Shakespeare

The Executive Soul

The soul of the executive does not and cannot reside within the corporate being. Why can't an individual human being make the corporate being his or her essence and live by its credo as life purpose? The corporate being is not a person. Executive life residing in the mode of a corporate being can be compelling and rewarding for the executive's ego given the power, recognition, and rewards that accompany a senior role. However, the corporate being is no more than internalized collective structures, values, and functions, personified and given life through the executive's behaviors, creating the end goals of the strategic mission. This is a commercial nexus between the collective and the individual. To be inspired and motivated in order to rise up to the executive ranks and receive its compelling rewards and power, you have to take these very seriously and believe them with a passion as if they were your own. The greater the commitment and the more strongly you internalize these collective values, mission, and role as your own, the more disconnected from your real self and the more likely the unconscious will be sending later messages of fear of retirement from corporate life. Obviously, it is always a matter of degree.

Many well-grounded executives have already developed a strong family, a strong conceptual psychological framework of objectivity, and an external identity outside of work, yet have still managed to perform well in the corporation. Yet even for this minority group, leadership requires more than a passive commitment. There is a psychological price to be paid for all executives. If they are to lead in the corporate culture, they must become to some degree a corporate being to be effective. In my role as HR executive vice president,

I followed up with many executives who had been involuntarily terminated. What stands out in my mind from these sessions is that nothing embitters executives more than the perceived betrayal of the company toward them. It is like divorce papers were thrown in their faces and their emotional well-being has been destroyed. The emotional bitterness that oozes from their pores is palpable. Although executive counseling is needed and available, it is often refused out of spite and pride. Clearly, the severance of the executive from the corporation is a destructive affront to the executive's corporate being which throws the individual into a personal crisis.

The corporate being is often an emotional relationship between the executive and the company. This emotional bond occurs because the executive becomes bound with the corporate culture and role, given the addiction to its rewards, power, and control. This bond is usually taken personally by the executive and referred to as a commitment. The typical post-termination sentiment of an executive after severance in my experience has been controlled anger. Common sentiments that reveal the broken personal bond are "I can't believe this after all I've done for this company"; "There's no appreciation for all I've done"; "This place has no heart. I thought it did, but this is a place filled with politics"; and "I'm going to sue the bastards."

Allowing oneself to become emotionally bound to a simple role is a trap: it vicariously fills real human needs of executives but in a seductively false manner. The bond simply cannot be reciprocal because the corporation and the role of the executive are not loving beings; rather, they are nonhuman entities and processes dressed up as jobs to take on human character. In fact, it is a key executive role to help personify as cheerleaders to bring the corporation to life, to motivate employees by inspiring them to embrace the company mission as living. Every company wants its customers to believe it is not just responsive and reliable, but that it cares about them in addition to providing products or services. Unfortunately, since the company is not a real person, it cannot really care about its executives, let alone the customers. Just ask a customer who has not paid or an executive who failed to make a profit.

In the simple analogy of a person in the lead role in a Broadway musical, we can clearly separate the actor as a person from the specific role played at that time. Executive corporate roles are no different except that they evolve and last for years. We allow them to take over and become our beings, our self-identities. The acting role has more of a script, but the corporate executive has a massive external structure of processes, a capital structure, cultural rules, values, and a mission, all of which create tight behavioral expectations. Once the person can no longer play that executive role, a replacement is immediately brought in because "the show must and will go on," with or without any specific executive. A commercial enterprise is a complex of jobs, orchestrated organizationally through process and structure. Such roles can be defined and learned as well as changed in order to continue operations so that the corporate mission and purpose can be met. The individual is not the corporate being or even the role he or she plays. The role is an external set of learned, mechanical behaviors, which can be modeled by the new talent. There are many trainees waiting in the wings in anticipation for the chance. The individual's being and freedom are essentially lost in or alienated by the complexity of roles orchestrated toward a greater economic end than any one individual could achieve in isolation. This alienation between the self and corporate role is essentially caused by the individual taking the role so personally that it becomes the self-identity in the absence of one developed authentically by that individual. The individual executive often believes that he or she is the role and cannot be replaced. Nevertheless, every executive gets replaced sooner or later—and surprise, surprise, the company rolls on and on, as companies are built to last beyond any executive.

In one role as the head of HR one day I was struggling and discussing the decision to leave the company with the CEO, he reminded me of the reality of leaving with the common metaphor for replacing someone: it takes about the same time to replace someone as it takes water to fill the space left by taking your finger out of a glass of water. You can look at this the way many executives do; fear of leaving is the same as the fear of being replaced. Paradoxically, this helped me finally decide to leave: if one can be replaced so readily, then it is all the more compelling to leave the slot and find a role less linked to a replaceable corporate role and more linked to one's personal, intrinsic meaning and passion. In essence if what was personally sacred to me was so easily replaceable then the real me was not needed. I sought after a role that was better aligned to my entrepreneurial passion, inner purpose, and talents which were not easily replaceable, where I could better integrate my inner and outer purpose. Nevertheless, many executives asked me, "How could you simply walk away from one of the best jobs in the industry?"

What about you as an executive talent? How easily is your role replaceable? Outside of the corporate organized roles and structures, your personal purpose and passion to accomplish a unique role are not replaceable! Your personal purpose and actions are sacred to you as an individual. Collectively your corporate being is merely a slot or job that can generically be filled easily. How can you better transform your role so it is branded around your personal talent, purpose, and mission?

The corporation is a well-oiled and organized machine. Any executive is easily replaced, even if at the time it does not seem possible. Many executives vainly try to overcontrol vital information and functions to defy their replacement without huge damage to the corporation; but this is short-lived particularly in today's computerization of all corporate data. The maze of structures, processes, and rules in a culture organize each executive in a job role. Here, the individual is limited bureaucratically and by organizational inertia as individual actions become collectivized through the mass interaction of procedures within the myriad of interventions and actions of others. Organized by a collective purpose, the corporate being provides a compelling surrogate purpose for an individual who has grown to love his or her job. Because many new hires into corporations are neophytes or apprentices, highly motivated to establish their careers given their hard work educating themselves, these recruits are easily imprinted by the corporate mission and role.

The reward of total commitment by the executive to the values and corporate mission is corporate and individual economic success, but the executive must pay a psychological price for living the collective culture. Personifying the corporate culture becomes the trap of hubris. Becoming a collective being desensitizes the individual from his or her own human being and full life potential. The price is one of becoming a neurotic executive.

The key symptom of neurosis is anxiety caused by the executive's ego repression. The real, authentic self and all of its freedoms and possibilities are pushed into the unconsciousness. This anxiety is very stressful but does not cause personal dysfunctionality. It is too seductive to lose oneself to power and control while being highly rewarded. Like heroin it feels too good to give up for personal reasons like one's personal meaning and mission that seem abstract and irrelevant at the time. The withdrawal fear of retiring is the unconscious sending the message of the need for the executive to change and prepare for retirement where one loses one's job. The unconscious is wiser and is telling the repressed executive to get a meaningful life. This executive denies through repression the self's personal freedom and potential to differentiate from the corporate role. Anger with oneself for denying this freedom is also repressed. The mechanism of denial and forgetting is repression, and a potential free self is pushed as deep as possible into the executive's unconscious so it seems not to be possible. This repression is the source of later anxiety. Like playing the lead role in a Broadway play, taking the role as the real self is self-deception. This leads to a false ego and repression of one's real self. One executive told me, "There's no way I ever want to retire. I love my job. I can't think of anything else I'd rather do. In fact I can't wait to come to work in the morning. I live to work." Another executive put it this way: "I'm totally committed to the company. I would retire if you could ever find someone as loyal as I am. I know you never will. If I ever left, things will go downhill. No one could ever figure out all the little things I do for the company. Don't worry. I'll always be there for the company."

How can repression happen to an otherwise bright and talented executive? The socialization process that leads to rewards is very compelling, particularly early in one's career when the need to succeed because of economic, social, and family pressure is huge. The career becomes the solution, but its side effect is the takeover of self-identity. Companies create unique tribal cultures to differentiate themselves from others as the better place to work. Enthusiasm, commitment, and passion for the company are rewarded as necessary traits to get promoted into leadership roles. This passion is possible because the company is able to give employees a sense of purpose and allows them to gain self-respect within the corporate culture. Consequently, as the career advances toward being an executive, the developing ego and self form their positive self-regard and identity by conforming to the corporate culture. This is continually reinforced and rewarded as the executive moves up the corporation's career ladder, emerging later as a role model for younger employees.

Tom Peters and Robert Waterman (1982) stated, "So strong is the need for meaning, in fact that most people will yield a fair latitude or freedom to institutions that give it to them. The excellent companies are marked by strong cultures, so strong that you either buy into their norms or get out. There's no halfway house for most people in excellent companies. One very able consumer marketing executive told us, 'You know, I deeply admire Proctor & Gamble. They are the best in the business. But I don't think I could ever work over there'" (p. 77). In other words certain company cultures that make meaning and purpose for so many of their employees repel others. Peters and Waterman go onto say, "For us, the most worrisome part of a strong culture is the ever present possibility of abuse. One of the needs filled by the strong excellent company cultures is the need most of us have for security. We will surrender a great deal to institutions that give us a sense of meaning and through it, a sense of security" (p. 78).

Most employees on their ascent are not fully aware of the psychological process they are undergoing, let alone the price that they may pay for embracing the corporate culture. As repression buries any disagreements or discomforts with the acculturation process of learning, any conflict is repressed so the individual can function as a team player, role model, and leader. This conflict is essentially between the individual's need for freedom and need to differentiate himself or herself by expressing differences with the company and those positions expressed by superiors representing the company. For example, this is seen clearly when conducting training programs for new employees and management. These individuals are amazingly more vocal in training programs or meetings when the superiors are not present. But many who want to challenge certain management practices or who want to openly disagree with certain policies become suddenly quiet, obedient, and visibly supportive once their superior management comes into the training room, or when they are later in the presence of senior management.

Fear also plays an important role in the executive repressing and losing touch with one's soul. Fear of job loss, loss of salary, or loss of status helps the executive repress his or her real self and assume the company persona. Initially, this is based on economics. There is a rising financial dependency that occurs with the rising costs of family life for the middle manager with mortgages, cars, clothes, and kids. This is consumerism at work insofar as the corporate being of the executive is driven into complete economic dependency through debt, new family needs, and consumerism. The rewards are rising but the vicious cycle of more consumption and more debt deepens the dependency, which then deepens the fear of job loss. Over the years, this dependency on the company evolves into the fear of retirement. This dependency process is not always recognized by the executive because it is repressed. There is an illusion of control as the neurotic executive has essentially forgone his or her freedom to satisfy security and economic needs. Even as the family expenses decline, the executive becomes more and more the consumer. The longer the executive is in this state, the more the executive's personal identity, values, and purpose will be based on the corporate culture. This becomes a personal barrier insofar as the executive increasingly becomes somewhat of a clone of the corporation. The executive, though, is rewarded for doing a good job fitting in, walking the talk, and getting promoted to higher responsibility, power, and authority. Such executives will retort: "So what's the problem? Is this not what everyone wants?"

This shows how important saving money is for the executive. The freedom to break away from the dependency on the corporate being to become oneself requires some degree of financial security. You can tell those executives who have thrown off their sycophantic shells, speak their minds in a fearless manner, and could care less if they get fired: they are financially independent to some degree and now will not deny their freedom to think and speak up regardless of the fallout. These executives have arrived. Having sacrificed consumption to reach this emotionally satisfying state of security is freedom to be oneself.

M. Scott Peck (1978) points out psychiatric problems are common soon after an individual has been promoted to a position of higher power and responsibility. The underlying driver of the neurosis is fear. In this case, it is fear of change, represented by the fear of handling new responsibility and power.

The fear of the executive's corporate being passes from fear of economic loss and security to fear of change of relationships as one assumes more and more power. This means one must personally become more assertive and show why one is more powerful. Former equals may ridicule this newly promoted executive as having "power gone to his or her head" and start to avoid contact with this person. This can become the next step in the formation of hubris as this newly promoted executive may reciprocate and try to demonstrate why he or she deserved to be at a superior level. The transformation of fear eventually shows itself as fear of retirement, which is a new form of fear of change. All of these fears are not experienced by the consciousness if there is a high level of repression and addiction to power, but rather shoot into the consciousness periodically as the unconscious signals a need to cope and adapt. Highly repressed executives will tend not to experience this fear until it is too late in retirement, when the corporate game is all over.

In essence the corporate being, and all of its rewards and success, will end at retirement. The executive has become the corporate culture, but the corporate culture and the role have not nor cannot become the executive. The corporate being will march on with no evidence of missing you, the retiring executive. The reality is that the corporation can only rent the executive's behavior for the years served. It's nothing personal, because corporate cultures are not people. When the executive is gone, the culture cannot miss the executive. Sadly, it is the executive who will miss the culture, like having one's heart ripped out, the more the executive has become the corporate being. Even more tragic is when the executive has internalized, through hubris, the materialism of the corporate being as the meaning of life. In this case, without having undergone the necessary process of self-differentiation from the corporate being, retirement will be empty.

What executive does not want to have it all? Many do, but having it all does not come from the depths of the corporate being, whose essence is the bottomless pit of consumerism. Having it all ultimately must mean understanding your authentic self and living it out in the limited time of retirement. Luckily, the Boomer generation more than any other have the economic foundation and education to be doing their own thing outside of the collective constraints of the corporation. Ultimately we need to ask, *how does my life make a difference to this world?* Making budget every year or overseeing successful product launches, just don't measure up to answering this question.

The Divided Executive Self as Neurotic

Our economic needs keep us in the tribe of collective conformity. Once we adopt the corporate being, it is hard to break free given the rewards and executive power addictions even though basic economic needs have been met. It seems difficult to believe that the executive cannot simply shed the internalized corporate being. The dilemma lies in the fact that such a phenomenon is unconsciously driven by the fear not just of economic need, but of loss of social status and self-identity.

What gets put in place is what psychiatrist R. D. Laing (1972) calls the "false-self system," which functions as personal conformity and compliance to corporate controls. Lang says, "One of the aspects of the compliance of the false-self that is more clear is the fear implied by this compliance. The fear in it is evident, for why else would anyone act, not according to his intentions, but according to another person's?" (p. 99). In other words, the corporate being represents our false self, which in fact is the executive neurosis. However, *only by understanding it we can overcome its power when we leave the company for retirement.* Only by bringing this phenomenon to the conscious mind can we begin to take control of the unconscious, fear-based corporate being. Only by becoming aware can we transcend this fear and prepare to move beyond our corporate identity for the sake of our own personal, authentic self-identity in retirement.

Overcoming this is not easy. It represents the struggle between the collectivity and the individual. Our Stone Age genes link us to the societal collectivity of our ancestors as we overcome our lower-level needs for survival in tribal cooperation. This is carried over into becoming our corporate being. Conformity to the corporate being is easier until we are forced into struggling to face the truth of individual thinking and self-differentiation and discovery in retirement. It is better to find our authentic individuality as soon as possible, well before retirement. Supporting Maslow's concept of our highest need being self-actualization, Carl Jung (1976) shows that human development eventually becomes the need for the individual's differentiation from the collectivity. The greatest danger is for the consciousness and the collectivity of the unconsciousness to become fused together with little hope of individual conscious differentiation. The collective exerts its force as it relieves man of its responsibility of personal freedom and differentiation. "Any large company composed of wholly admirable persons has the morality and intelligence of an unwieldy, stupid, and violent animal. The bigger the organization, the more unavoidable is its immorality and blind stupidity. Society, by automatically stressing all the collective qualities in its individual representatives, puts a premium on mediocrity, in everything that settles down to vegetate in an easy, irresponsible way. Individuality will inevitably be driven to the wall." Ultimately Jung says that "without freedom there can be no morality" (p. 101). The individual has far greater potential to be a person who can offer valuable work and achievement to society than can be ever represented by any job description.

The other controlling influence of the corporate being that is deeply rooted in our unconscious is not just our security and economic needs but our collective, primitive needs for tribalism. This social need identified in Maslow's Hierarchy of Needs is connected to our historical need for survival through the cooperation and hierarchy of the tribe, not just for food and shelter but for fending off other tribes in war and competition. The need for membership as part of our deepest needs for personal identity is fulfilled to a large extent through corporate identification, as evidenced by business cards with titles and golf shirts with logos used to announce membership. This control goes beyond just belonging. As a member, one has a set of rules for membership that, if not fulfilled, can lead one to be expelled, just like the Catholic Church excommunicates who do not follow its rules. As a consequence, the control of the corporate being unconsciously controls not just through the fulfillment of the ego satisfaction of being a member but also through the fear of expulsion or loss of membership. This fear can keep the executive in compliance long after his or her economic needs have been met and in fear of retirement.

The Neurotic Organization

Neurotic executives help create and perpetuate neurotic corporations. Not all organizations are neurotic. Jung (1976) suggests that the larger the company, the more powerful, bureaucratic, and authoritarian it is, the more it imposes its culture on the individual. Rigid institutionalization within a corporation does seem to cause its decline through a decline in individual creativity, internal challenge, and innovation. The more the corporate being controls the individual, the less innovation and creativity there will be within that corporation. Given the needs for renewal and regeneration, this creates corporate decline. General Motors used to be America's largest company, but in 2008, Harley as well as Mattel, the maker of toy cars, exceeded GM's market value (Berman 2008). When GM as well as Chrysler and Ford begged for a government bailout to save them from bankruptcy, it took Congress to dictate the rules for reducing their burden of bureaucratic legacy costs versus the newer Japanese lower cost producers. The corporate being of the heads of GM, Chrysler, and Ford failed to see the contradiction between arriving in Washington in their private jets and asking for a bailout. Everyone else could! The corporate beings of these company heads blinded by their corporate being failed to see that "the king had no clothes" because they had lost touch with reality through hubris. In fact in this case the "kings were actually beggars!" Judgments from corporate beings or culture lose touch through groupthink to drift into bankruptcy while blaming the economy.

Further, many of Peters and Waterman's (1982) excellent companies no longer exist or have lost their shine. Institutionalizing "excellence" is a contradiction, for it creates complacency. Such a culture is a corporate being that reinforces the executive hubris of "why change? We are the best!" This creates a lethargy and vulnerability to the smaller, more entrepreneurial upstarts. Too much time is spent looking within at how great we are and not enough looking outside at the competition. Gaining compliance, loyalty, and behavioral consistency within a corporate culture hardens the arteries, prevents cleaning out the "plaque" and maintaining a competitive edge through renewal based on individual challenge, creativity, and innovation. The neurotic organization is this institutionalization that demands individual sacrifice to the corporate collectivity. The corporate being of institutionalized excellence infects executives with hubris. This is neurotic because it is not only unrealistic and false, but it is the very kernel of that organization's demise. Being labeled as "excellent companies" was a death sentence for many.

Manfried F. R. Kets de Vries and Danny Miller (1984) describe how a culture of collective conformity is unhealthy not just for the executive but for the corporation. Healthy corporations need healthy individuals. The culture of collective conformity erodes the individual's effectiveness and enthusiasm for change and improvement. The inertia resulting from the culture of collective conformism also creates an unhealthy organizational climate for all employees with such an executive role model. The hubris of past executives and their success is institutionalized. New leaders are constrained by history and are crippled by the bureaucratization process of the corporate being. This leaves the great corporate legends vulnerable to competitive upstarts which thrive on change, creativity, and innovation. They create not only new discoveries and paradigm shifts but high priority ongoing continuous quality improvements before and after new products hit the market.

Thomas J. Watson Jr., who built IBM into a computer behemoth, built a culture that worked for a while. He chose certain rigid characteristics for excellence, like the blue suit that led the company nickname "Big Blue." This culture had to be completely unraveled later by Louis Gerstner to save the company. At the time IBM appeared to have a culture of unprecedented excellence, a bastion of stability and permanence. Yet one could argue that the IBM blue corporate being was actually built on insecurity and fear of failure. Tom Watson created and projected this IBM professional image. Yet according to John Greenwald (1998), Watson was tortured with self-doubt and depression. He cried when his father wanted him to join IBM. Tom had been a failing student, and it took three schools and six years for him to get through high school; according to Greenwald, he graduated from Brown University only due to a sympathetic dean. Tom Watson built the Big Blue rigid culture partly to ward off his own insecurities and fears of failure. There was nothing sacrosanct about this IBM culture, even though it became the most revered in its day. Without the culture of renewal, a company declines.

The point is there is nothing sacred about any corporate culture. It is only the creative freedom of the individuals who had the ingenuity to create such cultures that is sacrosanct as the basis for all organizations, but such structures need to be constantly renewed by ongoing improvements which adapt to environmental changes. It is the institutionalization process of the corporate being and its hubris which destroys such freedom and creativity for its successors. Corporations allow themselves to become rigid and their executives to become narcissistic by exalting the superiority of the past methods and their reputations like saints. You can see their pictures hanging in the halls and boardroom reminding new employees of their superior wisdom. Don't mess with the established principles of past success. New employees are encouraged to become fully annexed to the corporate identity through training and socialization. You are lucky to be here! This neurotic corporate being freezes creativity and initiative of new minds that have the potential for better.

This paradox of excellence is that the institutionalization of the past kills the future. "We have finally invented the very best buggy whip, with a resin based with a firmer whipping action which will drive your horse faster!" The unrealistic nature of institutionalizing this premise is essentially neurotic. The victims are the company as well as the executives, who learn to believe it and fall into the cement shoes of hubris. These companies lose their roots of the individual entrepreneurs who built the company on innovation, drive, and conviction. The collective hubris of mature cultures in large corporations causes individuals to lose their entrepreneurial drive in the rigid culture that rewards conformity to its norms of administering the past. This neurosis of the corporate being causes not only organizational but individual executive decline while exalting in their superiority.

Boredom: the Neurotic Malaise

The price the executive pays for corporate security is boredom. The same price is paid by the executive who does not challenge himself or herself to reinvent the business and remain competitive. Boredom is the inevitable result of a talented executive becoming noncreative, having to administer the past into the future. Career boredom is the reality of actualizing oneself in a corporate bureaucracy with a role that has a power base complete with boundaries, repetitious ritual tasks, and prescribed behaviors. The consciousness operates within the defined role in the corporate culture through the use of the professionally learned techniques of one's area of specialty. The only operational structure is defined through the corporate expectations and demands. The individual as a free expression of a creative self through feeling and inspiration of personal possibilities in life and career is repressed in order to attain and maintain the ego satisfaction of temporary corporate superiority.

Occasional mental flashes of career excitement felt by an individual executive who imagines leaving the corporate role for a new, entrepreneurial start-up soon become crushed by the fear of failure. This repression of freedom and an array of creative possibilities come and go in many executives' imaginations. Many executives have fantasized how to start up a new company and do things differently and better. However, these thoughts are dismissed by the security rewards of another pay increase, continual social recognition, and the increasing sense of normality of the corporation. I have often heard executives dream out loud about a start-up. However, it usually takes the form of *"we* could do that," not *"I* could do that." Such executives want, need, and assume support. I have also been approached by an IT-area executive proposing to outsource the function under his leadership, but nothing ever happened as he seemed to need encouragement, as if the company would set it up for him. The executive's self-talk may have been something like this: "I'd have to be crazy to leave such a job that many other of my colleagues envy. I've worked too hard to give this up. I know how to radically improve this operation, but I am too comfortable to champion the outsourcing as it will reduce my department, et cetera." The fact that I'm bored is only a sign of how great I am and that I'm due for yet another promotion!" Nevertheless, the repression of freedom permanently prevents the executive from overcoming the neurotic malaise of the collective role and life being played. The more successful the executive becomes inside of the neurotic corporation, the greater the buildup of the existential, daily boredom based on past nondisruptive routines, which are difficult to be reinvented even by the busy executive who is no longer working for security. The dependency on the corporation created through this arrangement is incongruous with the sense of the daily exercise of significant power. The powerful executive has grown beyond his or her needs for security and becomes bored with his or her own least resistance continued security-based behavior. Mentally tethered by their corporate being, executives dismiss their own creative ideas for operational cost savings and improvement as they ask: "why bother disrupting the operations and causing conflict? I will remain comfortable."

Ultimately, the executive becomes bored even with this power insofar as it seems more and more meaningless given the lack of challenge and personal engagement. Exercising power becomes trite because it resides not in the individual as personal power but is simply borrowed temporarily from the corporation. The executive's behavior is simply rented by the corporation to play a particular role. Real, authentic power of a leader is based on freedom, a personal creative vision, and meaning; however, the exercise of surrogate power for a neurotic executive becomes shallow, capricious, and meaningless. As it does not reflect the individual executive own values, the exercise of power is like following the corporate script of the corporate being. The boredom of exercising power emerges gradually, as the early exhilaration of being newly promoted cannot be sustained any more than the thrill of the next salary increases can sustain motivation for long. Gradually the schism of the surrogate power of the corporate being becomes a negative force alienating the executive from one's authentic self and possibility of personal power. The lucky ones feel this alienation and act on it. Those repressed executives who have totally become their corporate being are in for the retirement shock!

The weakness of power as a false motivator or addiction for the repressed executive comes through the executive's own growth and recognition that with power comes new responsibility for the duties of the role and more money. However, the duties or new responsibility does not come from the meaning of the executive's life but only from the corporate bureaucratic role definition of the executive's accountabilities. As a consequence, the executive will play the role primarily from conscious, technical skills and not from the heart. In essence, executing duties that one is contracted to do by the corporation produces boredom with enough repetition. The deep sense of responsibility is reduced to administrative definitions. The power that accompanies responsibility is idle and is exercised more symbolically than with personal purpose and passion even though there may be temporary demonstration of enthusiasm as the sycophant pays homage to the corporate culture as the essence of life. This boredom mainly affects those who have begun to see beyond their addiction to power, for they see power is empty from the point of view of their higher-level needs requiring personal growth, meaning, and the yearn for spirituality. The executive is bored with the role that can only meet his or her security, belonging, social, and esteem needs. Boredom is the unconscious message of the need to grow into one's higher-level needs.

The exercise of power in the neurotic organization is accompanied by an illusion of control. The corporation is really in control of the executive. The neurotic executive represses or hides this deep dependency on the corporation and can become addicted to power. The neurotic executive's conscious need to exercise power covers up the addiction and need to grow. The underlying, addictive, childlike dependency drives the executive to feel superficially gratified by the mastery and execution of power. Unfortunately, instead of fulfilling the executive's need for mastery and personal independence, it simply manifests itself as hubris. The more the executive has become aware of his or her higher needs, the more power is experienced as empty. The only real mastery comes with personal mastery of the self. This is only possible through awareness building by the individual as the repression is overcome, and the individual becomes truly independent and can creatively think independently outside of the corporate being.

Comfort and Boredom

The advanced executive will remain at the security, social, and self-esteem level of needs and is stuck there because these are the only needs that can be met playing a role as a corporate being and escape requires risking satisfying these needs. However, once the executive is reasonably economically secure and has the economic ability to address personal growth issues, there is no excuse to not move up the Hierarchy of Needs toward self-actualization. At this point, the executive has attained the emotional value and hopefully the satisfaction of having saved enough to overcome security fears and can afford to leave and do his or her own thing. However, many executives tend to avoid doing this because they fear change and are drawn to the comfort of the security of the role because they have no alternate life plan. Some end up saving even more for the future retirement as an end in itself. Without a life plan there will be never enough as you end up saving for the insatiable consumer needs of the ongoing retirement needs of one's corporate being. This forces the executive to stay in the well-paying job which can drive the executive deeper into boredom, as the main motivation becomes security and comfort. Not taking the risk of personal growth outside of the corporate being is based on the fear of failure and fear of change. What if I cannot find anything better? Setting new personal goals based on your own values as opposed to those set by the collectivity of the corporation risks losing your total focus on the job, and perhaps the job performance will slip. Feeling comfortable often leads to resistance to change, which leads to personal boredom on the job.

Unfortunately, this is the demise of many corporations. Too many executives are comfortable and resist change. This produces the hardening of the emotional arteries that is the seed of destruction for the company as well as for the individual executive. Comfort is a slow death. If the corporate culture seems dead and is not responding to the market forces of younger smaller companies, this is usually the root cause. Feeling comfortable is resting on the glory of past accomplishments and is also the root cause of the failure of the individual executive to grow and find new personal life beyond that of the corporate being. In retirement, this lethargy will lead to stress as comfort creates unbearable boredom. Comfort in retirement becomes the executive couch potato. Talent is wasted and reduced to a stressed-out vegetable. Becoming a spectator in retirement will lead to retiring from life, which emotionally and spiritually calls out to the retired executive to respond. However, having become a passive leader or a corporate being turning a deaf ear to one's calling results is a swelling of internal anxiety. This hyper-stress can lead to shortened life and retirement. The false self who failed to find real values and passions on the job as a corporate being will rot on the vine in retirement.

On the other hand, taking the risk of personal growth gives life to the executive. So much of an executive's talent and energy are not captured by the corporate being or job. And if they are not discovered by the executive in time for retirement, this leads to the stress of the boredom of retiring as a false self. One experienced financial executive once bragged and told me, "I am so much on autopilot I could do my job with my eyes shut. But you know, where else could I make this kind of dough?"

Ultimately, we must take risks to grow and to live. Finding our own purpose and passion based on our own experiences and talents is the foundation. The courage to be has no substitutes. We will never go beyond our economic need and reach our full potential without this personal courage to explore and to find ourselves outside of our contracted rental role as a corporate being. Nothing is more daunting than the challenging universe of discovering your own personal potential, but nothing is more satisfying than being successful on your own terms. Being successful as a corporate being will never allow you to go beyond becoming an economic being. Most executives have the means to be their own persons and to call their own shots, but have refused the freedom to do so out of a desire to remain in the comfort of the corporate security cocoon.

Dependency as Addiction

The neurotic organization is based on executive dependency on the corporation and its repression. This leads to addictive behaviors. Anne Wilson Schaef and Diane Fassel (1988) state that addiction is not just to a substance but can be to an organization as well. The organization "loves" workaholics and rewards them. Constant work can become the cultural norm for demonstrating one's loyalty. An executive's void of personal meaning is filled by the company. Again, the foundation of fear coming from the primitive hunter's survival need to fight the seemingly bottomless pit of scarcity helps make this dependency a lifetime arrangement. This primitive need can lead to an addiction. Addiction to a corporate being is similar to an addiction to a foreign object or substance, but in this case, it is to a foreign corporate being replacing one's self-identity. Schaef and Fassel define addiction as a dependency on something over which one has no control and we are fundamentally dishonest about (p. 57). For the neurotic executive, the loss of control is repressed and the dependency on the corporate being is covered up because this dependency is incongruent with the overt and conscious exercise of being a corporate leader with power. The addiction to power is the denial of the neurotic executive dependency on the corporate being. This is the false self of the neurosis and addiction. The tendency for this to cause executive hubris is high since the executive, through self-deception, denies the dependency on the corporate role and borrowed power, and sees it based on his or her own "superior" self.

A symptom of this addiction is the Boomer-created term *workaholism*. The executive may be at home or even on vacation with his or her family but has an irrepressible urge to pick up the laptop or Blackberry just to keep in touch and become renewed with the corporate "substance." This will actually momentarily lower the stress level of the executive workaholic who is at home or on vacation to "rest." Experiencing the stress of withdrawal from the corporate being is a clear and common sign of such a dependency and addiction to the corporate being. This neurotic executive has options but cannot be fully aware of them without surfacing the fear of withdrawal. Options include turning off one's laptop or Blackberry during family time or not taking them on vacation. Imagine that!

Just as for any addict, there is a shock of withdrawal from the object of the addiction. This will come when the executive retires. In retirement, the corporate being is gone, and the executive is left bereft of the meaning and purpose borrowed from the corporation. Because the corporate being is not a person and has no feelings, it can never prepare or help the executive with this loss. The corporate show must and will go on, even without the executive who is retiring!

Denial of Fear

The more the executive becomes the corporate being, the greater the hardening of the emotional arteries around power and money as the basis for social recognition and self-identity. As the collective power of the corporate being takes hold of the executive's identity, the more hubris forms in the consciousness, blocking the unconsciousness's warehouse of wisdom. As this is blocked, the fear is also blocked.

Fear is the unconscious message of danger. The unconscious is a friend trying to help prepare you for the danger ahead. We ignore it in order to pursue the more immediately rewarding conscious gratifications of the corporate being. Blocking the unconscious through repression prevents the self-preservation process of psychologically preparing for retirement. This preparation involves mentally abandoning our borrowed corporate being. When we are filled with the grandeur of corporate power, we view retirement as not real. Retirement is not something that seems to need personal Life Planning insofar as everything an executive ever faced on the job is readily solved with support systems. However, this is within the context of the corporate being. Retirement is then reduced to financial planning, which most executives think is within their control once their net assets reach a certain magic number.

In this way, the fear of retirement is blocked and repressed by hubris or corporate being. In its place we believe the supporting myths of retirement arising from the corporate being and culture. The corporate being is a cultural patriarchal system, protecting the collective economic interests of the corporation and its loyal employees. As Collins and Porras have identified (1994), the best corporations are built to last even though the most visionary leaders die. Maintaining a vibrant, consistent, and uniform culture based on a coherent vision is essential for the survival of the corporation, but not of the executive.

The executive is unbeknownst used temporarily but pampered with corporate rewards which create personal resistance and complacency from awakening to discover their own personal life mission or potential. This simply transfers such life issues in retirement.

In this way, the corporate being of the executive keeps the executive on course until the lights are turned out at the retirement party. The denial of fear coming from the corporate being prevents the executive from shedding the corporate being in preparation for the psychological needs of retirement. Hubris has no fear! However, what is repressed eventually must surface. Repressing the self is like locking vital personal secrets in your basement: they will eventually emerge since the basement foundation holds up the rest of your person. Losing an intimate connection with oneself is a sacrifice of one's own being for the rewards of the corporate being. Over the years, the personal sacrifice of one's personal freedom creates a neurosis that leaves the individual ill prepared for retirement and the shock of losing corporate being or self-identity. This repression of fear will eventually surface because the crutch of the corporate being, power, and control are not personally sustainable. This reality surfaces in retirement. It is a conscious shock of losing the executive cloak and personality of the corporate being.

The stress of undergoing this realization is much more traumatic for those executives who have psychologically adopted a corporate being as a pillar of their personality. The realization hits home that the power and control are lost along with the corporate self. This is why we call this *hyper-stress,* since the executive is the personal source of the problem. This contrasts with those executives who have chosen a more individualistic career path by their own free choice, even if it meant less money and power. This does not suggest that greater power and money equates with greater hubris. Many successful executives at the top are fully conscious, healthy, and well balanced. An inspirational example of such an executive is Thomas M. Chappell. While raising five kids with his wife, Tom was an active church leader, wrote books on business ethics and leadership, and started and ran his own business of natural personal care products, *Tom's of Maine* (www.tomsofmaine.com).

Such balanced executives often deal with the conflict between their own personal values and those of the corporate being through early retirement because their sense of self is well developed. Healthy executives are balanced in their lifestyles and tend to have strong, well-developed family roles or volunteer roles. Female executives are often better off in this regard. The balance and stress that they struggled to cope with in their careers becomes a huge advantage in the psychological preparation for retirement insofar as their self-identity is less affected by the hubris of the corporate being. I have yet to meet a female executive with kids who suffered from hubris. Also, the corporate cultures that attract women executives tend to be more balanced, allowing executives to have a life outside of the office. Nevertheless even women executives can have the fear of losing their identities in retirement, particularly if they have emulated their male colleagues. Many have foregone having kids or have had the extensive use of nannies to aggressively pursue their careers. In many cases women executives have embraced the corporate being as much as their male colleagues. Fear of retirement is more a function of the executive's lifestyle and corporate culture and has nothing to do with the gender of the executive.

Executive Questions

What should the executive who is securely working in a successful company do as early preparation for retirement? Here are some questions and actions to consider.

- Does your role and corporate success make you feel powerful and able to make things happen? Have you ever said about your job, "I love it!" Begin to differentiate yourself from the corporate being with the thought that you will leave all this behind in retirement.
- Does your role and company success lead you to ever say, "We are the best!" Corporate success breeds complacency and executive hubris. Separate yourself from the neurosis of hubris. The success of your corporation does not guarantee retirement success. In fact, it may be a barrier to retirement

success: you may have unrealistic expectations of continued success in retirement without undergoing personal change, as will be addressed in part 4.

- Are you feeling secure in your executive role but bored because you know you are capable of doing more and doing other things that you would find more interesting and challenging? How can you identify what these new activities would be?
- How would you define "retirement excellence" in your case? How can you start to change and make this happen?
- Do you simply assume that because you have been successful as an executive, retirement will be easy? Have you ever said to yourself, "I am excellent at my job!" This may be true, but it is unrealistic to think you will transfer this feeling into retirement. Remember how past corporate successes lead to a company and a personal belief in excellence based on the corporate collectivity. Also remember that such a belief can lead to a personal decline unless you have a change strategy outside of the corporate collectivity.
- Do you assume that the corporate excitement of success will be there in retirement simply because it is you? In your retirement, it will be harder to achieve the same feeling of success because you will lose the huge support of collective corporate being and all of its psychic rewards. You will need to change and develop a personal plan to have a successful retirement and to create new rewards and excitement.

This book will help you address these issues through gaining a new awareness by Life Planning as discussed in part 4.

Part Three: Executive Health

Men ought to know that from nothing else but the brain comes joys, delights, laughter and sports, and sorrows, griefs, despondency and lamentations.... And by the same organ we become mad and delirious, and fears and terrors assail us, some by night, and some by day, and dreams and untimely wanderings, and cares that are not suitable, and ignorance of present circumstances, desuetude, and unskilfulness.
—Hippocrates

Chapter 5: Sickness and Death: The Short Retirement

Except for an occasional heart attack I feel as young as I ever did.
—Robert Benchley

Overachievement

Successful executives got there through competitiveness, hard work, and continuous achievement. Rising up the corporate hierarchy to the top of your specialty with a company requires visibly supporting the corporate culture through dedication and commitment to the social mores. In other words, you will not get to the executive ranks without adherence to the values of the corporate being. These values often include being a workaholic. Working thirty-five to forty hours a week will not allow for career success in most North American corporate cultures. You will be perceived, rightly or wrongly, as not committed to the company cause. Even if you only do thirty-five to forty hours a week of actual work, you need to appear to work as much time as your boss does to get ahead. This expectation tends to attract overachievers to the executive ranks because, in general, they have been able to differentiate themselves competitively by burning more "midnight oil" than their equally skilled peers. Workaholics tend to received more promotions. Overachievers are often highly driven to succeed. Once the feeling of achievement is experienced and rewarded, there is a sense that even harder work will even be more and more rewarding. However, harder work leading to greater rewards will be affected by the law of diminishing returns. Personal sacrifices in other personal areas of your life will fail to make up for a little more corporate recognition.

The issue here is that the achiever can soon become addicted to harder and harder work in order to attain personal value. Work is not just a job for the overachiever, but it becomes life itself, and the proof of personal value if not superiority. The executive's inner values become driven by the trappings of the extrinsic rewards for the achievement. The executive becomes part of the neurotic organization by trying to live the corporate being as his or her internal self. Neurotically or erroneously, the executive equates external value and achieving personal success in ways espoused by a neurotic society—power, status, and money—with internal value. In this dissonant state, the executive can feel great while enjoying the rewards but also be cut off from the unconscious messages of stress and alienation. This association of overachievement with personal success transforms stress into the thrill of making a difference and meeting deadlines. The adrenaline of long hours and the thrill of contributing effectively sugarcoat the poison of stress! Such an association with the rewards of the corporate being is more than simple overachievement. Workaholism represents an underlying lack of well-being, which can lead to death well before retirement.

In Japan long hours of work are common. So is the phenomenon of sudden death for such workers. The term for death from overwork is *karoshi*, a term dating from the 1980s, when several high-level executives suddenly died without any history of illness. In 1990 it was estimated that 10,000 Japanese were dying from *karoshi*. The Japanese corporate culture of improving products and customer service through peer pressure to work harder was victimizing its managers and employees through overwork and stress (DeMente 2002).

Retirement Shock

The more the executive internalizes the corporate being and competitive requirements of working and achieving, the more the overachievement and the greater the rewards. Unfortunately, if the executive makes it to retirement, the withdrawal from living the corporate role can be more stressful than the workaholic lifestyle. The loss of rewards, power, and the social identity of the corporate being creates a psychological vacuum that can lead to depression, sickness, and early death. I have often heard managers and other employees who worked long hours say, "One day I'll be able to retire and just put my feet up." The idea of doing nothing and resting is a myth and dangerous. The shock involved in going unprepared from an overachieving life to nothing can be more stressful than being a workaholic. This can do real damage. Gail Sheehy (1977) points out that executives often do not have a choice of when they will retire given all the mergers, acquisitions, restructuring, and downsizings. Many are cut off before age sixty-five. She points out that there is a steep suicide rate for men between age fifty-five to sixty-five, "potential evidence that many retirees feel junked" (p. 499).

Retirement is very stressful for the workaholic corporate executive who has given his or her all to the company. The workaholic has lived to work instead of working to live, and now has nothing to do. This person has not undergone the psychological preparation for retirement. Retirement is often not just at the planned age of sixty-five but may happen any time and suddenly. Although the executive may be well-off financially, the retirement shock of hyper-stress may accentuate the sad irony of the shallow emptiness of the corporate being. Reality will require the executive to re-create his or her self-identity as a means of overcoming the stress of being left bereft of life as a corporate being. You cannot take the corporate being with you into retirement. It is only a borrowed identity based on your role, status, and power, which you leave behind when you retire.

Hyper-stress is the retirement shock of losing one's self-identity, which is a huge loss for the executive. Normal daily stress can be dealt with by avoiding or removing the stressors. However, when there is no external stressor of object to remove ourselves from, stress is more problematic. As a result, the stress is internalized as anxiety, given that there is no specific, externally perceived cause. Indeed the expression, "we have seen the enemy and it is ourselves" strikes home. The retired executive sees no object to avoid and to alleviate the stress, because it comes from oneself. The retiree feels victimized with no enemy to strike out against. The well-conditioned and developed corporate being in the new retiree is like the hunter waiting to go hunting. However, the former executive needs to redefine his or her self and change. To do so, the executive as hunter must now adopt the introspective skills and contemplative aptitude of a monk! Most executive retirees are not prepared for this. Still bonded to the action-oriented executive role, the executive can feel trapped and victimized in an inescapable, hyper-stress or retirement shock. According to Barry Sears (1999), extreme stress can cause heart problems stimulated by chemical imbalances in the endocrine system, which lowers the immune system's ability to fight illness.

Retirement from a specific position is hard to reverse given its perceived finality, even though without a new purpose and role in retirement many retirees seem to yearn to return to a similar role. One's job has been filled. It would be embarrassing to return the gold watch and try to return. Many executives, therefore, feel stuck and abandoned. Many make the classic comeback. In this situation, though the need to rebuild oneself when leaving at the apex of achievement is almost mentally unfathomable, it is necessary for the executive's well-being if not survival! The executive has trouble believing there is a need to consider retirement because he or she has been spectacularly successful. As a result, this need to change is usually met with denial resulting in hyper-stress. Frederic Flack (1998) says, " A pattern that researchers have established as significantly related to heart disease is finding yourself in a situation or a relationship that's frustrating, disheartening and demoralizing, and feeling unable to change the way things are, change how you experience them, or escape them" (p. 213).

Myths of Retirement

The corporate being sustains older executives through a simplistic belief system. The fear of retirement tries to forewarn our consciousness of the psychological need to prepare for retirement, but our corporate beings disarm and mystify this need through the myths of retirement. We will invoke and debunk such myths surrounding retirement.

The "Stress-Free Myth" is the conviction that we work hard and put up with stress as workaholics, and so eventually we deserve to retire and remove ourselves from stress. The cruel irony is that the existential angst of losing self-identity as accomplished executives is more stressful than being a workaholic. Overcoming this loss is difficult because of the addiction to work, power, rewards, and the creation of self-identity as a corporate being.

The "Hobby Myth" is that in retirement, the executive will have more time to pursue those activities that he or she never had enough time to do while working. This myth is dispelled when you discover that while a hobby functions as a stress reliever when one is working, it can become very boring when done full time. This introduces a new stress unless the hobby can be expanded organically into one's other talents and become a central part of one's life, perhaps becoming creatively and meaningfully engaged with others and making a contribution as an artist or developing a business or doing volunteer work based on the hobby.

The "Vacation Myth" is one that retirement will be like a great vacation. But an endless vacation can be empty and stressful without purposeful and meaningful activities, even if one has a great financial nest egg.

The "Golden Age Myth" is one that retirement is taken over by a fable-like storybook ending where you live happily ever after. The reality is the retired executive still has to get up each day, put clothes on, plan the day, and find worthy, satisfying and meaningful activities.

The "Successful Executive Myth" is that accomplished executives know how to be successful at anything given their track record of accomplishments. The opposite is more likely to be true, given that they have become dependent on the structural support of their corporate beings as the basis of their success. Many successful executives have a difficult time being "successful" retirees. They now must go through the stress of finding their real selves outside of their jobs. Michael Leonetti (2007) explains away the myth that success creates success and failure creates failure when it comes to executive retirement. CEOs should be more successful than janitors and professional athletes more successful than those selling food at concession stands. Physicians should be more successful retiring than orderlies. It is simply not true that successful careers lead to successful retirement, according to Leonetti. Why? It is because executives and athletes who earned high levels of success and psychic rewards in their careers find it hard to replace it in retirement. Those who earned lower success in their careers find the transition into retirement easier. Just like some so-called retired professional athletes like Brett Favre or Lance Armstrong call it quits at the end of a season, but after a boring off-season they keep coming back for one more shot at the championship. It's hard to replace what one has spent a lifetime developing as a skill and self-concept. Many "retired" executives I know talk a lot of a comeback. Others talk about new businesses and ventures. For them, the pursuit of hobbies does not provide a replacement for the excitement, rewards, and satisfactions of corporate life.

Corporate Loyalty

Executives usually feel the fear of retirement as the end of the life they have spent their lives preparing for. In contrast, they have rarely prepared psychologically for retirement. Fear is the signal of the need to change and prepare to shed one's corporate being for the new life of retirement. The problem is the executive's own internalized corporate being usually rejects this message because the corporate being is "built to last," and the individual tends to feel personally blessed by the corporate spirit as part of his or her addiction to power and control. Your corporate being makes you feel omnipotent: as long as I am a corporate being, I will last forever! Most executives have heard horror stories of other executives they know who retired, and soon after got sick and died soon after retiring. Instead of using the fear of retirement constructively, the corporate being rejects it. This rejection can take the form of feeling sorry for newly retired executives who are no longer part of the team. Another form is to distance yourself from the retiree since he or she is no longer in the know, not in the corporate being's inner circle of confidentiality, and has become a persona non grata. The retiree no longer is seen as relevant to the ascending careers of the insiders. Distancing from these retired executives somehow allows insiders to feel immune from the destiny that they fear. Retirement seems like death, something to be avoided at all costs. Actually retirement is a death of sorts, death of one's corporate being or self-identity. Avoidance, however, is based on fear, repressed in the unconscious. This fear begets hyper-stress, which cannot be overcome without a viable life plan.

The executive's corporate being has rewarded loyalty throughout the executive's career. In the executive's mind, continued loyalty to the company will maintain control. The corporate being creates a familylike sense of mutual protection and a sense of executive control. This is the myth of the corporate being personified by the executive. In reality the corporate being is not a caring person. As the executive becomes more expensive for the corporation to carry, since time has escalated the aging executive's salary beyond the value to the corporation, there comes a point when the executive's value proposition is not there for the corporation. In fact, as the older executive begins to block the career paths of younger executives, who are working around the clock and represent the new realities in the market compared to ways of the older executives, the executives gradually become too expensive for their value. Executives often sense this as the company builds new expertise around them. They may become dysfunctional behaviorally as their hubris interferes. As they resist, it becomes time for the corporation to push the executive into retirement—but nothing personal! I call this the "senior delegation syndrome." New vice presidents take on an expanded scope of work and begin to delegate to cope with all the new work. Many of the weaker ones do not expand the role with their new programs but rely on extensive reports from their next-level subordinates. In my experience, these subordinates often complain to HR that they are doing all the work and that the vice president really doesn't know what's happening. This is not often a fair comment. Yet when a new CEO comes in, there are interviews of those subordinates, and soon a restructuring is the result. The CEO often has a mandate to cut costs and wants to have direct reports close to the market. As a result, a number of vice presidents may be fired under these circumstances; some may retire if they cannot find a similar job, which is hard to do given their big salaries. Usually these executives are not willing to relocate at this stage of their careers and end up retired without having done any preparation for it. I remember the numerous resumes that I used to receive from downsized executives from competitors, who had apparently "retired."

Few corporations have the luxury of excess senior staff. Competitive pressures to keep costs down means executives who are not keeping on top of every detail and leading competitive change and renewal must go. A typical merger and acquisition with two hundred executives from two companies will be typically reduced down to one hundred and twenty-five. Such mergers happen suddenly and the restructuring happens at the fastest pace to quickly lower the cost of leverage of the acquiring company. Even in more stable companies few companies bother putting executives who have peaked out to pasture and keeping them on payroll. The corporation is ultimately a commercial machine that must increase profits and continue to grow in spite of its executives, who have shown years of loyalty. Corporate downsizings or restructurings are very common, and big salaries are often the target. The paradox is that as executives move up through hard work and are rewarded with more money and power, the more vulnerable they become. The higher their salaries, the more they must outperform those at a lower salary. This becomes politically difficult when one depends on those others and as one gets older. The executive loses security as soon as the executive's internal and market competitiveness is lost. Having become a corporate being for security is an empty exchange in the longer term. The quid pro quo of the corporate being—be loyal and follow the rules, and you will be secure—is essentially bankrupt.

Another vulnerability of established corporate beings comes from those leaders who come into a corporation from the outside, shake it up, and create a renewal from the old, staid, corporate, country club culture. This seems to happen more and more today with numerous Carl Icahn-esque shareholder revolts. A classic example of the breakdown of loyalty in a strong, "built to last" corporate culture is the old IBM, which had a monolithic, formal culture. Having missed the market change to smaller PCs, IBM moved to rid itself of its insulated blue-suit hubris through a cultural revolution leading to greater decentralized informality and improved customer service. This was led by a new CEO, Lou Gerstner Jr., who was an outsider from RJR Nabisco, American Express, and who originally had been a McKinsey consultant. The old IBM had built up a huge loyalty through its blue-suited corporate being that had all but promised job security in response to the competitive onslaught of Japanese companies, who had done the same for their employees. However, in the end, hundreds of very loyal executives were fired. These executives who had dreamed of retiring at an older age and spending their days on the IBM golf courses with other IBM alumni had their retirement myths shattered: the golf courses were sold off for a better return on capital by the company that had been "built to last." In this case, lasting meant gutting the company of its old-style corporate beings.

The Retirement Sickness

The retirement sickness is having the corporate being as one's self-identity but being unable to be that identity in retirement. The retiree exits the corporate stage after the final bow and applause with the proverbial gold watch. Now, all of the executive's high-powered energy, skills, ideas, and executive personality have nowhere to go. The executive is "all dressed up with nowhere to go." In fact, as an HR executive, I heard reports of terminated executives not revealing this fact to their families for several weeks, and getting dressed for work and leaving the house each morning as usual.

What happens when the executive retires as a false self, a corporate being? Most executives have had their egos pumped by the corporate values, culture, and purpose, which have allowed them to live the executive life of success. Although likely financially secure, this false-self executive is ill prepared for the emotional side of retirement. Psychic rewards have been high through recognition and rewards. This will end in retirement as long as the individual remains unchanged. The executive's corporate being or ego is not the real self; the real self must be found in order to achieve health and happiness. A new self-identity must be developed, from which new psychic rewards are possible.

The internalized corporate being repels the unconscious messages of fear of retirement through belief in the myths of retirement. From one point of view, the fear of retirement is like fear of death, because it is the death of the corporate being. However, the all-knowing unconscious mind is trying to help the consciousness prepare. This is difficult for the executive whose self-identity is the corporate role. In many cases, it takes the shock of retirement for the executive to realize the need to find his or her real self.

Wayne Dyer (1991) explains that the ego in itself is insane if it comes to believe it is something that it is not. It wants to prove it is what it is not by convincing others that it is something else. This is like the corporate being becoming one's self-identity. Dyer says, "As this insanity takes hold of life, you absolutely come to identify with this false idea of yourself. Unaware, you involuntarily join the rest of the world who also practice this insanity" (p. 172). The newly retired executive, who is still a corporate being and still wants to dress up for work, is going through temporary insanity.

The unprepared executive enters retirement with the unrealistic, false, or neurotic ego of the corporate being. The corporate behavior, values, and purpose will do this individual no good. The executive quickly becomes an outsider, ostracized from the new corporate secrets of the evolving corporate being, and is history. Many retiring executives take vacations with their new boundless time, but they must face reality when they return. With the corporate ego still in place, it soon becomes apparent that all the corporate stimuli, the constant interactions, the rewards, the news, the excitement, and the support are gone. Not only are these gone to a degree, but they have been completely swept away. This is difficult for the corporate being, which has the self-image of being a leader and creating action around itself like an orchestra leader. It is difficult for this individual to be accountable for this powerless state of affairs. Suffering this accountability is a positive step if the executive understands what to do to find himself or herself. Having always been accountable for external events was easy, but now being accountable for changing yourself can lead to hyper-stress and eventually serious illness.

The retirement sickness comes shortly after the shock of retirement as the executive ego discovers sudden powerlessness and uselessness. This withdrawal from the levers of power, its rewards and satisfactions in creating results, is a shock—it is a withdrawal from the addiction to the corporate being. Experiencing helplessness is highly stressful for the control freak used to having an organized power structure to get almost anything done. Now, of course, what needs to be done cannot be done by others; rather, it is up to the individual to transform oneself. Taking responsibility to reinvent yourself is extremely difficult to do for the first time, especially when any reinventing had been done through the corporate support system. Any executive whose identity is deeply bound up with the corporate identity will need to work to adapt and discover a new authentic self with new life possibilities and not just try to relive past glories.

Dying of Boredom

A common complaint I have heard from newly retired executives is boredom: "I'm not bored ... I'm incredibly bored." Going from the corporate environment, with great psychic rewards and a hectic atmosphere that is like being in the middle of a three-ring circus, to being at home day after day with nothing happening but a few domestic projects is stress shock. Boredom has its roots in the stress of sensory deprivation, of being without the high level of activity common in the corporate world. The myth of leaving the stress of the office behind in retirement is shattered by the hyper-stress of sensory deprivation and the lack of reinforcement of one's corporate being, which has become one's self-identity.

The problem is that killing off one's false self is not like swatting a fly; it is so stressful that it can kill the retired executive prematurely. This may seem to be an extreme statement, but let's consider that sensory deprivation has been used as torture to extract confessions from prisoners of war. In this case, however, the retiring executive with a strong corporate being not only goes through a high degree of sensory deprivation but must go through the destruction of his or her self-identity. Undergoing both together can be very stressful particularly because no one seems to understand. In fact, most people are jealous of your newfound leisure.

In addition, the executive was totally unprepared, given the internalized myths of the golden days of retirement. The shock and stress of retirement can cause serious illness by lowering the immune system's effectiveness. Naturally, if a retiree has a heart attack or gets cancer soon after retiring, people do not associate it with the hyper-stress of retirement. If the executive dies soon after retirement, paradoxically others tend to be thankful the executive had retired and had time off to do nothing but enjoy retirement given how hard he or she had worked before passing away.

Perhaps the highest level of stress is not the removal of the corporate stimuli or the rewards of the corporate being but the sudden awareness of the emptiness of the corporate being and the realization that your corporate being is not your authentic self. When the corporate party is over and it's time to turn out the lights, the corporate egos that we have developed have a difficult time. Worse yet is the hangover of stress caused by the fact that we have no choice but to overcome our addiction to our corporate being by dispelling the false self. Phillip C. McGraw (2001) says, "There is no greater stress than that generated by denying the authentic self. Because your life energy is being diverted and therefore depleted, you are compromised mentally, emotionally, spiritually and physically" (pp. 33–34). He goes on to cite the research on stress by Michael Roizen, which shows that for each year that you live with high stress, you shorten your life expectancy by three years. Not knowing your true passion let alone creating an outlet for it will cost you another six years of your life. If drained by conflict, you can lose another eight years (pp. 33–34). We aim to show you a way to overcome this in Part 4.

The retiring executive with a strong corporate ego takes the internalized corporate purpose, values, and meaning into retirement. This internal compass will fail the retiring executive as the dysfunction of the false self causes hyper-stress. The executive really retires like the empty shell of the famous character Willie Loman in Arthur Miller's *Death of a Salesman*. Willie was loyal to the company to the end, but he was fired because his sales style was deemed unsuccessful by the corporation. He died in the total frustration not of just being let down by the company but of being without a clue what he was to do without his job. He died because both his job and his self-identity were tied to that job that had ended.

Getting Out Early with a Life Plan to Rebuild

Entering retirement with a false sense of self is more difficult the older one retires. The longer you stay in the corporate rat race, the harder it is to find your real self. This could be called the hardening of the executive ego. Getting out of the corporate pressure cooker early may in fact extend your life if you rebuild your sense of self-identity. This is not so much because of the common belief that the corporate life is stressful, which it is, but because retiring with an entrenched corporate ego is a lot more stressful. The earlier in life that the executive can afford to get out to rebuild the self, the easier it would seem to be. This is not just because the executive is more youthful and more able to withstand the stress of the transition. More likely, it is because the executive who leaves early probably had less identification with the corporate being and wants out to pursue his or her own interests and passion. Executives need to consider exiting as soon as they can afford to take the transition risk to a more personally meaningful role. It is never too early or late to exit something that fails to reflect your real genuine values and self.

Sing (2002) provides results based on an actuarial study by Dr. Ephrem Cheng of age of retirement versus life span. "The pension funds in many large corporations (e.g., Boeing, Lockheed Martin, AT&T, and Lucent Technologies) have been 'overfunded' because many 'late retirees' who keep on working into their old age and retire late after the age of 65 tend to not live long enough to collect all their fair share of pension money such that they leave a lot of extra, unused money in the pension funds ..." (p. 1). He found that those who retired at an older age tend to die at an earlier age than those who got out earlier.

This seems to support our working hypothesis that existing as a corporate being is stressful because it is not your real self. The sooner you can get out and discover your real self, the lower the life stress will be and the healthier you will be. Getting out early reduces the executive's stress from a workaholic environment and allows him or her to have more time to find a new rewarding life. Further, those who leave with a false sense of self later in life are more identified with their false selves and tend to be less aware. These corporate diehards resist listening to their fear of retirement and fail to do something about it. They tend to succumb to the increased stress of retirement and withdrawal from their roles without overcoming the ultimate cause of the greatest stress of all: trying to act out a false self.

It is true that being prematurely unemployed can also reduce your lifespan. The experience of being unemployed is very stressful and can lead to an earlier death than for those who continue to work, according to Derek Cook and colleagues from London's Royal Free Hospital School of Medicine and St. George's Hospital Medical School (1994). All other health risk factors were neutral. Those who continued working had a stable lifestyle and sense of corporate purpose. This experience of being unemployed and wanting to work with no opportunity is similar to being retired by your company at the normal retirement age with no life plan opportunities to fill the time gap. The experience and stress can have a negative effect at any age if you do not redevelop yourself to lead a purposeful life to meet your needs.

I conclude that just as unemployment is a health risk factor, so too, is retirement, even at the normal retirement age if the individual lacks a replacement lifestyle, a life plan with a meaningful purpose. Without a life strategy, retirement is simply mental unemployment. As part of a strategic life plan, getting out early is an advantage allowing the executive to avoid the stress of being a workaholic. This also allows for the time needed to rebuild a more meaningful life. The key is to recognize the need and develop a purposeful life plan that supports your authentic self as soon as one can afford to leave the corporation.

Working Past Age Sixty-Five

It may appear that one solution to the stress of withdrawal from the corporate culture and job is the "die-in-the-saddle" strategy, but this only delays the shock and makes it worse when one is older. Executives continuing to work past sixty-five or the normal corporate retirement age may believe that they have a chance of living longer and outliving the retiring executive, but this appears to not be true. A rapid withdrawal from an addiction can kill due to the sudden psychological and chemical imbalances it can create, particularly later in life after being worn down by the rat race. Staying past retirement age may be a good strategy for the retiring executive who has a high affinity with the corporate culture and chooses to maintain a personal identity with the current role and corporate culture, but this is rare and may be possible only in a family-owned business where you are the culture. In my experience, it boils down to how much you control the culture of the corporate being. The more you own the business and the more the corporate being reflects you, the less the risk of having to leave and having to reinvent yourself. If you can stay and leave on your own terms when you want and still play a board role, then this may be your best strategy. If you have little control over the corporate being, staying after sixty-five merely avoids the issue of undergoing the stress of reinventing oneself, but it only delays it. It is better to get on with reestablishing yourself outside of your corporate being and regaining control over your life on your own terms, as early as possible in your career.

If you decide to work past the retirement age, try to do it in a semiretirement role. However, this is usually difficult for senior executives, given the nature of accountability and control. The new executive stepping in will want the whole job, not half of it. Perhaps the best way to position this strategy is to become a mentor for the development of a more junior executive. However, this will change the executive's status, power, and accountability, which itself may be hard for that executive and others to endure. Most executives would rather not lose face or status within the corporation, and so being there becomes an all or nothing proposition in their minds.

This is a serious issue for many executives approaching the retirement age and experiencing the fear of retiring and giving up their roles and rewards. Nevertheless, the strategy of staying on past the usual retirement age has serious defects. First, do you really want to continue and die in the job without having a chance to come to terms with who you really are outside of being a corporate executive? The role that was an economic means to security becomes an end in itself. This seems to be a tragic choice, like getting lost along the way. The executive who denies that this choice is tragic is so married to the executive role that he or she has repressed completely other personal possibilities for a life purpose and ends up with one that is merely economic.

Making this economic choice can make sense in a family-owned business where one can choose when to retire and, as the patriarch entrepreneur, may decide to stay on indefinitely because there may be no appropriate successor of age. Staying on here may be for the higher purpose of passing on a legacy to the family after a successor is prepared. Even so, this decision to stay on is done for the higher purpose of the family legacy of the business and not just for making more money for personal consumption. In most cases, however, it is the company that decides when you retire later in your career. Even if there is no longer a mandatory retirement age, given the declining performance and motivation that normally comes with age, most companies want to provide opportunities to the younger, aspiring executives, who bring in new fresh ideas at a lower salary.

Companies prefer not to lose these younger executives while waiting for the older executives to die. Consequently, the harsh reality is that the accomplished executive does not really have the choice of staying on indefinitely and avoiding the issue of undergoing the stress of reinventing himself or herself in retirement or semiretirement. This aging executive who wants to stay in the role wants to avoid the fear of change. However, when the inevitable retirement comes, the executive cannot take along the corporate culture and role. I can remember a case of an executive who was being terminated at the age of sixty-five. This executive did not wish to leave and retire and pointed out that he had the right to stay given the lack of a mandatory retirement company policy and similar legislation. The company felt a change would be better for the company and had waited and hoped that the executive would retire voluntarily. The company's employment lawyer, who was helping defend the company, put it all in perspective when he said, "No one owns their job!"

If an executive's personal identity is addicted to the role, ego withdrawal can be painful and stressful, often triggering illness. Anne Wilson Schaef (1987) says, "Like any serious disease, an addiction is progressive, and it will lead to death unless we actively recover from it" (p. 18). The more healthy choice is to overcome and purge ourselves of our false corporate being so we can be free enough to make our own choices.

Denial and Stress

Executives are used to stress in their roles—leading company changes, making tough decisions, negotiating and resolving conflicts under long hours, and traveling globally. This makes executives feel in control. Yet external corporate control from their power base is the opposite of personal psychological power over oneself. The executive's dependency on the power of the corporate being is based on a personal addiction to power. Addictions are based on a personal inner powerlessness over the self. Executives deny their own dependency on the external levers of power coming from their role when their hubris deceptively makes them feel that the power is rooted internally, not the authority vested in their job. Such executive hubris inflated with dependency on power proves useless in dealing with the withdrawal from power in retirement. You cannot delegate the solution to be solved by support staff. Retiring executives are not used to the kind of hyper-stress where they are not in control and personally are the target of the need to change. Having to change oneself means that the executive must change the very habits and behavioral patterns of one's corporate being, which were used to deal with the previous job issues. Hyper-stress is a more insidious type of stress because it involves changing oneself away from the dependency and even addiction on corporate power. This leaves the executive less able to deal with the new stress of retiring. The usual organizational support mechanisms fail. Those support systems have created a dependency and have become a barrier to developing inner power of the self needed to conquer the hyper-stress. For the executive who prides himself or herself on being in control, this dilemma is often dealt with through denial. The more the hubris involved, the greater the change required, and probably the greater the denial of the hyper-stress involved in retirement. This former executive will cling to the security of the past identity of the corporate being, which is the cause of the hyper-stress.

The only transition will be to try to live out the promise of the so-called golden age of retirement. Here, assuming that happiness is guaranteed, the retired executive acts out externally the perfect bliss of retirement. The props used are all the consumer items, trips, and experiences money can buy, which act to prove how great the retirement is. In these cases, stress is buried as much as possible in the unconscious. However, the cracks into the conscious begin to appear with the onslaught of boredom. Executives are comfortable with being needed and constantly being bombarded with requests, problems, meetings, and the need for solutions. They are the central control system of the corporate activities. In retirement, this suddenly stops, and there is nothing but their selves and no basis for action. Now, action reverses from external to internal, but executives cannot simply adjust to this reversal and become bored from the lack of external stimuli while at the control switch. Unless these executives become aware of their pseudo-corporate selves and get connected to their passions based on their authentic selves, bottled-up stress will likely kill them as manifested through some well-known disease, and well before their time. Like any contradiction, one way or another, the false self must die.

Change is difficult. Major change occurs when we work to change or try to change our fundamental thinking and sense of identity, which includes even how we deal with change itself. This is stressful. Reinventing methods is difficult, but reinventing ourselves is stressful. Nevertheless, doing so helps overcome the hyper-stress of the false self in retirement. The need to change your self-identity can help save your life. Hyper-stress involves the helplessness of not knowing what to do to solve this dilemma. However, this can be the basis for learning more of ourselves if we do not simply deny it and replace it with superficial activities. Reinventing yourself around who you really are and what you love to do is the simple solution to relieving stress through the joy and passion of pursuing personally meaningful goals. Since stress seems to contribute to many illnesses, we need to better understand the drivers of stress to be better able to master it in our own ways.

Let's more thoroughly explore the potential stress pathways of the retiring executive. Only by fully understanding the potential for retirement shock and stress can the executive prepare for it and avoid it. We will later show the answer to the stress problem lies in finding ourselves and our passion.

Chapter 6: Executive Stress in Retirement

It is not easy to find happiness in ourselves,
And it is not possible to find it elsewhere.
—Agnes Reppler

Fear of retirement is the executive's intuition of a future major life change and its accompanying stress. The degree of stress depends on how the executive perceives this event based on his or her situation, psychological state of mind, and degree of preparedness. The main determinant of retirement-related stress is the degree that the corporate being has been internalized into the executive's personal ego. The more the corporate being has been internalized, the greater the change and stress to follow. The degree the executive represses this fear prevents preparation for retirement. Each executive is different in preparation for retirement. In general the more repression of such fear and the greater that one identifies with the corporate being the less prepared and the greater the retirement shock this person will face. The inverse is also true. However, the dilemma here is the more this executive is prepared for retirement the less he or she may be willing to be committed to the rigors of the job and be able to fit in without appearing to have quit and stayed. In my experience this state often leads to the premature termination of the executive as they have started to show a lack of anticipatory enthusiasm for the company's future. Personally, I have experienced the early stages of this state. Whenever I felt I was not being challenged and slipping into auto-pilot boredom would result. It would be time for me to move on and leave the company for a new challenge. As we will see, in order to prevent the retirement shock looking at it as a new challenge will help be proactive and figure out a new personal plan.

Some of the retirement stressors are based on the following dimensions: loss of your structure and role, loss of control, loss of your social status, and loss of some social support and personal relationships. All of these are offshoots of the fundamental loss of power and control that is based on your self-identity as a corporate being.

Loss of Structure and Role

The first change impacting the executive is the experienced loss of the job itself. This is an obvious fact of retirement. However, the actual experience of losing one's role has a high personal impact because of the realization that means giving up part of oneself … and a very important part! Retired executives often complain about missing the structure of the job and of corporate life. An executive's role is demanding in that the work week is structured with endless meetings, reports, e-mails, business lunches, and the unexpected events and crises that only specific executives can resolve. This structure of the role also extends into evenings and weekends as most executives bring home their laptops or Blackberries in order to keep on top of the issues they champion. Things happen so fast that an executive can be out of touch by the next day if he or she is not globally connected electronically after hours. This structure compulsively takes control of the executive's life. You cannot lead if you are out of touch or not up to date with every latest detail.

The executive does not typically experience a lack of freedom in this system; rather, he or she experiences the exhilarating sense of being needed and being able to orchestrate global events twenty-four hours a day. The executive can choose to reschedule or cancel meetings and choose when or if to respond to e-mails or voice mails. But this level of control is confused with freedom. Although there is perceived flexibility and freedom within the corporate work structure, the overall structure itself is not flexible and controls the executive's life. Often it is the complete loss of this overpowering structural framework which fills one's life that the executive misses the most in retirement. This all-encompassing structure, which determines corporate life, is really the controlling macroframework of an executive's microchoices. Losing this structure for the freedom and unstructured life of retirement can be stressful. This explains why many retired senior executives are offered the greatest "perq" of all: an office at corporate headquarters. The idea is that they can hold court as philosopher kings, rather like emeritus faculty at a university. However, in my experience most other executives shun this opportunity to be coached by a retiree unless there is political advantage.

In one case I experienced, the retired executive, the former CEO, who had been given an office at head office, was moved out to a remote location because he was meddling in everyone's business: no one seemed to come his way to request his coaching. His traditional style and methods were out of sync with the new CEO. Since having a retired executive around is often disruptive to the political hierarchy, it is wiser to look upon an executive's retirement as the absolute end of his or her role.

Those executives who seem to make the easiest transition are those more individualistic and entrepreneurial executives who may have hated the corporate structural intrusions into their lives as well as the constraints of their role. These mavericks would typically do things their own way, reaching their goals in a more creative way. If these types make it to the retirement age within a corporate framework, they will be more likely to genuinely see retirement more as a liberation from the structure than a loss. They will be free to pursue those things they really value. These individualists typically retire early with fixed ideas on what they want to do.

Loss of Control

One of the hallmarks of the executive's work life is that there is both accountability and authority over the work of others. As a consequence, even if things do not go as planned, there is still a sense of control to delegate and make changes. The executive has the internalized sense of basic control over his or her work environment. It would not make sense to move executives up in a hierarchy without giving them greater control. The logic is that this assures the planned outcomes for which those executives are accountable. An increase in control comes with increased accountability.

This is important in regard to the executive's ability to deal with stress on the job. Companies are stressful environments, so the sense of perceived control acts to lower stress. The executive can delegate to subordinates and mentally off-load a huge part of the stress. If the subordinates do not get the desired results, then the executive can make changes and reorganize.

Control over a stressful situation acts to reduce the stress. A sense of control, no matter how real or apparent it is, acts to reduce stress and increase performance. The executive's support system not only reduces stress but acts to improve performance. For example, the senior executive who may not fully agree with the sales director's tactics for a certain market segment may think, "I'll give him a shot, but if I don't see results in the first quarter post launch, I'll reorganize and take this market segment away from this individual and hire someone from the competition I know who is more experienced with that market segment."

The inverse is also true: without perceived control, stress increases and performance declines. In my experience, employees and managers often lobby for more power. Without the control, they believe they have all the accountability but not the authority, which makes the role seem futile. This is, in fact, the dilemma of second-tier management, and why that role is more stressful compared to those of the executive, top-tier management. Such middle-level managers who report to the more senior vice presidents often blame any failures that they have on the fact they were not given the power, authority, or support to get the results as assigned. On the other hand, the vice president may have justified this on the basis of wanting the individual subordinate to prove that he or she could rise to the challenge and get real results given the uncertainty and stress. In fact proving oneself can be a rite of passage for many middle managers to the executive ranks.

Peters and Waterman (1992) report psychological experiments showing that performance in control groups exceeded the performance of other groups when the control groups knew they could reduce the stress of the exercise they were doing by pressing an on-off control button. The performance was superior in the groups that knew they could use the control button—and in most cases, they did not even bother to use it.

We can conclude not only that stress lowers performance, but also that the lack of control over stress amplifies the destructive force of the stress. Conversely, having perceived control over stress lowers the damaging impact of stress on performance.

This is significant in regard to the retiring executive, because the executive loses his or her power base structure and sense of control when retiring. As a consequence, the same types of stresses will be more difficult to deal with. The executive will be more irritable because of stresses that previously seemed innocuous are more invasive without that control structure. The executive in retirement will spend more time at home alone, without the support structure and without a well-defined span of control, whether real or assumed. If there is a spouse at home, this can lead to increased stress and marital discord, because the spouse at home may resist losing previous independence and freedom. This spouse must now cope full time with the former executive, who is used to delegating and controlling the behavior of others to get things done.

For the retired executive, the most stressful aspect of being at home is suddenly adapting to having no corporate structure. There is now complete freedom without any meaningful tasks or projects and even without the domestic skills. Too many basic choices can be very stressful. Further, it leaves the executive too much free time to think about his or her life, which now seems vague, without direction and structure while still thinking within the structured framework of the job. This lack of structure makes it difficult for the executive to know what to control—or how. Now, the requirements for what one needs to do must be dealt with internally, without the usual corporate structure. The executive has internalized the external corporate purpose and mission, but this corporate map is now useless domestically while planning to do dishes or clean or landscaping or whatever and leaves the executive lost and unfulfilled. It is much more stressful being at home full time, trying to find an internal compass and sense of control, than working in a structured corporate job which gives purpose, mission, a span of control, and a strategic map from the corporate being.

Loss of Social Status

Along with the loss of control and power is a similar loss of social status. The executive has been rewarded throughout his or her career with higher levels of accountability, and social status comes with the territory. Such an increase in status is internalized by the executive as the normal expression of his or her career and personal growth. The newly achieved status that accompanies greater power and a higher organizational level is not experienced externally as a trapping of a new responsibility, but rather internally as the actualization of one's true being or potential being actualized. The congratulatory comments resulting from a promotion are often from sycophants and customers hoping to gain leverage by being connected to the new power and status of the rising executive. However, in retirement, this is reversed. This loss is hard to take for the executive corporate being who had internalized the previous status as an expression or proof of his or her true personal value. Those lucky executives who take the status as a simple burden of power often get out early.

The first support group to disappear in retirement is the sycophants. These supporters of power no longer see any value in or have time for an executive with no real, current power or social status. They will move on to where they can gain greater leverage. This starts to happen just before retirement. Since upcoming retirement is a late indicator of loss of power and social status, the executive will tend to fear and avoid thinking and talking at the office of his or her age and retirement plans. Executives who have internalized their rising power and status as being who they really are, or deserve to be, will suffer the significant stress of loss of social status in retirement. They are shunned in retirement through the lack of recognition from the same people who used to build them up. The more the executive has become a corporate being, the more this will be taken personally as a stressful loss. Other support groups—colleagues and industry officials—will fade away as the currency of the executive becomes out of date and less valuable for their own needs.

The executive tends to internalize social recognition as social status in the ego, even though it is merely an incidental function of the corporate culture supporting the hierarchy. In this way, his or her social status is very much who the executive becomes. It is not just a structure but the actual person interacting with others. This is leadership in the mind of the executive experienced through the level of social stratification attained. Given the executive's personal experience of being recognized day to day in this way, the executive becomes his or her social status, and that executive's sense of personal meaning and life purpose becomes dependent on retaining that social status.

The fear of retirement stems from the unconscious anticipation of the shock of losing this social status. Paradoxically, the more the executive is aware of this reality, the less the fear, and the more the executive is able to plan for such losses and become more retirement ready. Understanding of the loss is better before retirement than after, for that allows the executive to proactively develop a realistic life plan and move on with grace. However, in my experience, most executives are so immersed in their roles that reality is repressed and experienced as a distant fear. As any corporate role is assumed, we unconsciously know we cannot take the trappings of power and status with us into retirement. Although all executives know this factually, most have not consciously thought through what this implies personally. Interestingly enough, those who have consciously thought this through may quickly lose their interest in becoming a corporate being or a serious player. These individualists may soon plan for an early exit to some other career choice not built on the temporary social status of the corporate being. In essence, the corporate being is an empty shell, pretty but empty.

Loss of Social Support and Personal Relationships

The specific part of the loss of social status that is most personal is the loss of the retiring executive's personal corporate relationships. Within the hubris of the corporate being, the executive comes to feel that these relationships are true friendships, including those of the seemingly loyal sycophants. The executive spends more time working than at home, and these corporate relationships become a "work family." In reality, they grow and function in the same corporate world sharing the same battles and confidences.

However, since the corporate being is not a person, these are not real friendships as such. Nevertheless, given the executive's personal alienation from the corporate being, he or she usually refuses to completely adhere to the corporate role and often crosses the line of one's role and risks being a real person by making real friends and even having "flaming affairs" at the office. Such deviance is driven by the impersonal nature of the corporate being, which restrict the executive's inner desire for the intimacy of friendships. This helps overcome the personal alienation of being an impersonal corporate being. While this is a common fact of office life, it is dangerous for the executive to make real friends at the office. Other colleagues will shout foul as they perceive that the executive's personal alliances will favor the new friend or cronies over them in salary increases, promotions, and opportunities, not to mention of gaining the advantage of insider information. Such a backlash is common and routinely undermines such an executive's credibility. Although human, transgressing away from the executive's role as a corporate being can lead to a conflict of interest. Many senior executives have lost their jobs over the loss of their corporate being's objectivity, simply because they craved the opportunity to express subjectively their real feelings at the office. However, favoritism can destroy an executive's power. This dilemma is the real self of the executive rebelling against the impersonality of his or her corporate being. It is personal power trying to come out beneath the veil of surrogate power. Hubris often deceives the executive into thinking that his or her surrogate power is real personal power. To prevent this conflict friendships are usually discreet as those executives do not want to be labeled as subjective and biased toward their office friends or cronies. The number one rule for learning to be a supervisor is: do not make friends with your subordinates. This may be easier for colleagues at the same level to do, but even so, you will be called on from time to time to make decisions for the best interests of the company, which will go against such a friend's vested interests. The executive role demands impartiality and objectivity. Further, forming alliances based on friendship often end up being cliques. The politics of cliques usually self-destruct as turf wars as new cliques are formed to combat other's power and influence. The corporate culture cannot allow small cliques to form alliances that have greater loyalty to the part than the whole organization. Relationships between executives cannot place individual ties ahead of that to the whole culture, so the corporate being must be the essence of these relationships. Exceptions of friendships, affairs, or alliances are self-destructive for the executive when exposed because he or she deviates away from the duty of the impersonal, neutral executive role. The corporate being is essentially defined roles, processes, techniques, structures, rules, and procedures bound together through values with a strategy and mission. Relationships cannot become true friendships on the job without causing friction with the essence of the corporate being. However, executives are very human and often try to do both to some degree given the conflict between their role and their human needs.

Consequently, although these relationships appear and feel like friendships, they are not. Executives are human and often deal with this reality not by playing by their corporate role but by projecting and labeling such relationships as more than functionary. The shock of retirement is partially the awareness that such relationships are not real friendships or sustainable on the basis of the corporate being. Former close confidants who were corporate beings together in the same company may find that they do not have enough in common outside the corporate culture for the friendship to survive in retirement. The corporate glue that brought them together is gone in retirement. As an example, one fellow comes to mind. He was a popular industry icon, rising up from a pharmaceutical sales rep to vice president of HR. Given his experience in several companies, he was instrumental in bringing new key executives into the company. This was appreciated given the fact that the company now led the industry with rapid growth for numerous years. I replaced him when he retired. He moved out of town but made trips into the city to visit family members that still lived in the city. Whenever he did, he came to the office and walked around to catch up with everyone. He would usually try to get the old group of colleagues together for lunch. He just assumed that they would want to be like the old days. However, he never could get many interested in this because of their shifting priorities and for them rehashing the past and listening to his retirement stories seem intrusive on their time and priorities at the office. I noticed that many former colleagues would either close their doors or simply come out and quickly greet him, wishing him well but explaining that they were off to a meeting. Having more time than he expected, he would always end up in my office, and I never had worked with him. He would ask all sorts of things about other executives and even give me unsolicited advice, most of which did not seem relevant. I'm sure he found me evasive: if the other executives did not wish to disclose their most recent situations, then I certainly wasn't going to reveal them. Soon, he came in to the office less and less. After several years of not hearing anything of him, I heard he had died. Many executives who had avoided him were dismayed that they had not even known; they would have liked to have gone to his funeral even though it was out of town.

The typical retired executive, aware of the loss of status and power, has no option but to retreat, for there is no basis for asserting power and influence in that corporate domain. Pride and hubris force the executive to reevaluate the situation by stepping back. In this early stage of retirement, the executive may plot a comeback to an imagined social status. More and more, the occasional lunches with former colleagues will fade away as the retired executive feels as if he is wasting their time. Because the retired executive has been replaced, the situation has changed, and information is confidential, the retired executive becomes an instant dinosaur with no social status within the corporation. The new executive who fills his or her shoes will have a fresh mandate and approach, and will not want to appear dependent on the retiree. Most executives want to bring in change and at least create the optics of improving the old ways. Most new executives communicate how they will improve the weaknesses of their predecessors as a means of consolidating their own power and establishing their own leadership brand. Everything previous relationships for the retiree were based on as corporate beings is now gone. The language of the corporate being is current data, tactics, and strategy; trying to keep up such relationships based on insider confidentiality is futile. The retired executive can no longer be trusted with current confidential data because he or she no longer shares the interests of the corporate being. Current executives would question why the retired executive would need to know current, sensitive information. Consequently, there is a shared exercise of mutual distancing from each other. Corporate executive retirement can feel like personal estrangement and isolation if one fails to replace its social rewards.

This isolation and estrangement creates stress for the former executive who ranked high in the corporate social order, even though the departed executive understands the need for distancing. There is a defensive mechanism of the corporate being toward anyone who leaves the company. The retiree knows that whenever an executive leaves, there will be a circling of the wagons around the information that does not get out even to former executives who previously were in the inner circle. Now, however, it feels different for this retiree because he or she is on the other side of the confidentiality fence and must be excluded for the protection of the corporation. Even though the process is understood in a factual way, it will feel like being excommunicated from the corporate being of the company. This is very stressful insofar as the retired executive is still that corporate being psychologically. The stress of this isolation can cause the executive's pride to plot a comeback or more positively a reinvention of the self separate from that former corporate identity. Part 4 explores this healthy alternative of reinventing oneself.

Social isolation is caused by the fact that the newly retired executive is the corporate being but with no outlets or limited connections to be what she or he had become. The normal sources of social relationships, social status, information, and power to do things are reduced if not gone. These can't be replaced simply by joining the local organization or club. In essence, this isolation is part of hyper-stress insofar as it is more than being isolated from people and normal social interaction. It is being cut off from one's corporate being, culture, rewards, and meaning that were established within the corporation.

Leisure: the Joy and Pain

Corporate beings are programmed to work hard for the golden age of leisure. I can remember distinctly a head of automotive manufacturing explaining this philosophy with the story of a colleague from his former company. He said, "Life's a bitch. A fellow I used to work with worked his butt off and saved a nice nest egg for retirement but before he could retire and enjoy it, he has a heart attack!" Unfortunately this myth of working hard for a golden age of leisure is often an empty promise. The loyal executive who has worked hard to be able to afford this life must be able to afford the lifestyle of leisure. The idea that leisure is the purpose and meaning of retirement is a false promise and a dead end. Leisure as advanced consumerism is really the ultimate goal of the logic of the corporate being. The executive retires to the rewards of hard work and the toys of leisure. This reduces the executive to a retired corporate being. The ultimate meaning of life becomes an extension of the executive's power and status as the rewards and savings allow the executive to continue to differentiate his or her station in life through a higher level of conspicuous consumption: the bigger boat, better cottage, exotic vacations.

Of course leisure cannot be just playing with the tools of our hobbies: boats, fishing gear, antique cars, golf clubs, planes, and the like.

Leisure also allows relieving, relaxing activity to counterbalance more purposeful and more engaging pursuits and goals. It will always remain an escape from a more serious pursuit that we believe in. Leisure is just too trivial to become the purpose of our lives. For example, golf by itself can be empty without companions or without the social interaction at the nineteenth hole. On the other hand, if you teach others the techniques of golf, the purpose becomes more elevated than simply trying to hit a ball into a hole. Meaning is bestowed through benefiting others. Helping others improve so they can receive recognition will be appreciated and provide recognition in return. Practicing your hobby proves worthwhile, particularly when you get the recognition, the applause, or the trophy. The piece of metal called the trophy is worth very little money, but it is worth a lot emotionally with "your name on it." When we are stressed out from working, a life of pure hobbies feels compelling, but this is only because it seems a great diversion and relief from the stress of work. Inversely, try the hobby or hobbies full time without the need for the diversion. The hobby by itself can become the new source of stress that will itself require a more meaningful diversion. If the hobby no longer provides stress relief or diversion from work, it becomes a full-time, futile pursuit of the trivial. The myth of retirement as the life of leisure is the false promise of consumerism. How can this be? Any retirement based on the trivial pursuit of hobbies ends in boredom. Pure leisure is ultimately narcissistic consumerism. Executives who have had a rich work life of intellectual challenges will never feel rewarded or happy pursuing the trivial full time.

Hobbies are essentially learned techniques played with tools like golf clubs. The meaning of an executive's life in retirement can never be reduced to just catching the biggest fish. Consumerism, in fact, embellishes the myth of leisure, implying that the better the tools, the better the technique, which leads to the ultimate implication: the better your life can be. Having a better golf swing or winning will not make your retirement better. Essentially, the pursuit of hobbies is a mindless activity and can never replace the challenges of work. Consequently, the pure pursuit of hobbies becomes boring and meaningless as a full-time retirement lifestyle. It is our corporate being retired as a false self, playing out the corporate myth of retirement. One executive I know joined a prestigious golf and country club at a significant cost several years before retirement with the view to it being the hub and focus for his retirement, given the golf and social activities. Within a few years after retiring, he had not renewed his membership and lost his large nonrefundable equity deposit, saying it was just too boring to be doing the same thing with the "old retired fogies."

Essentially, fun is not sustainable full time, but like laughter or humor, it bursts out of the mundane or routine. Trying to make fun, laughter, or humor routine, loses its essence as meaningful spontaneity, and it is no longer funny; pure hobbies cannot provide the richness your life needs for a unique and original individual purpose and meaning. This is why pursuing hobbies as a primary activity without others is not only less fun but lonelier and more boring. As others help give us meaning, so one of the clues to finding our real meaning is through our connections to others and their needs. To transcend the superficial limitation of hobbies and trivial pursuits, we must find our own authentic purpose and meaning in the context of others. We must overcome the corporate being's myth of the meaning of retirement as leisure and consumption, and do the work of individualizing ourselves to separate our self and life from the collectivity of the corporate being. The corporate being is conditioned by the group-think process and a prescribed model of behavior that does not think for the individual but for the collectivity.

Overcoming the collective consciousness of retirement requires new, original thinking, new work, a new "job" based on our own higher need for self-actualization through listening to ourselves and our dreams, unconscious messages, intuitions, and hunches. Doing so may at first seem awkward and difficult, but the emotional rewards by far exceed what the life of pure leisure will ever be able to deliver. Thinking for ourselves will always remain a very unique and difficult challenge, because corporate beings do not think for the individual but rather for the corporate collectivity. For the newly retired corporate being with an internalized corporate purpose or set of professional techniques to follow, there is no roadmap to learn to discover and to think originally and creatively. Doing so involves the most difficult challenge of all: our own limitations. This is not corporate leadership but real leadership of the self. Overcoming the existential boredom of our false selves as corporate beings by finding our own unique purpose in retirement is necessary to allow us to transcend the superficiality of hobbies as our corporate being's definition of retirement. Imagine being condemned in retirement to a lifetime of triviality; that's what the myth of the retirement as leisure in effect does, however unintentional.

We are ultimately free to choose. Although we have gotten used to following the corporate collectivity as corporate beings, we need to rediscover ourselves through our own creative freedom. As corporate beings, we have achieved the corporate success through the collectivity. This does not reward or allow for the individual to fully differentiate himself or herself as a unique, free person, separate from the corporate being or job, without conflict and without shortening a career in that company. However, this may actually be a blessing in disguise. There is no roadmap for finding yourself because each individual is unique. What makes this most challenging is that we cannot follow others but must invent our own way. Yes, executives have worked hard and now deserve their retirement. However, if we settle for a retirement of leisure, we will cheat ourselves out of possible emotional rewards. Leisure in retirement cannot replace the power of the corporate being. We need something as powerful. We can find it beyond the power and addiction to the corporate being through our newly discovered, overarching meaning and personal purpose.

This issue is more severe for executives because they have been in high-psychic challenges and reward roles. Executives will be hit by the boredom caused by a retirement full of trivial activities more intensely than those who may have held less mentally challenging roles. As a consequence, this wall of stress caused by the boredom and the challenges of escaping it are of a different magnitude for the executive. If stress gradually increases without a solution, it can undermine the executive's health.

Trying to Buy Satisfaction

The well-heeled retiring executive with the means to buy anything may be heading for the boredom of advanced hobbyism. More toys in retirement do not make for a more rewarding hobby, nor do they allow for the escape from existential boredom with life or boredom with oneself. As affluence can lead to boredom and stress, so it can lead to sickness. Lots of money allowing consumption as an end by itself is an empty proposition. Without individual differentiation and self-discovery to set one's purpose, having and spending money can lead to the despair and nihilism depicted in Jimmy Buffet's popular song "Margaritaville" in contrast to Jimmy Carter's commitment to Habitat for Humanity. The point is to base your purpose on your values and meaning beyond trivial, activity-based hobbies. Only by finding new work beyond pure consumerism and the trivial nature of hobbies can the executive used to being challenged transcend the boredom. Severe boredom leads to hyper-stress, meaninglessness, and retirement despair.

Consumerism is a unique issue because in retirement, the executive as a corporate being may rely on buying to overcome the rages of retirement boredom. Isn't this the golden age of retirement? This seems to be why it is all worthwhile, from the high rewards of executive life to the transition to "success" in retirement. This is a vicious circle insofar as the executive inevitably becomes bored with one set of toys; it will feel as if those toys are not that good anymore. The remedy seems to always lie in having to buy the latest and greatest tools of one's favorite hobby. This cycle will continue to repeat itself, supported by feedback from one's envious fellow retirees. Unfortunately, this means of finding your retirement joy and meaning through consumerism fails by creating renewed stress, if not despair. This is a case where "less is more."

Philosophers and psychotherapists refer to the three modes of existence: "having, doing, and being" (Jean-Paul Sartre, p. 557). As long as the individual has stayed in the collective mode of the corporate executive role, life will be based on mainly "having and doing." However, once retired, most of the busy life of corporate "doing" is over, and one is reduced to the primacy of "having," which is essentially consumerism. This is an empty value to spend one's retirement in, especially if "doing" is reduced to the triviality of hobbies. As the corporate being is a false self reducing our potential to "doing" and "having", the only way out is to reinvent yourself by discovering your real self or authentic being and reviving your passion. This way, "having" can be supplemented with meaningful "doing," resulting in a new vibrant sense of "being." This is the only way out of the debilitating ravages of stress caused by the boredom of not being fully connected to your inner values and purpose.

The so-called guarantee of the corporate retirement myth of the golden age is a dangerous one for the retired executive: money will not buy satisfaction and happiness, nor will it buy meaning and peace of mind. What money cannot buy can lead to the ravages of hyper-stress. Gabor Mate (2003), who studied the relationship between stress and disease says, "The executive whose financial security is assured when he is terminated may still experience severe stress if his self-esteem and sense of purpose were completely bound up with his position in the company, compared with a colleague who finds greater value in family, social interests or spiritual pursuits. The loss of employment will be perceived as a major threat by one, while the other may see it as an opportunity" (p. 31). In part 4 we will explore a strategy for how you can develop a personal solution for finding happiness through a renewal of meaning and purpose, thereby overcoming the vacuum created by the loss of your corporate being.

Repressed Anger

Politically astute executives have played their corporate role well enough to survive the corporate jungle or the rat race. Being agreeable when necessary but showing enough initiative to be considered a "leader" deserving of promotion is a psychologically difficult balance for the executive. This requires a significant degree of self-control. When the boss disagrees with you or when certain positions are not politically wise to take, it usually forces you as an executive to put your position forward in a mild, muted way to gauge possible acceptance. This requires you to perpetually repress your ideas for those of the corporate being. Any feelings of personal anger at constantly having to conform and agree against your own thoughts or at having to constantly compromise must be repressed. Open disagreements embarrassing corporate executives' genteel, political demeanor in a meeting usually can be a career-limiting move (CLM). Executives are quite aware of all the CLMs in their political corporate culture. This leads the individual to a difficult choice, one of compromising one's own original thinking for the security of the collective thinking of the corporate culture. If the individual has no issue with the conformity factor, then this individual may be a person with less creativity and leadership to begin with. This person may be happy just fitting in and offer little real leadership potential. However, for the talented executive with imaginative potential and high energy, continually having to compromise and censor thoughts to be politically on the right side is exhausting and demoralizing. This executive will also have to repress any frustration and even anger to avoid open conflict, and will have to mentally dismiss the issue so as to be able to continue to function smoothly as part of the team. This is even more challenging for the executive who must not only show unanimity but lead his or her part of the company accordingly. The compromises required out of fear are palpable: only the fearless few are psychologically secure enough to overcome this. *Groupthink* is subordinate sycophants routinely agreeing with the boss or corporate policies, and the "if it ain't broke don't fix it" philosophy prevails. This is common in most companies but limits creativity and motivation and contributes to the decline of large successful companies as they become vulnerable to smaller entrepreneurial upstarts with a freer culture of communications.

In my personal career, this need to compromise myself for the corporate being was in varying degrees one of the reasons that I had decided to engineer my exit as the executive head of human resources in four different multinationals in the pharmaceutical, financial, computer, and automotive industries. As the head of HR, I believed it was always important to open up the pathways for discussion and debate to create an open, free-thinking culture that allowed individuals to be entrepreneurial in their own ways in their own areas. In these personal cases, it was a common factor in my leaving, believing that I could be a better change agent externally as a consultant than internally. Whenever I had to choose between articulating my thoughts accurately on what I believed were important issues, or following the corporate thinking, I always had an overwhelming need to speak up or write down my views regardless of the recipient, thinking it would help the company. Most executives tend to tactically modify their comments to fit and to support the prevailing opinions of the next level executives. Luckily, my ideas were usually seen as creative fresh thinking, but when they addressed a sacred cow or an ego issue, they could be seen as not just unwanted but construed as insubordination. This could easily lead to resistance based on, "who does he think he is?" My colleagues usually appreciated my lead as breaking the diplomatic ice for them. However, my issue was never being able to devote my mind to becoming a dedicated corporate being who knew his place in the hierarchy. Although I was as diplomatic as possible, as a dedicated change agent my ideas for improvement refused to be constrained by the fetters of the corporate being.

Perhaps my academic training and pedagogical assumptions led me to believe that the truth was to be sought at all costs and was a liberating benefit for all. This pursuit of organizational objectivity led me to often refuse to compromise on important issues in the face of higher-ups with greater power. I became aware that higher-ups do not always want to be "liberated" by my analysis. Political alignments and egos were often more powerful than my dogged attempts at reform in the hopes the climate would become more democratic. It may also have been my emotional conviction that real power lay within the value of an idea and in situational thinking, and not in formal positional power. However, I never seemed to lose sleep over reactions, and a "let the chips fall where they may" approach always felt good. This was always my way of trying to prevent the groupthink that constrains original thinking in many corporations.

Unfortunately, most executives believe that their organizations are different and have a free-thinking creative culture.

Ultimately, I could only play the corporate being role within my own values, which was of course, a contradiction. I truly felt that if I could not express my thoughts freely, this was not where I wanted to work anyway, and so I had nothing to lose. I always felt that I always had other more rewarding career options and that I would never sacrifice my original thinking for any job. This is perhaps what led me to pursue writing as a way of reaching a wider audience. Whatever it was that led me to feel suffocated by many corporate beings, I proudly lived to write about it. I knew myself and learned that being willing to reflect my views objectively and transparently had its downside. In fact, whenever I was asked for my weaknesses in job interviews, I candidly admitted that I was not a good politician, and that if I ever got to the point where the leadership did not encourage open, creative thinking on key ideas and policy that I would have to leave. This is perhaps why upon leaving those companies I have always felt liberated and excited by the creative options possible on the horizon. I will help you address the executive need to become yourself and re-create your life in retirement in part 4.

What about you and your relation to your corporate being?

- What ideas have you dismissed because you were discouraged by the corporate culture?
- How often have you compromised your innovative ideas to fit in with your peers' ideas?
- How often has the boss said that your idea does not fit into the new head office initiative?
- What ideas did you feel a passion for but could never get any traction inside of the corporation?
- What ideas did you feel were the real you, ideas that you could base a start-up on?
- What ideas fit your calling in life but do not fit the corporation?

- How has the rejection of your ideas affected your motivation to do your job and commitment to the company?
- Have you compromised your values and beliefs by backing away from your creative ideas for job security?
- How does not following your creative thinking and your dreams make you feel about yourself?
- Do you ever feel like you are "rotting on the vine" inside of your corporate box or corporate being?
- What's the worst-case scenario if you stay as a corporate being and deny your dreams?
- How can you ever be fulfilled and happy if you don't listen and act on your inner calling, your special purpose and meaning in life?

One of my favorite stories pertaining to this is that of Thomas Siebel, who founded Siebel Systems in 1993. As Siebel told his story, he had angrily quit Oracle because Larry Ellison, the CEO of Oracle, did not support his idea of customer relationship management (CRM) software for call centers. Siebel developed this idea into his own multibillion-dollar company, beating Oracle to this market segment, which turned out to be huge. In the end, Oracle bought Siebel Systems in 2005 for $5.8 billion! (Kerstetter, 2005). Not bad for following your own creative ideas and dreams in the face of rejection.

Part Four: Transcending Fear with Love and Passion

A thing of beauty is a joy forever:
Its loveliness increases; it will never
Pass into nothingness; but will still keep
A bower quiet for us, and a sleep
Full of sweet dreams, and health, and quiet breathing.
—John Keats

Chapter 7: Finding Oneself

It is well with me only when I have a chisel in my hand.
—Michelangelo

Music saved my life!
—Lenny Kravitz

It is never too late to find or reinvent yourself; it can save your life! M. Scott Peck (1978) talks about cancer cases where surgeons opened up a patient, found the patient riddled with cancer, and just closed the patient up as there was nothing they could do. The cancer was inoperable, and the patient was given six months to live. Yet miraculously five to ten years later, the individual was still alive without a trace of cancer! "[T]here are indications that one of the similarities in all those rare cases is a tendency on the part of the patient to make very profound changes in their lives. Once told they have a year to live, they seem to say to themselves, 'I'm darned if I want to live out my days still working at IBM, what I want to do is refinish furniture. That's what I've always wanted to do....' So after they make such decisions and such changes in their lives, their cancer goes away" (pp. 54–55).

Nothing is more stressful than not being your authentic self. Finding ourselves and doing what we really want to do not only lowers our stress but reduces the cause of most illness and disease. Does it make sense to live as corporate beings to save for a "successful" retirement of prosperity and consumption when we may be cutting our retirement life in half? By removing stress from your body, it can better heal, according to Dr. Ben Johnson (Byrne 2006).

Given the addiction to the corporate being, we need psychological strategies to wean ourselves from its all-encompassing power. It is important to recognize it early as a dependency on a false self and prepare to get off it. We need to raise our consciousness on the issue in order to psychologically prepare for retirement. You will not be retiring as your corporate being, so you need to find your real self that you want to retire to!

Community Participation

Addiction to the corporate being and its system can best be overcome through activities within the context of community involvement. Reinventing yourself and overcoming the ravages of the addictions to power, money, and your professional techniques are difficult. Exorcizing your beloved corporate identity and replacing it with your authentic self cannot happen solely through the transformational powers of individual counseling, but only through the power of action and community involvement. Anne Wilson Schaef (1987) points to the futility of treating individual addictions in the isolation of one-on-one counseling. She consequently gave up being a psychotherapist to become an organizational consultant and healthcare trainer. She advocates the success of the Alcoholic Anonymous social model for overcoming any addiction. Only through social support and connecting to a new social system can we transform ourselves from corporate beings to new self-identities based on new social roles. If we are to become our authentic selves, we will need a new community or social system to support this new process of reinvention of our selves. Otherwise, we will never conquer the power that the corporate executive identity has over us. We will simply languish in the stress of its absence, as a form of death before our time.

New activities, based on a renewed sense of purpose and meaning, are necessary within the social context of a focused community or subgroups that share our newly discovered values. This could result in a new set of activities as a volunteer or as an entrepreneur. It could also be combined with family or hobbies. Finding ourselves has both a thinking and self-awareness process. To become yourself, you need to apply the insights through the activity of social involvement. Your new purpose needs to connect with others and a new social system. Your individual purpose must connect to a social purpose. *Don't forget that your corporate being was formed through the social system of the corporation and professional associations.* When you retire you lose this corporate community and will languish in isolation as a corporate being like a lost dinosaur looking for its herd. Your only way to overcome being reduced to the stress of a deprived addiction to one's corporate self is through finding your new life mission and joining a compatible social network or community with compatible and supportive values and goals.

Corporate Being versus Authentic Being

Our corporate being has collective values and has shaped us to fit into a collectively defined role. Our identity is recognized from the perspective of this role, or the required behaviors needed to fulfill a specific corporate result. This slot would be filled quickly if you were not there by the many suitors to the role. It's nothing personal, but these willing executives strive for promotions and are happy to get the chance at a higher responsibility and salary.

On the other hand your authentic being is unique. God made you unlike any other, with special, unique talents, and as such, your authentic self can never be replaced. Your unique blueprint is very personal. Your individual identity is sacred. We all adapt to the external corporate being and internalize it, but we are our authentic beings and can never be co-opted by the collective corporate being. George Orwell's "Big Brother" in his classic book, *1984,* tried to standardize people based on the totalitarian governments policies through "watching" its citizens behavior to ensure compliance and robbing them of their freedom and creative differences. Similarly, our corporate being is like the little "Half Brother" of "Big Brother," watching through peer pressure and through our own internalized corporate standards to conform to the corporate mores. Executives lead to create this corporate being hierarchy of conformity through rewarding teamwork and groupthink. Our corporate being culture has a cloning effect like the old IBM's "Big Blue" personality.

Yet as individuals, we shall never feel more comfortable and stress free as when we are our authentic selves. We never feel comfortable with the standardized ideal of the corporate being we chase as we pursue the next promotion because the corporate being is a false self which really is a fictional self designed to cover up our personal weaknesses just as Thomas Watson, Jr., used the "Big Blue" standard to cover over his own insecurities. This is the executive neurosis. You can be fired or replaced from your corporate beings, nor will you ever be able to retire to it. However, you cannot be fired from your authentic being, for that is who you are underneath. It's the "diamond in the corporate being rough." You just need to find it! It is who you need to retire to in order to overcome the addiction to the corporate being and the stress of being what you are not. You are only truly happy at home without stress by becoming yourself in your authentic self, the alignment of your real values, talents, and passion. Your authentic being is based on your inalienable freedom and creativity.

A good place to start to differentiate yourself and find your authentic being is by recollecting your experiences of not feeling comfortable with your corporate being. Reflecting on the times that we used the corporate talk of conformity or 'groupthink' makes us feel ashamed or wasted. Times when we may have inwardly disagreed but nodded in complete agreement make us feel dissonant as our body language contradicts our mind. Re-thinking and reconstructing such corporate events and personal behaviors help us to see how we sacrifice ourselves by failing to take up these opportunities to think creatively and help create new value.

Do a Reality Check

- How do your personal values differ from those of the corporation or those values you act out daily for the company?
- What would you have done differently or better to reflect who you really are?
- There is always a gap between our thinking and what we say. What are those gaps between your inner thoughts and your official statements on behalf of your company role?

- Are you allowing yourself to be victimized by you corporate being by allowing it to dominate your behavior?
- To what extent do you fit into the company? To what extent are you a corporate clone?
- How do you really feel about this when you look in the mirror?
- Are you happy to live out your days as a collective corporate being?
- Why not?

Differentiate Yourself

- From a bigger picture, look at your life and ask, what is my purpose and what are my values?
- Can these really be fully met within the confines and conformity to our corporate role? Probably not. We are bigger than any collective role! Our full potential will never be fully developed or actualized within the corporate role.
- What were your dreams when growing up? Have you become those aspirations or not? Is your corporate being your personal dream or nightmare?
- How do you want to be remembered after you die, as a corporate being? Probably not!
- Do you want your life's best achievements read out at your obituary to be "always met budget," " rose to the VP level accountable for six hundred people," "made $,$$$,$$$.$$"?
- In your last stage of life what is the final value that you want to create?
- Can you reach this vision or value in your current role within this corporation? Probably not.

Obituaries of great corporate leaders do not talk about the great deals they did or "killing" they made in business or the unbelievable feats they accomplished against the competition, but rather of how they showed compassion to others and added personal value to others, of the charity work and foundations they left. Why do great corporate leaders like Bill Gates leave the corner office early and turn to philanthropic purposes? It is because ultimately the corporate being is empty, a false self that needs to be re-created by the values that represent the real self.

We move up Maslow's Hierarchy of Needs as we satisfy each lower level of need. As we do, new, higher levels of human needs open up and must be satisfied. Our corporate being has been successful at satisfying our material needs and vicariously some of our social and esteem needs, but it has not allowed us to satisfy our highest need of *self-actualization.* To do so, we need to develop and live out our potential as unique, authentic beings, separate from the collective corporate being.

Becoming self-actualized may seem unreal, abstract, and vague, but it is the opposite: it is your most personal satisfaction and fulfillment. *Your self-actualized person is your real person, the one original you long to be and in fact love.* In contrast, the corporate being is a standardized role for you and your replacement, representing appropriate executive behaviors for that company. As a cookie-cutter template for what you need to do or be as required by your job description of the corporate being the executive leader helps to lead others as a commercial team to win in the marketplace. Given the collective nature of the role, you are easily replaceable. But as you are unique and special compared to others, your authentic self allows you to free yourself of the constraints of the collectivity and conformity to the success criteria of a corporate being. Freeing yourself allows you to explore, search for, and find your unique potential, talent, and creative originality, which can never be fully met by the corporate role or career. Abraham Maslow (1954) gives some indication of the qualities that characterize a self-actualized person. In many ways, the qualities stand out in stark contrast to the qualities that characterize the corporate being. Maslow's concepts are summarized and italicized below.

- *The self-actualized person is creative and is not constrained* by the *conformity* of the corporate being or its groupthink ideas. This individual is original and comfortable being different.

- *The self-actualized person is spontaneous*, responding to the person's original thoughts or feelings, and is *not constrained* by what is politically safe in that corporate culture.
- *The self-actualized person is cooperative* versus displaying the competitive traits of the corporate culture seen as superior to beat the competition and even to protect one's inside power base.
- *The self-actualized person prefers decentralized organizations,* allowing for the *creative free flow of ideas,* not the confidential containment and protection of information in the corporate hierarchy.
- *The self-actualized person is democratic* versus the authoritarian qualities of the corporate being needed to protect turf or empire.
- *The self-actualized person is non–power seeking* versus the addiction to power of a corporate being, who seeks formal, positional power at the expense of personal, creative power.
- *The self-actualized person recognizes the value of others regardless of rank* versus the corporate being that bestows greater personal value to others in proportion to their level in the hierarchy.

As the authentic person grows to discover personal and authentic values, talents, and roles as differentiated from the corporate role, this person becomes real, shedding the superficial power and role of the corporate being. Greater inner power is found in the real self and with non–power based, authentic relationships with others. The self-actualized person finds the solace and fulfillment of choosing to be free of the constraints of corporate roles to pursue his or her own values and dreams creatively, whether entrepreneurially, socially, artistically, intellectually, or spiritually. The key is that the impetus comes from the well of free self-discovery and the person's unique values and talents. *The self-actualized person is responding to his or her authentic inner calling, not to the corporate boss!*

From Fear to Love

For the executive who is pragmatic and results oriented, the status quo is not enough if it fails. Nothing fails like trying to live out the corporate myth as a corporate being. It fails because it is not just unrealistic but impossible. Retiring into the stress of the withdrawal from the support of the corporate being is like a major demotion. The fear of retirement repressed by the idyllic corporate myth of retirement soon will reveal its ugly head after retirement as boredom and stress take over leading to possible morbidity and premature death.

Finding your real self is simple, but this can be deceptively difficult for the executive entrenched in the corporate being. You will not find yourself by using the usual executive or professional techniques, but only through exercising the freedom of getting back in touch with your dreams and discovering your originality, your unique values, experiences, talents, and life purpose. As you retire from the corporate being, instead of being a has-been leader, you have the chance to reinvent yourself by reshaping and rebranding yourself. You are no longer a rented agent, your skills bought on the market by the corporation to play a specific role. The psychologically therapeutic bridge to your authentic self will conquer the fear of retirement and later stress and boredom. Paradoxically, the authentic self has greater personal power as it emerges with your real values and taps into the personal power of your natural passion. Discovering this new power creates harmony within you, overcoming the fear of losing the artificial, borrowed power of your corporate role. This is the happiness and joy of being yourself, overcoming the stress of your false self. Love of retirement replaces the fear of loss. Ahead are the questions, structures, and awareness building to help you make this inner passage to your originality.

Relearning Yourself

This inner passage of self-discovery you owe to yourself. Growing away from your corporate being starts with the need to relearn yourself. I use the term *growth* because this is genuinely personal growth. Here you are not trying to find a new stereotyped collective personality that you like but your own unique originality, what makes you different from everyone else. This can be rewarding and fun! Try it!

You thought you knew yourself, but this was you in your corporate power base of specialized control. You accepted your new corporate successes, power, and authority as evidence of your natural superior self, but now you must prove this standing without your corporate, well-recognized status and support, not to mention the power base and authority that came with your empire. As you enter so-called retirement, you may not be fully prepared from an emotional point of view, to knowingly be a king with no clothes!

Personally, as a management consultant and VP, HR having designed, facilitated, and managed corporate training and development programs in many companies and industries, I have come to understand the limitations of such leadership programs. Academic training is often seen to be general with limited value to specific companies. This is why most of my training was customized. It also had a higher value and paid more. Leadership training ideally works within the framework of corporation's culture and business model to facilitate the business executives to achieve greater personal execution and commercial success. I realize now that much of my work in-house and as a management consultant trained employees to become managers and to lead by becoming a better corporate being. Corporate training may make you a better corporate leader but may restrict your preparation to be your authentic self in retirement.

Here's a chance to return to relearn who you are, to regain your sense of self. Instead of learning the collective rules and corporate methods of success, you now must learn your own values and personal style and methods of expressing who you decide to be as an original you, for success in retirement on your own terms.

Your roots: Relearning yourself involves a deeper kind of introspective thinking of your whole life story including before and outside of your career. Start with your childhood and then do the same for your preadult years and remember who you were.

- Who were you, and what was your sense of self? What happened? Did this get lost?
- What did your parents think you should do? Did you follow or overcome their vision? How? Why?
- What were your favorite activities? What skills and aptitudes did these develop?
- What were you good at and not so good at? Did you pursue what you were good at, or did you work to improve your weaknesses?
- What were the five best things you accomplished? Your real talent may be hidden in what you were best at.
- What were your dreams of your future? Did you follow and fulfill these dreams? What happened?
- What were the critical events that shaped your future? Was your future more shaped by external events or by your own design?
- Did you have goals and a life design? What happened?
- Did you get lost on the way "to the circus"? How can you get your own life design back on track?

Your corporate being: Define what you became in your corporate career and as an executive leader.

- What are your company's success criteria? Do you feel successful personally if the company succeeds? Why the gap?
- What are your company's values and culture? Do you know the values, or do you have to look them up in the corporate report? Is there a difference between the published corporate values and those practiced?

- Do your personal values differ from those of the company? How have you coped with this difference? How do you feel about adapting to this difference?
- What do you love/hate about your company? Remember this is a private thought, and it is not being asked by your boss. You have nothing to lose and everything to gain by being honest with yourself.
- What are your performance success criteria? Do you agree with how you are rated at the company? Do you feel that your performance success represents your personal success, or is there a difference?

Your personal success: Identify areas of your personality not known by your company, and personal success that has never been known, identified, or rewarded by the company.

- Name and define those areas of personal success that are different from your performance success. Why do these successes fail to fit your corporate being? How do you feel about this?
- Name three great things about you that your boss does not know or even care to hear about and which may not help your next promotion. For example:
- "I love painting scenery, but I never seem to find the time in this job."
- "I keep dreaming about buying a ranch in Montana."
- "Due to a scheduling conflict, I've decided not to be at the Annual Meeting this year, I've made it to the national bowling competition in Buffalo and I'm goin'!, I wouldn't miss this for anything. It's my dream, my passion. In fact it's going to be covered by TSN!"
  Now, how does that feel? Saying these things may be a "strike" against your future corporate success, but you have "spared" your emotional integrity to your dreams. This is a personal, emotional win that differentiates you and helps you break out from your corporate being. It feels real good because this is the real you. What's more important now

that you are financially secure, you or your job? Besides given your experience, they are probably lucky to have you. How will you break out?

Re-cap: Your emergent aptitudes, aspirations, aptitudes, and values, particularly those that were unfulfilled by your corporate roles need to be identified.

- How do your personal characteristics differ from your corporate being?
- What do you like best about these nascent traits of yourself that have not been expressed, fully developed, or allowed to emerge in your corporate roles?
- What do you like and not like about yourself as a corporate person? Given the personal qualities that differentiate you from your corporate personality, why can't you express them or actualize them within the corporate values or role you play?
- Given these personal qualities, what other career choices and roles could you have played?
- What kind of person do you want to be when you "grow up" in retirement? Don't forget your corporate being will fail you in retirement.
- Are you having fun in your role as a corporate being? What's missing, and how can you add fun back into your life?
- How do you fall back in love with yourself and life? Remember if you can't love what you see in the mirror, you won't be able to love others and allow yourself to discover and follow your passion.

The corporation found you and made you into a corporate being, role, and executive leader. That was exhilarating, but that was then; is this the real you now? You cannot take this role or being into retirement. Only you can find yourself. Yes, your spouse and trusted others can be very helpful. Finding yourself may be an instant "eureka!" or a gradual experience of trying new things. Even better, you probably already know who you are and what you want to be and do, but your job never allowed it. Making the leap may be based on one big, obvious decision or small, experimental decisions. Finding yourself will be part of your rejection of your corporate being. Both your corporate and authentic beings cannot co-exist in you without personal conflict and high stress, which threaten your health. You will need a higher personal purpose beyond the job to find yourself. You will also need that higher purpose to be beyond the pure leisure of hobbies or consumerism of retirement. This requires *a new vision based on what you love about yourself and how you can create new value based on your unique talents.*

Creating new value depends on your own unique values. So your retirement value-added project must be distinctly designed for you by you. Do you know your real values? When asked in interviews, executives most commonly give their version of general social, family, religion, and country values. Although this is fine, it is vital for any executive to drill down into his or her experiences and find more specific personal values based on what is it in childhood experiences that makes him or her unique as individuals. Every one of us has different experiences that have created hardship and struggle. Such childhood-based real life failures and triumphs create a passion for certain things. These experiences are vital to discovering the roots of our inner, most compelling unique values. Often these do relate to family but can lead to other causes. One executive who had excellent financial skills realized that she had turned her back on the family farming business. It turned out that this did bother her enough to refocus her family values to begin to offer help to her younger siblings. She was not sure quite how, but she became excited about the possibilities for agriculture given the new age of ethanol and bio-fuel. Another executive was born in China and decided that his underlying, strongest value was to coach new Chinese immigrants on how to achieve success in North American business. He also could see the value in forming these new relationships in order to form possible entrepreneurial opportunities.

Such living values go beyond the general social values of family, country, or culture and open the door to specific personal actions based on gaining valued results based on your own talents.

Look inside your diverse, corporate roles; you will find there are elements which did fit your true aptitudes and talents, or you never would have embarked on such a career. There are also many hobbies or personal activities that also fit your best talents and aptitude as well as your values. Since retirement needs to be low stress, the new role or roles that you need to create for yourself need to be optimal fun. This must be more than the trivial fun of hobbies or "bored" games, but connected to your visceral passion and deeper need for purpose and meaning in the community. You want to be able to get out of bed early in the morning with a new zeal and purpose to add new value and yet still have fun. How can you do what you love? This is the same as doing what you find fun in—but with a valuable purpose.

Becoming obsessed with a new purpose is different from the workaholic's addiction and fear of failure because it is freely adding new value based on your personal mission, not the company's mission. It is personally meaningful because you have chosen it freely as a value of love and not because you learned it from your corporate role and are doing it out of fear of failure. Discovering yourself can lead to being the passionate volunteer or the entrepreneur who creates new value for others in the community. This new, purposeful activity is based on the joy of your newly discovered purpose and your real talents. This personal vision is found inside you and is based on love. Actualizing your dream can only be achieved outside yourself in the community as you apply your talents to a new entrepreneurial venture, social or community cause. You will achieve what you personally love as opposed to reacting to the fear of failure as a corporate being. For example, the executive who loved to bowl followed his dreams to the national tournament; he might have become a national celebrity, which may have catapulted him toward opportunities leading to a role that better suited him and was what he loved. He could be using his unexpressed artistic skills to make designer bowling balls, or using his promotional skills to work for the promotion of bowling for youth and the retired. The point is it takes real courage, but you can be more successful by following what you love and dream about than following the collectivity or the extraneous demands of your corporate being.

Rediscover Yourself

One way to relearn or rediscover your self is to draw three circles. First, draw your *skills circle*. Your skills represent the specialized, technical and organizational skills of your corporate self. These come from your education and training as a professional.

Next, draw your *talent circle*. This represents your inner talents that your corporate role never could encompass. Remember you are much bigger and better than any job! For example, you may have greater leadership skills developed through community volunteering than you will ever be able to express in your job. You may plan to run for the town mayor as an exit from the company. You may have developed great photography, writing, painting, musical, or computer skills, or a unique combination well beyond your limited job description. What you consider as talent must encompass your potential, not just your actual demonstrated skills. You may not have spent enough time nurturing or bringing out this talent. However, such a talent is real, given the feedback of others and your intuition for developing and performing this ability. More time may be necessary to practice and develop your potential to bring it out. By overlapping this talent circle over the skills circle, you can compare what they have in common. Your talent may have diverged from your skills and may have little in common.

Finally, draw your *passion circle*, which represents those activities for which you have a personal passion. You never seem to have enough time to do these activities, projects, or creations. These are personally satisfying pursuits for which you feel total joy and the fun of doing. Pursuing this activity and process raises you up emotionally, connecting you naturally to your holistic nature and purpose. It inspires you. It is so uniquely creative that you feel that you can do it in your own way and add value. This will allow you to differentiate and uniquely brand yourself.

Put this passion circle over the other two and see what they have in common. Most importantly, specifically view the difference with the talent circle. It is possible that you are talented in something, but for whatever reason you do not have the passion for it. Passion can change and may not be identical to what your talents are. There may have been a recent life-changing issue that you may feel a very strongly about. However, they are usually quite close, given the highly reinforcing and rewarding, integrated nature of following and performing your talents. It is vital to have the passion for something to even be able to develop the area as a talent. Passion is necessary to develop and to sustain your talent.

To get to the essence of this exercise, carefully look at how your passion circle diverges from your talent circle and particularly your skills circle. Your corporate being is probably very similar to your skills circle, but your job is likely too narrow to capture your full talent. Your talent circle is probably bigger than the limits of your job. However, you may not have any passion for certain talents you have. For example, you may have been forced by your parents to learn to play the piano. You may have kept it up at church as an organist partly out of keeping your parents happy, but now that your parents have passed you have no passion for it and decided to be only a part-time organist. Talent without passion will be like pushing rope! This is why the passion circle is the most important. If you have the passion, you can overcome many obstacles to achievement. Issues and projects that you have a passion for will need some skill and connection to your talent to form a new inspiring personal retirement project. If you have the passion and the talent in a specific area, this can be the basis for your new life plan in retirement.

It is usually beneficial to get input from a significant other who knows you well to help you develop a life plan. *Reality testing* is vital to ensuring that your new life plan is achievable and realistic, and that it will be consistent with their life priorities. Obviously, what you have gained from the thoughtful comparison of the circles is to see how much your technical and professional skills are really reflecting your true talents. Finally, do these technical and professional skills reflect your real interest and joy of working or creating? Often they do not line up, and so it becomes a new opportunity to plan your life in a new direction. However, it is possible that the circles overlap quite well, and your talent and passions lie within your technical and professional skills. It is common, though, to be bored with the skills you use routinely on the job and to feel you would rather do something new and exciting. Here you need to find the talents that you can sustain by identifying your passion. If you do happen to love your skills as an activity, then you need to focus on how you can transform your role in retirement and still use such skills outside of your corporate being and its stress-laden workaholic environment. For example, an executive with accounting and financial skills could become a tax or financial planning consultant based in a recreational location or cottage. A well-respected professional could also serve on boards, become active in nonprofit organizations, or write professional articles for a professional association. The important point is that you must plan for a vibrant life outside of the corporation.

A former colleague and a vice president from the pharmaceutical industry had a plan to get out early and retire to his hometown, a farming community, and simply put out his shingle as a chartered accountant to pay the bills. The area was a fruit-growing agricultural area, and a demand for wine led to many farmers to convert to growing vineyards, including his late father. His mother had rented the land to other local farmers and moved into town. It didn't take long for the former vice president to be doing a lot more than income tax for locals. Before long, building on his father's relationships, he was doing a number of small business taxes, began to provide financial corporate consulting, and began to serve on the board of the largest winery in the region. He said he just loved going back to his roots and helping the families he knew as a kid, not to mention being able to care for his ailing mother. He said he regretted not getting out years ago because this was much more relaxing, rewarding, and fulfilling. Besides he reported that he was having more fun than he ever did working.

His profile and skills were business finance. However, he was bored with doing finance inside of the corporate role with all the pressure and having to answer all of the "dumb" questions from the corporate headquarters. He also preferred to live simply in the country and ended up moving back to his family farm after rebuilding the farmhouse. Finance, it turned out, really wasn't his calling. His calling was to complete the work his father had begun in fruit farming and raise it to a new level by turning it into a winery with the farmer who had rented the land, who was someone he had known in high school, a son of one of his father's friends. Although bored with corporate finance, he loved farmers and had a passion to help them, which had developed when he was a child sitting around the family kitchen table and listening to his father figure out how he could pay the bills and support the family. This was probably why he had gone into finance and accounting initially as a way to help his family. His skill was finance, but he was bored with doing it in the corporate environment. His talent was applying finance to help others and his passion was to use his talents in the family business. His calling was to help the farmers from his community to complete his father's work and potential. It was that simple.

Every case is unique. Every case is simple if thought through. Don't overcomplicate the process as executives are prone to do, with the acquired complexities of their previous roles. *You are unique and need to find your own singular calling.* The corporation won't do this for you. You have the responsibility to yourself to do this. The following questions are designed to help you do it.

Your Real Talent, Passion, and Calling

- What *skills* do you need for your corporate role?
- Do you have at least one skill that you are *bored* with using?
- Could you combine this skill with something like a new project to make this skill more interesting to perform?

- How are your skills bigger than this role?
- Can you name one new dimension or application that you could add on to use more of your skills?
- Why are your *talents* bigger than your job skills, given the narrow limits of your job description?
- Differentiate why your *talents* are organic and personally unique and why they will never fit the standardization of your job description, or why many others could do your job but no one else has your combination of talents?
- How do your *personal values* differ from the corporate values?
- *Beyond the narrow scope of skills,* how would you describe the talents that you have developed in your personal activities and overall life?
- Can you compare your talent to the corporate role and ask yourself why your corporate being fails to fully tap your talents?
- What do you enjoy *playing* or working at more than anything else?
- What are the activities that you have the most *fun* with and don't get bored with through repetition?
- How could you combine your talents within the context of your *preferred activity*?
- How would you define your possible *talents of joy*?
- What stirs your *emotions* and gets you *excited* to act on something because it is important to you?
- Can you name three *causes* that you care about more than the corporate mission?
- How could you use your talents toward one of these causes?
- What activity or cause could stir your emotions and *passion* to create results that fit your talents?
- What *unresolved issues* do you have in your life, and how could your talents resolve them?
- What are your *personal values* and purpose outside of the corporation?
- Given your talents and passion, what could your *life's calling* be outside of the corporation in retirement?

Finding oneself is like finding the perfect role that fits your talent. This is inspirational. In retirement, you will be free to do what you couldn't do in the job box. However, you need to determine through self-introspection, career analysis, and Life Planning what that is. The sooner you do this before retiring the better. Identifying those activities that for you are *labors of love* is the key to identifying your real passions. Exercising your passion is healthy and creatively rejuvenating, the opposite of burning yourself out through stress. Reaching outside to apply your talent to a new community, group, or social cause through passion is the basis of self-actualization.

Self-actualization is far more than finding yourself; it takes you beyond yourself through purpose and adding new value to others. Self-actualization occurs through new, focused creative activities, which can be entrepreneurial, volunteer, intellectual, artistic, and/ or spiritual. Whatever it is you end up doing in this process, it will be unique to you, allowing you to fully express your full potential in your environmental situation. It will allow you to overcome your false self-stress of being in the state of a collective corporate clone to attain the special, full individual being that God made you to be. God even made each and every snowflake distinctly beautiful and unique. Imagine the total state of natural boredom if every snowflake was made from a cookie cutter mold in the sky to be identical. We need to break out of the stereotyped corporate clone through expressing and actualizing what make each executive uniquely talented and special. This special being is happily distinct and unique from every other person that ever existed. It is not being different for its own sake that matters but using our special sacred distinctness to finally and fully be and actualize ourselves. Self-actualized people have shed the fear of nonconforming of the collective corporate being. This will create new joy and fulfillment to the executive as he or she escapes the clone role of the job box but given what it creates for the individual will blossom to others and add new beauty and love to others making the world a more creative kinder gentler place.

In essence, you need to start by identifying your unique talent and special calling, and then determine a purpose and meaning for applying your God-given talents. Finally, you must look for new opportunities to apply these talents within your community, friends, or other outside groups. *Only through reinventing yourself within a new social system will you transform yourself from the confines of your corporate being to the freedom of self- actualization.* This will allow you to escape stress and hyper-stress to the joy of self-discovery and the passion of creating and actualizing new personal value.

Further Education Creates Options

Retirement is no time to begin or to redo your fundamental education or even to redevelop your basic skills. However, lifelong learning is a key to health, an essential part of the dynamic life plan of the so-called retirement years. It is also the chance to fine-tune your talents. Typically, the workaholic corporate life has not given you enough free time to fully develop your talents in areas where you have a passion. Further education at this stage can reinforce what your talents are already. It is difficult to develop new talents at this stage in life. The point here is to reinforce and bring out your existing latent talents left dormant and underdeveloped by your corporate being.

For example, you may have already studied music as a kid and may have been in a band in college, or may even have sung in a church choir. You may have also quietly written poetry but never bothered showing anyone. You love expression and music. However, you may have spent your career as an accountant or lawyer, perhaps partially influenced by your parents or others who made you believe that you could never earn a living in music. You believe the talent is there waiting to be actualized. You may have a passion to set up a new band, sing, compose, and even record some music. You may choose to take some musical composition courses in the area of your musical inspiration. Similarly, you may have been good at art, drew periodically, and dreamed of doing more, but you became an engineer for security reasons. Now your passion is driving you to paint. You may choose to enroll in art workshops in your areas of interest: wildlife, outdoor scenery, abstract painting, or others.

Retirement does not necessarily mean stopping work. For that reason, further education can help you learn how to set up a small business or consulting practice, how to sell and distribute your newly created music or paintings. Now if you follow your talent, work will be fun as you follow your passion. You can do it part-time or full-time depending on your own motivation and internally driven passion to complete the project. You are in control. You are the boss. Instead of being stressed out or security bound, you feel a new, giddy sense of freedom with a personal purpose, destiny, and calling.

Another major personal option of your life plan may involve travel or working in the Sun Belt at least in the winter. (Chapter 11 will more formally address Life Planning.) Taking English as a Second Language (ESL) training and certification courses can allow you to visit many exotic countries and do some work teaching English. This can help you pay the bills and travel longer, and the interactive social experience of befriending the locals will vastly enrich your traveling experiences and personal meaning. Traveling is a lot more than seeing geography, historical sites, major cities and tourist traps, et cetera. Other courses that allow you to travel more would be courses that train you to be a tour guide. You could work with travel agencies or even use your original language skills if you are fluent in more than one language. This could be an excellent way to see the world in your own way and have a real adventure.

Hobbies can also be combined with travel or living in the Sun Belt. For example, avid golfers can take courses and get certification from the Golf Teachers Federation and use their talents and passion for golf down south all winter. Working part-time allows you to afford the Sun Belt lifestyle. Similarly, those with a passion for fishing can take boating and hands-on fishing courses to qualify to lead fishing expeditions. Qualified sailors can likewise become certified to be chartered for all kinds of expeditions and adventures. Using your corporate communication, inter-personal, and managerial skills combined with a hobby or passionate area of interest can put you into business on your terms. This way you are being paid to follow your dreams. The list of combinations of interests goes on and on. Almost any hobby can be combined with your corporate skills and further training to allow you to set up a small business locally or follow your passion to travel. The only limits are your imagination.

The favorite part-time work that many CEOs and executives embark on is serving on boards of other companies, foundations, or charities. This often involves travel and allows them to use their executive expertise and business contacts to further the work of the organization. Getting on a board requires networking and figuring out the unique value you have to offer. Getting to know the board members of a company that interests you before you retire will help you in this planning process of finding an opportunity.

One highly respected CEO of a pharmaceutical company had a passion for cardio-vascular (CV) drugs given his experience as a pharmaceutical sales representative promoting such medicines to heart specialists. The company was successful selling such CV products partially because of his personal relationship with the specialists. In retirement, he carried this passion for helping patients with heart problems and for dealing with the physician specialists into playing a prominent leadership role as chairman of the Heart and Stroke Foundation. This visible leadership role led to his appointment to the board of a CV biotechnology research company. His retirement role was based on his networking talent and relationships in the CV community and his passion to help solve the disease that took his own father's life. He meanwhile had time for his grandchildren and socializing around his hobbies.

Volunteering

Finally, all of the above can be done through volunteering. All of your talents can help others as a volunteer. Developing skills through teaching anywhere in the world can bring the greatest satisfaction through helping others for free. Check out the range of opportunities at <www.volunteer.com>: you can find travel-oriented locations through religious organizations, World Vision, Doctors Without Borders, the Red Cross, and countless others. You have more skills than you realize. Most have been highly developed and usually learned from expensive university degrees and corporate training. It is a shame to let these skills fall into complete decline and be wasted in retirement. If you do not need the money in retirement—or even if you do—volunteering your affordable time is a very rewarding choice. Volunteering is the best activity for developing and maintaining a high self-esteem. Ultimately making a difference for others and adding value for others is what life is all about. Adding value for others beyond our own self-interest is a basis for self-actualizing ourselves. This satisfies our highest spiritual need, taking us beyond security, owning, and consumption.

The Hierarchy of Self-Actualization

Reaching your highest potential is to self-actualize yourself. In order to do that, Life Planning needs to be based on the structure outlined below. Chapter 11 provides some examples of Life Planning around these three Modes of Life (Having, Doing, and Being).

The terms *Having, Doing,* and *Being* are useful as a basis for Life Planning because they describe our life modes. They are compatible with Maslow's Hierarchy of Needs but simpler to apply to Life Planning. For example, our lower-level needs like security and safety relate more to Having, and our higher-level needs of self-actualization through intellectual, art, and spirituality relate more to our Being dimensions. We will build this framework into our Life Planning framework as illustrated in part 4, particularly chapter 11.

In preparation for your own Life Planning you may want to consider the following dimensions and questions.

Having: Consumption

- 101 things I want to buy, try, consume, eat, drink, or own before I die.

Doing: Actions

- 101 things I need to do, see through travel, or experience before I die.

Being: Purpose

- How can I make a difference for others?
- How can I grow, discover, and understand to create new value?
- What purpose does my life serve?
- What value can I create artistically, intellectually, spiritually?
- How can I change the world to make it a better place for others?

Finding Purpose: From Fear to Love

Finding your purpose builds on having determined your talent and turned your passion into your calling. Now we need to position this into your life as its overarching purpose as a basis of prioritization to begin to organize and to enable you to self-actualize your life plan.

To escape the corporate mission of our internalized corporate life, we must re-balance and reinvent ourselves by our new guiding star or purpose. Determining your talent needs to be linked to what it is you have a passion and need to do. What is the legacy and unique difference you want your life to have made? Today is the first day of the rest of your life: what is your life's unfinished business? Is it sufficient that you were a loyal corporate executive and will be remembered mainly for doing a good job? If you were a real leader, you probably want to individualize your life and have a personal purpose different from the corporate mission.

The very best indicator of the new shining star you need to follow is not your past skills but the purpose for which you have a real visceral passion. Your individual purpose is very personal and in essence incompatible with the collective purpose of your corporate being. Often in corporate life, individual passion is turned off because any ideas that do not fit the corporate culture or strategy are discouraged, and no one wants to be too different. The nail that sticks out gets hammered down! The mavericks are pushed down or out as creativity and passion is often replaced by fear. Fear of appearing different and not fitting in or of losing out on the next promotion drives behavior away from our real passion. As a consequence, passion lives submerged in our "basements," only allowed out in a timid manner when it happens to be aligned with the collective mission. This dulls your real passion. You need to decide if you want to live in retirement for the internalized corporate purpose and mission or on your own terms for the personal purpose of you passion. *Do you want to die for the collective mission of your corporate being or for* your *own personally created and discovered special life purpose?*

Passion, though, resides only in the individual and cannot co-exist with the fear of disagreeing or of being different. Passion resides only in your freedom to choose, to think, to be honest with yourself, and freedom to be yourself! As a consequence, your passion is the only pathway through which you can find your new purpose. However, this is not so simple because the corporate being has repressed individual passion. Transcend the collectivist corporate being for yourself by creating your real purpose and passion. The courage to be different because you are connected to your real passion and true beliefs leads to the conflict and destruction of your corporate being and perhaps your future security and promotions. Awaken yourself to your full potential! So what—you are bigger than any job! The end of corporate life is the beginning of your real life in retirement. However, fear can periodically resurface as the fear of retirement or fear of giving up the security blanket. There is also fear of standing up and becoming your real self with your own individual purpose. This is to be expected. Fear will linger as we risk failing to find ourselves. To be ourselves is one of our greatest challenges.

Shakespeare said it best: "To be, or not to be, that is the question." This revealed that the challenge of "being" was not just a centuries-old problem but perhaps the most fundamental one for the human condition. Finding what we love gives us a huge edge as we pursue what our passion is. Getting back in touch with yourself or finding yourself is very much a process of getting in touch with your feelings, getting in touch with what you really love, getting in touch with your inner passion. It is finding the *simple truth* of what is really important to you beyond the clutter of power addiction and consumer promises of the corporate being. This allows you to conquer your insecurities. Finding the courage to do so will not just help you leave the corporate role for retirement but launch you on perhaps the most exciting chapter of your life!

Chapter 8: Personal Change

Success is not the key to happiness.
Happiness is the key to success.
If you love what you are doing, you will be successful.
—Albert Schweitzer

Can you retire from your corporate being? You can retire on paper, but your corporate being is your adopted self and will not go as easily. Even though it is your false self, you will need to do some work to redevelop yourself. Life Planning is empty without personal change and transformation. This is why we call it *Transformational Life Planning*. The problem is that you may not be your corporate being factually but emotionally; you still have a corporate being hangover! The corporation rented your false self for a fee over a period of time expiring at retirement. Post-retirement, you are in a double bind of despair if you long to return to the corporate being identity out of addiction to that role. The stress of being a past memory of a corporate being destroys your future and probably shortens your life. Embracing the past as a has-been is very stressful for an executive who has been a champion of creating change and a new future for others. The healthy thing to do is to undergo significant personal change and create a new, robust future for oneself. This is your last chance to be great!

Don't mentally leave something to retire—go toward something new! Changing oneself will not happen automatically just because you retired or even if you underwent some mechanical step like moving to a different part of the country. Change is difficult but necessary. Retirement is a factual change that happens to you. Avoid becoming a victim of this external event. Take control by changing internally and taking charge. A positive change must derive from a new, fresh vision of what you want or need to be. To be healthy and lower stress, you need to become the real you.

To begin the process of mentally conceptualizing a life plan to self-actualize this real you, ask the following questions:

- What are your most powerful inner needs? They must be palpable and based on your passion. You must feel the painful gap between what you are now—exiting the corporation—and what you see as the real you. Desiring to be something you are not yet is the beginning of the long and exciting journey ahead. You have retired from your corporate being, not from yourself and life's wide open possibilities.
- What is your most important vision and the state of personal being you want and desire the most for the rest of your life? Taking up your freedom with the courage to be involves personal risk as you move from the security blanket of your corporate being image toward your real, naked authenticity.
- What are the most personal dreams you have for yourself that fit your unique values and personal meaning as well as your talents? Do remember all of the lost dreams that you have had for yourself but became too busy to attain? Which dreams will allow you to attain your full potential?

To achieve your dreams, it is vital to start climbing now. There is an old Chinese proverb that says, "Great journeys begin with the first small step." As you mentally set your target and physically validate your desire by moving toward your goal, those first steps may be the hardest but the most important. Momentum helps to fulfill the prophecy of the vision. Motion is the key to the positive reinforcement of your personal progress in your new journey to actualize your dreams. You will never get to the top of the mountain with a few big steps. Small, sustained steps allow you to better overcome obstacles and enjoy the view on the way to your personal greatness, your authentic self.

If you are lucky, you will get a head start: many Boomers are getting out early or transitioning from the corporation with part-time work.

Many professionals, managers, and executives are getting out so they can set up their own part-time or full-time businesses in the type of work they love. Many are doing so to find that precious extra time needed to pursue their dreams of advancing their skills in hobbies so for example they will be able to sail to exotic locations, et cetera. They are setting their lives up on their own terms, what, how, when, and where they want! Getting out early opens the mind to new vistas of opportunities which were blinded by the corporate workaholic pressures.

Gail Sheehy (1977) comments that envious executives complain that civil service employees are lucky: they can accumulate twenty years of service in time to retire on a pension in their forties, which is enough time to launch a second career or combine a paying hobby with loafing on a beach. Increasingly, more executives are taking early retirement so they can do what they really like. Providing that there is not a huge drop in income, the sacrifice is more than compensated by the satisfaction of doing what they really want to do!

Life Planning: Not Retirement Planning

Retirement is a negative word connoting a retreat from the real world of work and a passiveness defaulting to a mythical golden age of healthy, carefree leisure and ease. This naive assumption by itself can lead to the hyper-stress of a short retirement. Life Planning is a renaissance of your life and all of its full possibilities. Life Planning can open up your unique talents, passion, and potential never captured in your service to your corporate being. Life Planning is not a retirement from the corporate being but a psychological transcendence beyond it to a better, fuller life for your potential new career and new life. In essence, Life Planning is all about life, your life and how to expand your horizons beyond your impoverished, in-the-box corporate being. It is all about transformation and expanding life not retreating or retiring from your full potential and your dreams. Life Planning is all about attitude, the positive adventuresome attitude of self-actualization as opposed to the dismal, defeatist attitude that diminishes one's potential by retiring from something and living in the past glories of one's corporate being. Your life mission is not complete; neither is the work to get there.

Attaining your dreams is a labor of love! In many ways, this kind of work can be more challenging but much more satisfying than achieving the goals of your corporate role. Inside the corporation you get lots of training and practice at strategic planning and even career planning, but not Life Planning. Why would this be? It is because Life Planning is counter to the corporation, as it can lead executives to the realization that they are bigger and better, with more options and potential than can ever be packaged into their corporate being. Life Planning is self-discovery and as such is dysfunctional to the corporation, for it could lead many talented and high-performance corporate beings to become disenchanted and leave the company to do other work that is personally more satisfying. Life planning raises too many fundamental human issues: Who am I really? What are my talents? Is my personal potential possible to reach within the constraints of this corporate role or being that I play? These issues cannot be meaningfully answered by your boss or even human resources, given their own roles to represent the company and to optimize the corporation's performance, profitability, and short-term output. This is why Life Planning is not promoted by the corporation and is replaced superficially by career planning and later by retirement planning. The corporate myth wants one to assume that the retiree had a fulfilling career, therefore what else could he or she ask for but having been a well-paid executive in this great company? All corporate cultures want their executives to believe that this is the place to be. Given the fundamental personal change potential involved in Life Planning, this is why we describe it as Transformational Life Planning in chapter 11.

Transformational Life Planning opens up all the possibilities of reaching your full potential not met when you were a corporate being. Retirement planning assumes you have met your full potential as a corporate being and all you now need is enough money to live the golden life of hobbies and consumerism. Assuming a hobby or consumption can fill your entrepreneurial, intellectual, or spiritual needs is an empty proposition. This leads to the dead end of the despair and boredom of leisure and consumption. The missing ingredient is the need to pursue your passion; this does not exclude hobbies or consumption, but they cannot be ends in themselves without being integrated to the primacy of your life's higher purpose and meaning. Setting your charter for the rest of your life requires specific plans based on the above-identified skills of joy, activities of passion, personal meaning, and a life's purpose. What are you willing to give to ensure that your life makes a difference for others in these areas of your passion? Retirement without a life purpose and plan is mindless. A plan based on your passion and personally identified meaning can be exciting and lead to satisfactions not experienced as a corporate being. Self-actualization can lead to new satisfactions, aesthetic, intellectual, and spiritual, as well as those of personal leadership or altruism. Getting to this new life plan is not easy, for it requires emotional, mental, and lifestyle changes. Change is never easy, but this is your last chance to be great!

Despair and Hope

As I have shown, the myth of retiring into a golden age of blissful leisure is really pain, despair, and emptiness without replacing your corporate being with your authentic self. The inner joy of finding yourself and becoming personally great is not possible while the corporation or profession has rented your leadership or technical behaviors. In retirement, there is no guarantee you will find yourself either. Unless you change your self-identity, you will wallow in the despair of losing your corporate being, your professional image, and your social status. Being a has-been is not easy for the ego that has experienced boundless success. This is why so many successful executives and athletes revert to the "come-back," which seems easier than trying to remake oneself. The more a high-profile executive or athlete has identified with the corporate role or sport for self-esteem, the greater the despair in the loss. This is particularly aggravated by the heights and glamour of the adulation, applause, and recognition, all of which create a sense of invulnerability of the ego beyond the role itself. Such is the seductive trap of the corporate being, which leads to self-deception. Yet the best can still come with the hope and vision of Life Planning. This hope lies in the transformational power of finding your authentic self rooted in what you value and have a passion for. Yet the biggest resistance to undergoing Life Planning may be the ego, which resists admitting the need for the corporate being that felt larger than life itself! Reexamining their life and rebuilding it is for losers, not them! But the reverse is true, and this book aims to open new thoughts and possibilities for all retiring executives.

Pain and despair can be your friend in motivating you to recognize the need to say good-bye to your corporate being and get on with changing. Otherwise, the pain will hang around as the retired corporate being mourns the loss of its role for an unnecessarily long time, creating undue stress and anxiety. Executives are winners in the corporation, but retirement is an entirely new game. Becoming a winner in retirement means no longer mourning the loss of the executive role and the state of having been a corporate icon in your mind and becoming what you want others to remember you for. Unless you recognize the pain of not changing, you will fail to find the need to transform yourself. The sooner you recognize the superficiality of your corporate being, the sooner you can prepare for being your real self after this role is finished.

It happens to every executive: we all leave our jobs either before or on the normal retirement date. A few choose to hang in there after this date until they lose it and are asked to leave. It is better and healthier to take control of the situation as early as possible so you are ready when the time comes. Often this preparation leads you to get out before your designated retirement date. It can also lead to a perceived decline in your commitment and performance as you become less identified with your corporate role, its sense of urgency, and the absolute value of its goals. Given the need to prepare as early as possible, it is important to have become prepared financially.

However, being asked to leave has its financial advantages insofar as you will get a salary package versus a gold watch type of gift at the designated date. This needs to be planned out in advance by the individual. This is an example of personal Life Planning not retirement planning and why you don't want to do Life Planning with the company. Here, the individual executive proactively decides when to leave and does not assume the corporate retirement date. Ideally, the executive takes control of the future and leaves with a new, robust purpose and vision for a new, active life unlike the aimless passivity of leaving with only a good financial plan and a hobby mindset.

The retired executive who recognizes the need for radical personal change may also despair because this time the type of change is vexing. There are no meetings and no strategic planning process to create a new, forward-looking business plan of change. Change management works in the collective context of the company and creates a naïve sense of confidence for the corporate leader entering retirement. However, being an executive you are a change agent or leader, changing processes and others, but this is starkly different from changing yourself, the change agent! There is no collective support or prescribed process to undergo. The retired corporate being has no support; the executive is on his or her own. In this case, the tools one would use as a corporate being are useless personally. They are insular and part of the corporate collective thinking process. The collective thinking processes are business tools of discernment that entrap the individual into the corporate collective. They do not allow for self-reflection or personal discovery. Psychotherapy is not taught at business schools or at in-house corporate training and development programs. The closest such programs would come to psychology would be programs on how to deal with and motivate others, so they are converted into corporate business tools or processes and socialized into the corporate being. How to manage your self is not taught, except through time management and conflict resolution, again all part of being a better corporate being and growing your skills and career. The process of gaining self-awareness and getting in touch with your subconscious is not taught in business school. This lack of self-awareness training reduces the ability to personally take control and meet your higher-level needs in self-actualization. This is due to the corporate bias for learning and following business techniques, like optimizing sales, margin and the bottom-line. Management training teaches you how to get a margin and a bottom line not how to get a life. You will know how to get a better return on capital employed not a better quality return on life lived. The intrinsic need for quality mapping through transformational Life Planning requires your resolve to see things from a peaceful distance through introspection and meditation not possible in the frenetic rat-race. Failing to get in touch with your authentic being leaves you with the self-deception of collective hangover of the corporate being in retirement.

This lack of empathy, support, and need for the retiring executive was the inspiration for me to write this book to offer you the awareness building and coaching to make this positive transformation.

The retiring corporate being as an executive role does not have the basis of self-awareness to undergo the self-discovery process needed to transform the self from despair to hope. This is not part of the job nor does the corporation initiate it because no one sees it as an issue within the corporate culture. The executive must do this as a person outside of the role but is usually too busy in the maze of work overload. The corporate being is not a person but a collective process and structure that the executive is caught up into in work. The executive as a human being can develop self-awareness only outside of the corporate being. This is possible through Life Planning and finding the time and mind-set to do it. This involves fundamentally taking charge of your life and abandoning the cradle-to-grave security mind-set of the corporate being. As a consequence, many corporate beings despair in retirement by the lack of joy found in the corporate myth of the golden years of retirement. They often wait for something meaningful to happen between golf games or between casino visits. Since most things come at the corporate being from the outside, the issue is being able to move from external reactivity to following your internal compass. Authentic personal meaning can be found only from the inside out. The result of being caught waiting for something meaningful to happen externally in retirement is a lot like being in

Samuel Beckett's play *Waiting for Godot*, where people wait for God to somehow come and give them meaning, but nothing happens.

Kill Your Corporate Being

Despair is the retiree's friend if the realization and awareness surfaces that the corporate being internalized by many years in corporate life brings no joy in retirement. There is no future in the past! The value system of the corporate being is dysfunctional in retirement. The pain and despair caused by the retired corporate being can only be turned to hope and joy by mentally killing off your corporate being as part of your personal transformational process. The motivation to do so is the pain of carrying this false self into retirement. Your corporate self was less than the full you. It worked as the role you played in the corporate "play" for your career and financial rewards, but now the play is over. It is insanity to continue that role mentally or wait for its cues because they will never come. The audience is gone! Playing to an empty house is meaningless. It is time to move on and find your own authentic role. In this case, you will not play the role or job: you will be the role! Being yourself has the promise of being not just meaningful to you but fun as well.

Until you "kill" your version of your corporate being, you will never move on. It is a false foundation upon which to build your retirement. The corporate myth of retirement was a false promise. To take control, the first step in this distancing process is to gain the awareness of what you have become as an executive corporate being. Once you become aware of who you are and its limitations, you can begin to ask who you really are and what it is you want to be given your real values, beliefs, and passions.

One example of an executive who "killed his corporate being" was a former CEO of a pharmaceutical company. After a merger with another company, he elected to leave with a sizeable package and to return to his hometown. As an expression of his freedom and joy, he shaved off his hair and wore very casual Western attire, including the boots. He also bought a pickup truck and hung out with old buddies at sports bars. He volunteered to coach the local high school football team and rejoined the church he went before university days. Those who knew him were shocked at the change. He rejected the business suit and donned the casual jeans look and lifestyle as an expression of his freedom but re-established his roots in the nutrients of his childhood soil. He eventually spent a year building a huge cabin in the mountains and then returned part-time to his family construction business, which had been taken over by his brother. He reports that he never was happier getting out of the corporate "b–s" and doing what he wants to do whenever he wants to without any pressure. He goes fly-fishing at the cabin whenever he gets the urge. It's allowed him to clear his head and make decisions based on what he values and feels good. He loves wiling away the hours with his fishing buddies telling stories. He particularly loves the fact that he does not have to impress anyone anymore, but he is free to be himself, go back to his roots, and contribute to his community with no career pressure. Sure, his savings helped him afford the luxury of being free the way he wanted, but he did not miss his old corporate lifestyle, including its seven-figure salary. He says he could never go back even though he has had calls from executive headhunters. In fact, he definitely under-lives his money. You can't tell him apart from the locals. However there is a big difference: he recounts that when he left his childhood community for university, it opened his eyes to a new world of opportunity and success. Yet as the expression goes, "you can take the boy out of the country but you can't take the country out of the boy." Now he says he has gone full circle. "I became successful as a CEO but so what. Now my opportunity is here in my community. My roots are here and I have never felt so good in business as I do here … nothing could pull me out of here!"

Personal Change Process for Retirement

Life Planning is idle without a personal change process for retirement. The biggest danger of Life Planning is it becomes only a plan: there is too much resistance to change or an unwillingness to pay the price of actualizing the life plan. To create a dynamic life plan is one thing; to learn it and fine-tune it so you can actually live it and create a new, authentic self-identity is quite another. To do this, you must go through a personal change process.

Before you can rebuild your own new visionary and creative house of hope and joy, you need to tear down the old collective rooming-house foundation of your corporate being, which is only a standard job box conforming to all the corporate cultural rules of "turfism." This is like a standard cookie-cutter series of boxes for corporate beings for what you need to do and be to become successful in the company. Not stepping into the turf or boxes of other executives means that you also must fend off their intrusions. The rule of the turf means you must always spend energy to survive the rules of territorialism. This means that your creativity and energy must be boxed up to avoid conflict or get used to attack any other executive intrusion that would undermine your department's credibility and method of operations. These rules are the standard foundations of the collective, not the creative, personal, value-based foundation of self-actualization. You need to first get out of the emotional, intellectual, and spiritual poverty of the standard row housing box foundations of the corporate being to create and build your own architect's new designer home. Only by tearing down the barriers and limits of the mental box of your corporate being can you escape its tether for a new, changed, more creative future.

You need to discover your innate freedom to escape from the straight-jacket conformity of the corporate collectivity to design and create the fresh, new life ahead. The more one feels comfortable with the corporate identity, the more difficult is the road to personal self-actualization. You can only creatively self-actualize yourself in life postretirement if you escape from the belief in the superiority of your corporate being. Feeling superior in retirement is simply the hangover of the hubris of the corporate being which uses fear to paralyze your full potential as a person. Remember the story of the tethered elephant that would not leave the tree it had been tethered to for years—even after the chain had been long since removed. Its mind was still tethered. It is time to move on mentally, emotionally, and spiritually.

The personal change process for a proactive retirement is in three stages.

Stage One: *Melting Down Your Corporate Being.* Clearly, you cannot become self-actualized as a unique individual or allow yourself to think creatively outside of the corporate box until you melt and dissolve your personal executive identity. This will free you up for new opportunities not possible while in the mental executive box. This stage is not only mandatory but necessary to move forward after retirement. Getting out of the mental box of your corporate being is the only way to advance to Stage Two of the retirement proactive change process.

Stage Two: *Visioning and Rebuilding.* Here you begin to imagine new opportunities that fit your talents and passion and begin to act, experiment, and conceive concrete scenarios. Here the new person emerges with a new transitional mental vision, a new look, a new talk, and a new walk. You will start to believe in the change process much more as others react to you in a fresh, new way. You become liberated and fully connected to what you really want to do when you finally grow up. Stage Two is still provisional and tentative as you feel out the different scenarios and options of your vision. The vision may have been with you for a while, but when you apply it in Stage Two, the practical reality may change your vision and lead you to fine-tune it. For example, if your passion for breeding, raising, and racing horses leads you to realize that the opportunity is in Ocala, Florida, and you live in Chicago, you may start investigating moving. However, if your spouse objects to moving, you may revise the vision and plan to partner with farms that have best programs and then travel down periodically or rent a place in Florida. In effect this Stage Two is fine-tuning and molding your best life to actually take effect as a new, permanent lifestyle in Stage Three.

Stage Three: *Actualizing.* Here your provisional planning of the last stage takes effect. You now live your vision and love it. You feel free and fully integrated with who you are and why you are doing it.

Transformational Life Planning must involve this personal change process. Although you have developed a full life plan on paper in Stage Two, it must involve action in Stage Three to actualize it. It cannot be just a vision or an idle plan, but it must be a catalyst in killing or melting down your corporate being. This does not mean that you have to quit your job prematurely. You can mentally start to differentiate yourself from your job. Stage One in Life Planning is not finished however until you have dissolved your corporate being: it is over and you can't go back. The end of the Stage One will be the mourning of the loss of your life as a corporate being. Stage Two is the heart of Life Planning, the active, transitional experimentation through trial projects with your planned lifestyle. This will involve time as your final new life emerges only through action as new life experiences and undiscovered opportunities emerge. Stage Three is the best lifestyle that emerged as you live your dream. There is nothing profound in this; it simply implies that if you don't change your behavior and act differently, you will never shed your corporate values and self-identity to discover your authentic self. This behavioral change process can be fun and liberating. It is quite simply compelling emotionally to connect with the real values and life of your authentic self.

Life Planning is unique to each individual. The only common features would be to anticipate the reality of major life-altering events such as the death of a parent or a spouse, planning around the new presence of grandchildren, possible illnesses depending on your history, sale of your house, starting a new business, and travel. For example, grandchildren or elder care of your parents may influence where you plan to live, the amount of travel you do, and even when or if you sell your house or where you plan to work a small business. Life Planning is planning to follow your passion and meaning, but your plan must fit the reality of probable life-changing events. Travel is one that often fits the early retirement stages better given family and medical factors, which tend to become more tenuous in the later stages.

How do you inspire yourself to create a life plan and avoid the traditional passive retirement? Imagine the executive corporate being who goes home after a retirement dinner, fails to remake his or her self-identity, and lives the rest of his or her life in the past. This is sad but inevitable if one proceeds in this way and fails to undergo the change and transformation of Life Planning. This is also very stressful to live a false self that is impossible to actualize. Entering the proactive change process for retirement is the solution; it can lower stress and increase your zest and passion for life beyond what it was as an executive.

You have the answers locked up inside of your mind and heart. Use quiet times to read about your heroes and the possible lifestyles of others. Use your imagination and intuition and begin to listen to yourself. The following questions aim to stimulate your imagination to inspire you to create your own life plan.

- What are your inner signals, the gut-feel messages that you get about yourself? Listening to oneself is new to the corporate being who has been rewarded for listening to one's boss. Now you need to break free of the collective consciousness and reconnect to yourself through your feelings, inner thoughts, intuition, and passions.
- What are your longings and desires?
- What new results would you love to create that you feel strongly about?
- What are the causes you care about but never thought to do anything about because your life was too busy?
- How do you feel about yourself in different situations and new roles?
- How do you dream about yourself and what is possible? Begin the process of imaginary projection. This means to picture yourself in new scenarios and roles. How does it feel?
- What are your realistic options?
- What would you prefer to do?
- How can you see your new future in this new role playing out?

- What is your life's calling? How can you plan out a response?

Further, you need to ask yourself, what are my real talents? As discussed above, your talents are often different from what your professional skills were. Your skills are typically specialized or technical to have fit into a professional job, but your talents go beyond this connecting to your passion and meaning. For example, your skill may be accounting, but your passion may be to help build your daughter's new business. Or your skill may be corporate training, but your passion is to help build a transitional coaching and training center for disadvantaged youths.

Ultimately, your life plan needs to tap into everything that matters to you, not just your fragmented skills. Bear in mind your old corporate being internalized the corporate meaning and mission around your skills but this was extraneous and not the real you. Now you must fill in the meaning and focus on the soft issues of what are your values, purpose, and passion as a new framework for your skills. Integrating your skills with your new personal mission will become your ultimate talent. In retirement such a new, visionary plan can also include hobbies and leisure, but now within a new framework of your meaning and purpose.

Change Barriers: Time, Speed, and Complexity

The *time barrier* is the first barrier to clear when you move out of the corporation. This represents the "future versus the now" mind-set. Executives have a strong, futuristic orientation, planning strategies for one to five years out. This involves a strong conceptual ability to envision an evolving strategic implementation, its financial results, and all the changing resource commitments. The executive's role is to manage what does not yet exist. The executive's present is the future. The more senior the executive role, the longer term is the future orientation. This requires a comprehensive staff. Comprehensive reports as well as feasibility marketing studies are necessary. Living in the future is high on anticipatory stress.

This futuristic orientation is not useful for the retired executive insofar as there is no planning staff, data, or budget, let alone a product portfolio. Most important, a future orientation is very stressful. For the retired executive, the present is indeed now and not the future, but it is difficult for an ingrained futuristic mind-set to focus and get in touch with the simple here and now. Yet, if the retired executive cannot make the transition to the primacy of the "now," it is because the thinking is too cluttered with the complexity and hypothetical of long-term scenarios of what-ifs. Life is lived in the series of moments called "now." Reconnecting with the now requires having purged the corporate mind-set for a new, simple, personal self-awareness. A useful, proven technique to clear the mind is meditation. Many executives have successfully used meditation, yoga, and prayer to heal the mind and body of the harsh impacts of stress. The habit of taking on all of the accountability for the next five years of results needs to be purged through a daily quiet time of uncluttering of the mind. Although I do not aim to provide guidance on techniques of meditation, yoga, or prayer, I do suggest reading the many good books on these subjects. As your life is only a series of nows, it is important to reverse the long-term primacy of future and ground yourself back into the concrete reality of the present because the executive need of creating a future no longer exists. Always keep in mind, life is fragile and can end at any unexpected time. As you age, the long-term future shrinks in its potential. Embrace the beauty of the moment by making the now the primacy of your thinking. Slow down and catch the beauty and possibilities of the moment, and there are a lot of them. Stop to smell the flowers before you are feeding them!

Stress is created by the executive still in the future, no longer able to ground himself or herself here and now. This problem is similar to the executive on vacation, unable to get his or her thinking out of the future into the moment to completely connect with the kids playing on the beach. Vacation is supposed to re-charge the batteries by temporarily letting go of the corporate pressures but the corporate being cannot insofar as it is the executive's self-identity. As long as the future is dominant, the present is illusive. This becomes the retiree's problem with becoming bored so easily in retirement. There are lots of "now moments" but seemingly, no future. The present is boring when compared with the complexity of anticipating the future and its long-term payoffs. However, happiness is the ability to focus on the now. The future is anticipatory stress. While obviously both the present and future are always used by the executive and retiree, it is an issue of the need for the dominating priority and creating a balance. Only by grounding yourself in the reality of the new present can the retiree create a realistic future. For example, Stage Two of Life Planning change is possible only after mourning of the loss of your corporate being. This brings the mind back to the reality of the here and now and provides the basis for action. The increased connection to your own reality helps you avoid being lost in the abstract future of the corporate being. Reconnecting to the concrete here and now allows you to enjoy the present as a priority, to smell the roses and the people in your life.

Connected to the barrier of time is the *speed barrier*. For the executive, speed is everything as *time is money* for the corporate being. This means it is very productive to maximize electronic communications for connections to all possible data. Having increased data saves errors in assumptions and keeps the executive up to speed on what has changed. Because things change rapidly, one can become obsolete and redundant without staying in complete contact with all of the players in any business dynamic. This is the essence of the rat race as every executive tries to stay one step ahead of the changing information and trends in his or her area. Technology of communication is basic to keeping up. It becomes addictive as one has the urge to protect one's situation from eroding. Failure to keep up is fear of failure: not having complete data can be embarrassing and a sign of not being in control, not being in touch, representing a fear of appearing incompetent. Most executives experience this as a somewhat exhilarating race to be globally connected, but it is nevertheless based on fear, fear of being left out, fear of falling behind, and fear of failure. As information comes from everywhere, being technically connected is essential. This then takes over the executive's life: it is an addiction to needing a data connection to feel alive or to feel a connection to the universe and to feel the self-esteem of power and control. This of course is illusory. It might be called techno-neurosis, for we allow this technological connection to the world to replace our real sensory connections to our most important world, our immediate world of real people, the here and now. I actually had a CEO who wisely refused to own a laptop or Blackberry and got all the information he needed at the office, in meetings, or by phoning. He religiously separated his private time from his corporate time.

The retired executive needs to reconnect to the immediate sensory world in order to reclaim "the now" as the priority basis for a meaningful future. This is the opposite of the corporate being which makes the future the priority basis for the present. The retiree must redefine reality based on what is possible to interact with as well as control. It is important to escape the frenzied world of new data in order to discover what is meaningful for life. Speed kills! No matter where you are, in a meeting or working alone, take a time-out moment, take a deep breath, focus on something beautiful, be thankful, and then ask yourself why you are doing what you are doing. Connect it all to the richness of the present and your life purpose. Slowing down is a faster way to allow yourself the solace to ask yourself what is meaningful for your life and to elevate yourself to a new level of thinking. Tapping into your spirit and meaning takes a careful, introspective form of meditation and thought. This will is not possible in the corporate world of ongoing reactive communications data filled with incompleteness and the demand for more and more data. More speed and more data lead to the illusion of understanding and wisdom, which can only be found in deeper thought which cannot be rushed. This is not to suggest that the executive operates at high speed and the retiree must simply slow down. Rather, I am suggesting that the executive is robbed of the wisdom to be gained from introspective and deeper, creative thinking by being overloaded and engulfed by the water hose of the immediacy of ever-present data. The retiree has the luxury to get away from the need-or-speed to think beyond the surface data overload and feel the connection with the underlying present meaning.

The bias for focusing on the future and trusting in speed to get there is the territory of the corporate being and its contagion and fear of falling behind in the corporate tribe. This reflects only a shell of your authentic possibilities. Imagine rushing through the Louvre museum of art in Paris to see each and every piece of art in a day and actually thinking that one has "seen" the art. Rushing into the future prevents the possibility of wisdom in the present. Like the peace and tranquility found through the example of solitary fly fishing in a mountain stream, each of us needs to reclaim our future through living our real present on our own terms at our own speed. This is not the traditional retiree slowing down but the retiree getting off the frenzied treadmill of the corporate being so we can move "faster" toward a less stressful, meaningful future on our own terms. Doing so allows you to conquer the future by going at your own pace. Great missions can be accomplished through many small steps, while taking the time to ensure you are on course. As an example, picture the greatest sages or spiritual leaders like Buddha: are they frenetically doing e-mails, going through thick reports, looking at their watches, speeding in traffic, or calmly and deliberately thinking deeply about life's issues?

Also connected to the time and speed issues is the dimension of *complexity*. The executive who can manage greater complexity rises to a higher level of authority, status, and accountability within the corporation. The corporation is highly complex with many moving parts. The more one can manage such complexity, the higher one can go in the company. The goal of management training and education is to develop such competencies so middle managers can be successfully promoted into more senior executive ranks. This cycle again is linked to the future orientation and speed dimensions insofar as one must be able to manage this higher complexity without compromising significantly on the time and speed dimensions. It is unforgivable for the marketing executive to have the right product but being slow and too late to launch and missing a real opportunity of capturing the market advantage of the first to market.

However, in retirement this bias toward and need to deal with high levels of complexity creates increased boredom that can be very stressful, like forcing a chess champion to play only checkers or a PGA golf champion to a lifetime of mini-putting. The type A executive, who thrives on and has grown to master complexity, will not fare well in retirement where the business complexity is removed. The executive who has grown into a complete corporate being will be thrown into hyper-stress with the removal of all of the challenges of complexity and executive stimuli.

The cure for the retiring executive who has had a typically highly complex role is to get into the introspective process of connecting with oneself as a human being. This can be even more complex from a more psychological dimension, but it is not based on frenzied retrieval of business data. Conquering your inner life complexity may require that you get involved in stress-relieving and awareness-building processes like meditation in order to spiritually connect with yourself. The other vital connection is for the executive to learn the art of reducing complexity to simplicity. Reducing life itself to simplicity is a good start as it allows you to connect with what is really important to you. Reducing one's own life to simplicity means to begin to connect with the here and now. Executives are more than capable of doing this since they often stop and reflect on why they are killing themselves: "It's all for the money!" However, the whole point of Life Planning is to go beyond this mind-set of the corporate being, and to stop and set your own meaning and definitions to take control of your life. Beginning to connect to the reality of the present and create a future meaning and new purpose for your own life is a start in overcoming the penchant toward the busy complexity of the workaholic. You must conquer complexity though the reflective process of discovering simplicity, by beginning to reduce all the unnecessary complexities to their simple truths in your own life's mission. This is part of planning for the rest of one's life. Again, this is not to suggest that the life of the retiree is simple versus the complex life of the executive. It is the reverse. The executive's complexities are based superficially driven by an unwieldy, constantly changing corporate data and role mandate. Finding your authentic self in retirement reduces the deeper complexity of your life to the simplicity needed to do Life Planning.

Beginning to find the simplicity on the other side of life's busy complexities will give you the tranquility of purpose. It allows for the wisdom of what is really important—to emerge and for consciousness and full understanding to take control of your life plan. The executive needs to conquer the need for the superficial task complexities of corporate life and slow down to reflect on what is really important for the rest of his or her life for a focused meaning and understanding. *Less is more!* By discovering the simple truths for one's life in Life Planning, one can enjoy a richer experience of life's complexities, like the deep inspiring insight in a moment of the universe's complexity in viewing a simple rain drop on a rose!

Other Challenges to Changing

The major barrier or challenge to changing is *complacency* due to fear. The corporate executive has been given the comforts of financial security, the rewards of social recognition, and ostensible personal success. Being seduced by the comforts of success creates resistance and fear of change, even though retirement itself takes the corporate being away. Since you are soothed by the corporate myths of retirement and supported by the knowledge of the retirement plan as having enough money, why do you need to change? Old mind-sets persist even in the face of losing your corporate being and its reward foundation that provided comfort for so long. This transfer of comfort to the new boredom and stress of retirement is really the fear of change, or complacency. "I've got it made in the shade!" Why change when life has been good?

Consciousness of the new reality of retirement is necessary. Recognition of the emptiness left by losing one's corporate role and life for retirement as well as awareness of the fact that the corporate being was a false self helps create a sense of urgency to find your real self in the wake of the end of corporate life. It's important to find new, meaningful activities based on your own personal values, talent, and passion. Finally, it's important to become aware of your own underlying freedom to choose to be and do whatever fits your new vision. Complacency is a defense of the status quo and covers over these fears: fear of change, fear of failure, fear of being bothered, fear of finding oneself, and others. As long as the retired executive lives defensively on the powder keg of repressed fear, the malaise and boredom of retirement will dominate. Retirement stress will gnaw away and undermine the potential for happiness and longevity. The transition from fear to love and passion for your new activities is founded on your new power, the personal power of your rediscovered freedom to choose your new activities, your new goals, and your new self. This new power of freedom was always repressed by the false self of your corporate being, which defined and led you through the corporate mission, job objectives, and the group thinking of corporate political hierarchy. Your personal freedom is more powerful for your psychological need to self-actualize your potential than ever was your executive positional power borrowed from the corporate hierarchy.

Never having to become yourself as long as you are a corporate being creates a collective mind-set and a fear of abandoning its comforts of conformity. "I'm right because everyone else says the same thing." It takes courage to break out from this collectivity mentality in retirement, since your financial plan or retirement plan creates complacency based on "what else do I need if I have the money?" A retirement plan that is no more than a financial plan becomes a poor replacement for your possible authentic life plan. Sure, your financial planner will ask you what you want to do in retirement before working out the cost and financial plan necessary, but this usually trivializes the radical nature of Transformational Life Planning.

Your retirement planner may create a financial plan so your money lasts until the actuarial average life of 82.5 years. However, this age expectation may become a self-fulfilling prophesy and limit to your life: you subconsciously do not want to outlive your money in the lifestyle you are accustomed to. Retirement planning is reduced to the quantitative biases of the corporate being because the retirement planning industry is part of it. *However, the risk of underliving your money is far greater than outliving it!*

Discovering your real passion for life after you exit the corporation may extend your life well beyond the actuarial average age because of the health benefits of doing what you love. Once you discover your real life passion and purpose, the money needed for the consumerism lifestyle you have become accustomed to as a corporate being may be not needed. If you discover your real passion is in a new entrepreneurial business, your retirement earnings may exceed your expectations, particularly if you are pursuing your dream or new idea. Don't forget Colonel Sanders, who had such a passion for his secret recipe that he started his business after age 65, and Kirk Kerkorian has such a passion for deal making through his Tracinda Corporation that he is still doing deals at ninety years old. Clearly, both are optimists and resisted complacency through the challenges of following their dreams.

Becoming your authentic self takes courage. This courage to be is all you have to help you avoid the malaise of underretiring to the myths of the corporate being. It also requires individual integrity to differentiate yourself from others based on the self-discovery process of finding your real values and setting your own voyage and future mission. Taking charge as a self-manager is necessary. No one else can do this thinking for you. You must be self-motivated and driven to set your own course outside of your corporate role. The radical nature of the change process makes this more introspective and intense because it is personal, and no one can do it for you. Conforming to someone else's plan is like creating a new corporate being, and nothing can substitute for your own personal passion to pursue an idea. Your best partner may be your spouse or a significant other insofar as many of your future goals will involve and affect them. Through visioning, scenario planning, and self-talk, you need to create a new life plan by defining your new life purpose so you can take control.

Re-Brand Yourself

After you have overcome your resistance to change and have a sense of your new self-identity based on your new values and meaning, the best way to kill your corporate being and make the leap into your new sense of self is to re-brand yourself. This assumes that you have accepted and embraced the ending of your corporate being and are now moving on to the second stage of *visioning and rebuilding* mentioned above. Re-branding yourself is the open declaration of the end of your previous self as you start to act and look like a new person. This is the envisioning and transitional stage to your final new, authentic self.

If you are serious about making a transition to the new you, you need to change your image. The new image needs to say to the world and to oneself, I'm my own person. What new look best allows you to say, I'm an artist, a musician, a sailor, golfer, world traveler, birdwatcher, gardener, etc., or a combination. The key to the re-branding and your new thrust to self-actualization is a new positive image. You move beyond saying, "I'm a retired executive." This is a negative self-statement because your life is based in the past with no future in sight. Instead, you need to be able to say not what you were, but what you are and will be! This must be created and supported through the following:

- *New Self-Vision.* Your new future needs to be created through scenario planning, prioritization, experimentation, and decision making.
- *New Self-Talk.* Your boss is gone; you are your own CEO and self-manager. Take control and plan yourself out to your new dynamic future.
- *New Walk.* Define some new behavior changes that signal to you and others that you are different and boldly changing to a new life.
- *New Image and Style.* Creatively change your image, dress, style, and body language to reflect your new self-vision and life goals.

- *New People*. Bring new people into your life who would support and share your new life goals.
- *New Organizations*. Develop or join new organizations relevant to your new life plan in order to develop a social system that supports your new life.

This is still the transitional stage two of your Life Planning but sends the signal to everyone and especially yourself, I'm changing! A newly chosen image is only a catalyst to help you take control as you move toward your new life's activities. Taking control allows you to lower stress as it focuses your energy outward toward your new purpose and goals. As you emerge with your final sense of self-actualization, this look will become more personally defined and original and not based on the transitionally chosen   stereotyped image.

The best way to re-brand yourself is to find a new hero or heroine in the area of your new inspiration. Research the life and the lifestyle of these new heroes. Read their biographies. Try to understand how they got where they did and why. What were their reasons? Do you share their passion for their pursuits for excellence in this field or hobby? Can they represent a new role model for you? Do they give you new ideas for becoming what you value in their lives, and in yours? What is their demeanor and look? What elements of this are you comfortable with and suit you? This is not to suggest that you even know your future heroes or heroines. However, it is vital to find them because they can become a new inspiration for the new you. Nor does it suggest that you should copy them. Picasso learned his early techniques from others but transformed them as he self-actualized and differentiated himself as an original artist with his own personal, unique style of artistically expressing his subject. Similarly, Tiger Woods learned techniques from others, and as he internalized them and practiced, he adapted them to his physique and transformed them into his own leading talent. The point is to gain a new role model or role models, internalize them, adopt those elements experimentally that suit your own personality, talent, and values, and then create your own new lifestyle, role, and panache different from what they have done. Doing so will speed up your learning as you fit these inspirations to your talents and underlying passion, for they will provide the first transitional step as a role model for you to create yourself as an original! You must mould the clay into the new authentic you, an original and not a copy. Do not make the mistake of thinking you can become a new authentic person by copying. After learning from your role models, it is vital to self-differentiate by adapting the learned techniques to your own talent, values, and style. Don't make the mistake of stopping with a transitional learning phase of internalizing your heroes, their best practices, and their style. You must self-differentiate by transforming such inputs creatively into what makes you unique and passionate for certain values. Only through a practical behavioral evolution will you get to your ultimate self-differentiation and sense of the real you, the person that you love to be and feels so natural to you. This stage two of transitional *visioning and rebuilding* continues until your experimentation and rebuilding becomes your original authentic you. Here you enter stage three of self-actualization. Here you emerge with a new, positive self-identity different from your corporate being and even from those you have identified for inspiration. Emerging into the final stage is based on picturing yourself in a positive, inspirational way as you master your new role and self-identity.

Remember you are never too old to begin again. In this case, think of it as becoming the person that you were really meant to be. No person was born to be and die as a collective corporate being. Accepting age as a reason not to lift yourself up would be a self-fulfilling and self-defeating prophesy. If you say you are too old to do certain new things, then you are right. If you say, I can do it regardless of my age, you will do it! You will be right either way. *Attitude is 90 percent of successfully actualizing your dream!* By remembering that life is the journey not the destination, you will become a more interesting person through the creative process of reinventing yourself. You will love yourself more and become capable of loving others at a higher level.

Early stages of personal change can feel awkward, but ultimately the ugly larva emerges as a beautiful butterfly! In this case, the final judge is you as you shed your corporate being's restrictive shell for the being of your dreams.

Chapter 9: Happiness and Health

Q: Why do you write?
A: Because I love it and I need it.
—J. K. Rowling

Men grow when inspired by a high purpose, when contemplating
vast horizons. The sacrifice of oneself is not very difficult for
one burning with the passion for a great adventure.
—Alexis Carrel

If you observe a really happy man you will find him building a
boat,
writing a symphony, educating his son, growing double dahlias in
his
garden, or looking for dinosaur eggs in the Gobi desert. He will not
be
searching for happiness … as a goal in itself.
—W. Beran Wolfe

I shall be telling this with a sigh
Somewhere ages & ages hence;
Two roads diverged in a wood, and
I took the one less travelled by,
And that has made all the difference.
—Robert Frost

Why not do your Life Planning around those activities and projects
that are based on your unique real values and passions? Be different,
be yourself! If you do so, you will be happier than if you follow the
retirement crowd of former corporate beings who still follow the
collective values of consumerism. You may not be able to optimize
your happiness if you follow the template of collective wants of the
traditional retired corporate being. Fulfilling your highest needs is
to attain the satisfaction of being your authentic self. This means you

need to figure out in your own way the intrinsic difference between your authentic needs in contrast to the plethora of wants that are the hangover from your corporate being. Money will never satisfy your highest needs. Just look at the narcissistic lives of many high-paid movie stars, entertainers, and athletes, who use their money destructively to consume their endless wants while failing their real human needs. Money as a foundation will satisfy your basic security and some of your social, and self-esteem needs but not your self-actualizing needs. Assuming the lower needs are satisfied, self-actualization is of a different higher order and cannot be bought.

The Currency of Happiness: Needs versus Wants

The corporate thinking fails to distinguish between needs and wants. Any company sells their new and older products by convincing consumers that they need the products even if they have never heard of them before. You simply cannot be satisfied with your life unless you try our new soap, cream, soda pop, diet, cell phone, car—and on and on. Even if you had wisely bought last year's product, this year's version is even better and so compelling you have to upgrade. Once the consumer buys the new product, the consumer justifies the decision through feelings of satisfaction and being ahead of the crowd because he or she is able to luxuriate in the latest and greatest version. Ask anyone who just made a major purchase if they like it, and it is a given that they love it because the consumer needs to reinforce the decision. This increases demand for the product or service through word-of-mouth testimonials. Statements that someone has the latest version and how totally awesome it is seem to validate the purchase and enhance the buyer's image by being wise enough to identify with the leading brand release. Demand is driven by creating wants regardless if we need the product or not.

Economists do not distinguish between needs and wants since they reduce everything to demand. Differentiating between real needs and wants is too psychologically complex to figure out because it involves qualitative values not easily reduced to numbers. Economics only measures consumption. Trying to separate out needs from our impetuous wants cannot be measured, given the philosophical issue of what is a real need versus a mere want? It is easier to simply call everything demand but this is misleading. The bias in economics is reflected in the corporate being. Value is reduced to the principles of consumption in the business language of the corporate being! We need to shake this illusion or bias of collectivity. In the corporation, the thinking of a demand-based value system denies that there is any higher value than consumption: the more consumption, the better the society. The more one can conspicuously consume, the better the life or better the person. These economics of the corporate being have a legitimate place and are important for a sound economy but limited as a basis for planning retirement. Corporations create jobs and wealth necessary for society's material needs to be met. Yet, the corporate being's values are based largely on the good of greater and greater consumption. The point is that you will never reach self-actualization through consumption or being part of this tribal and trendy thinking of collectivity but only by getting to understand your authentic needs. Economics only measures numbers. Your self-actualization goes beyond quantity for quality, like art surpasses number painting.

To what extent have you been able to separate yourself from the corporate being, where more is better, and truly learn your *authentic needs* from the typical executive *demand* in your corporate culture?

- Have you ever felt the peer pressure to buy a new car or SUV to match or exceed the image of other similar-level executives have bought or leased, knowing full well that if you exceed the luxury image of your boss, it could be a career-limiting move?
- Have you ever said to yourself or your spouse that you were going to pay more for the new luxury vehicle than you can afford because "it would actually be a good investment in my career." If you look more successful you will become so, besides you don't want to send the message that you are any less than your peers?

- To what extent are you driven by the thought that investing in the right luxury house in the right neighborhood regardless of the debt and affordability creates the right connections for increasing career success?
- To what extent do you increase your respect and defer more to another executive because that executive drives a better car than you? Do you assume that he or she must have more power and influence than you?
- Now that you have retired, to what extent do you feel it be a fall from grace to be seen in a lesser vehicle or house than your former luxury models? Would you worry about others thinking that you have come down in the world?

If you answered yes to these, it is a sign that your corporate being is alive and well, even in retirement.

The problem is that we tend to confuse satisfying wants with satisfying our needs and falling into the collective economic determinism of the corporate being. If we understand and identify our real needs for self-actualization, we would be able to prevent reducing our authentic higher needs to the wants of consumption. Being inundated with advertising from the corporate machine persuades and determines our consumer behavior. As the latest car model is unveiled from under a cover with the backdrop of flashing strobe lights, smoke, and mirrors and breathtaking music and half-naked dancers, one would think it was the second coming of Jesus himself! However, such collective determinism cannot understand or deal with what it cannot quantify. It cannot quantify our higher needs but only simplistically reduces everything to demand. It fails to understand human freedom, where the individual can escape such collective determinism for self-determination based not on mass wants but on the individual's unique and sacred higher needs. Corporate advertising tries to make believe we can satisfy our highest needs through their new anti-wrinkling skin cream. Retirement planning usually reduces Life Planning to the financial planning needed for the corporate being consuming in retirement because retirement planners are essentially numbers driven. As the human spirit is freedom to be oneself allowing the collective determinism of the corporate being provide the basis for your retirement reduces your authentic needs to the wants of consumerism. This is why I aim to help you differentiate your retirement through Life Planning and by doing so base your financial needs on your authentic needs, not the wants or demand of the corporate being and by doing so needing less money in retirement as you spend wisely.

While consumerism is a perfectly legitimate strategy from the corporate perspective in order to maximize sales and profits, it is our own problem and limitation if we believe the many daily advertising and marketing hyperboles that we face. It is up to each of us to rise above these influences to establish our real authentic needs and purpose. It is on this foundation of our authenticity that we can gain control of our wants. This allows Life Planning to overcome the bias for financial planning and retirement planning. The traditional retirement planning industry usually reduces Life Planning to the financial planning needed for the corporate being consuming in retirement. Paying experts for a financial plan is like buying a vacation that you can afford without knowing where you will be going. Financial planners are essentially trained in finance, accounting or, economics tend to put the cart ahead of the horse. Ask your retirement planner if he or she is trained in psychology or finance. The change is in the introspective process of getting to understand your genuine needs. Putting the numbers together after the fact is easy in comparison. This is why I will help you prevent this. Only through an in-depth Life Planning process will any financial plan make any sense. Don't let your life plan be reduced to a financial budget!

The Hierarchy of Wants

> (I can't get no) Satisfaction
> —The Rolling Stones

Once our basic needs are met, if we allow the hierarchy of wants to take over, we lose touch with our real values and allow consumerism to replace our authentic needs to grow. Why bother with the pains of growth when I can consume and look successful? However, embracing the social symbols of success is not the real success demanded by our highest needs and is inauthentic. We must learn to get to know our real needs and learn how to keep ourselves from confusing wants with our higher needs.

A possible hierarchy of wants is bottomless because the more we consume, the more it fails to satisfy our real needs, and the more we want in order to make up for the lack of satisfaction by wanting something better and better. In other words, the addiction to wants is neurotic insofar as it is a false promise. It can never satisfy you to the level of its promise, and it forces you to go deeper down the spiral, depending on money available. The insatiability of living a life valuing the social wants of consumerism is in fact the highest level of the false self. The person allows the artificial product image to become the self-image to enhance the person's value. Turning your back on yourself and your higher potential to creatively and freely choose your own being as unique allows the collective consumer value system to determine your self-identity. The frustration of insatiability speaks for itself: it simply does not work. This is not so much a moral issue as a pragmatic reality: consumerism fails to achieve its claims and satisfy our higher-level needs. Life is more complex and cannot be dealt with through the corporate being, which is the philosophy of consumption. Consuming fails to achieve its promise because it is our neurotic means of unrealistically trying to fulfill our real needs through new wants. It is designed to fail us, and because it is unrealistic, it is essentially a driver of new stress, which leads us to become dissatisfied, leading to a new round of superficial consumption.

Nevertheless, from our days as a corporate servant, we have come to define ourselves by our role and see the monetary rewards as the scorecard defining our success and worth. We turn ourselves into the "quantitative being" by measuring our value by the rewards, as the company does. In effect, *we reify ourselves by allowing the belief that our self value is our net worth*. In every economic downturn or recession there are always examples of suicides of rich corporate beings whose self-identity and personal meaning was sadly tied to their lost fortune.

Self-Interest

There is no question to the economic benefit and the driving force of self-interest. Adam Smith's *The Wealth of Nations* showed how it is the most effective mechanism for a flourishing economy. However, at a certain point of material success, it is simply not in the individual's self-interest to spend more time accumulating more. One of my personal heroes is Bill Gates. I remember he was interviewed once on TV. To paraphrase, when he was asked about his wealth, he said that he may have unlimited resources, but limited time. At a certain point, money has a diminishing marginal utility for personal happiness. This means that once you have enough to fulfill your material needs, money has less value or impact on your life and satisfaction than other pursuits. Time is finite, and so human beings can attain greater value and satisfaction by differentiating their activities through a higher purpose. This is why Bill Gates chose not to spend all his time making more and more money, but to spend his time with his wife and manage the Bill & Melinda Gates Foundation, which focuses on saving children's lives in Africa. When Bill Gates walked out of his CEO office for the last time and turned his talents to a higher purpose is an example of self-actualization. Attaining self-actualization is in one's self-interest! Self-interest is usually limited and captured by the corporate being as having merely monetary value. However, in retirement an executive has the opportunity to pursue the satisfactions of his or her higher needs. This is our ultimate luxury: the pursuit of the loftier needs of happiness—beauty, truth, justice, art, love, and service to others. *Pursuing them is in the retiring executives' self-interest because they are the currency of happiness!*

As an executive about to retire and explore the options involved in Life Planning, consider these questions:

- To what extent do you feel the need to spend as much if not more for your retirement lifestyle?

- To what extent do you feel that your retirement would be a failure if you couldn't continue to make lots of money in new commercial pursuits, even if you are financially independent?
- To what extent do you feel that your retirement will be successful if your net worth rises?
- How would an extra million add to your retirement satisfaction?

If you answer positively to these, bear in mind that once you have attained the satisfying state of having your material needs fully met throughout retirement, more money will not increase your satisfaction. If you want to pursue happiness as most do, the ongoing pursuit of money will not give you the highest joys of self-actualization, our highest need.

In other words, moving toward self-actualization is not the pursuit of a former "sinner" now awakened and becoming a chastised, altruistic philanthropist; rather, it is the pure pursuit of your self-interest for happiness and health through altruistic goals of service to others, art, music, justice, and truth.

- What difference do you want to make for others in your life?
- What difference will your short existence here on earth mean?
- How can you make this unique difference, given your unique, God-given, and developed talents?

Self-actualizing answers our deepest needs because we now have the foundation of having met our lower-level economic needs through our professional and executive careers. The corporate being has been the *ultimate servant* but makes a *poor master* in retirement!

A great purpose can be large or small. Small steps can be huge. Big goals like creating new social organizations that help to solve social problems—global warming, poverty—can be broken into small, bite-size pieces and attainable steps. Simply creating a new awareness of issues to change behavior through education in small ways can make big differences. Finding new ways to create mutual interests beyond tribalism can alleviate social, cultural, and national conflicts, and can save lives and avert wars. Small acts can become big acts as change happens more from the ground up as others follow the emotional logic of a well-defined purpose. If you look around, you will see many examples of the self-actualizing person seeking to create new value for others.

One example is that of a retired CEO from the credit union industry who joined an initiative as a volunteer to set up nonprofit credit unions in Africa. Because of poverty, many people there had the desire to work and create value, but they lacked the basic tools, resources, and seed money. The project helped get aspiring entrepreneurs and farmers started to grow an initial crop and protect it through fertilization and irrigation systems. This began a positive cycle of self-sufficiency as a percent of the microloans provided was given back each year, which in turn helped other farmers, trainers, and irrigation and fertilizer specialists get microloans to better support the farmers to continue to expand an agricultural system of wealth creation. Based on this modest wealth creation, new credit unions formed and helped provide an economic infrastructure that was not there before. This, in turn, allowed for better education and health care systems. There are now about eight thousand credit unions in Africa. Having developed a passion for creating this value and difference for the people of Uganda, this particular retired CEO now makes speeches and does fund-raisers, knowing that every $1,000 will not be simply spent for an immediate gain but will provide the start for a new, virtuous cycle of wealth creation by unleashing human capital, which is the real wealth creation of any economy.

Happiness and Money

"I need a bonus so bad it hurts!" said one executive to me when the calculations for that year's bonuses were being made. This is a typical, pent-up joy factor for executives, like the anticipatory excitement of playing a slot machine. They live for the big deals, the big payoffs, and the big bonuses. Executives are bonus junkies. In the rat race of competition, the executive needs a clear sign of personal success. This is why the bonus is so addictive. However, the bonus hit wears off quickly once it is spent or assimilated into investments. Like the hunter's kill, the bonus is the chance to "eat what you kill" and is a necessary pillar of the makeup of the corporate being as essentially an economic being. Happiness for the corporate being is associated with successive bonus hits and salary increases. Unfortunately, the happiness is not sustainable, salary increases and bonuses are short-term injections not sustainable motivators. Nor do they create more job happiness. Last year's hit had long since worn-off and the withdrawal symptoms and the hunger for more has long since set in. It is often reported that salary increases and bonuses do excite the recipient, but the value and satisfaction of it wears off in a matter of a few weeks. Frederick Herzberg (1968) showed how money was not really a motivator but only acted to prevent the lack of motivation when pay and benefits were perceived inadequate.

The lack of ability of money to offer real happiness is clear. It is better thought of an addiction to the excitement that money hits bring. In essence, the corporate being is a money junkie longing for more and more. Its hunger for money based on the fear of scarcity is insatiable: there can never be too much. In fact, it's not the money so much as the addiction for more money. Each year's salary and bonus need to exceed the last to make the executive ecstatic. Otherwise, it's like going backward. For the corporate being, it's really not the money passed a certain point: it's about winning and acquiring the symbols of success. Otherwise, how would the executive know if he or she had been successful?

As team of psychologists from the University of British Columbia and Harvard Business School found that participants in a study on money and happiness that individuals got greater happiness after receiving a bonus from the manner in which they spent it. Those who spent it on others received greater happiness than those who spent it on themselves. How the money was spent was a greater predictor of happiness than the size of the bonus. So those who spent a small bonus on others received greater happiness than those who received a large bonus and spent it on themselves (Fox 2008).

Money allows us the security to find pleasure and the adventure, which may lead to happiness, but it is not the money in itself that gives us the meaning or happiness. Charles J. Doane described, and I summarize, a man who built his own sailboat with available, low-cost used materials. While many boat projects lie idle in boatyards each year, this man returned doggedly to continue his work. He dreamed of going down along the coast from Maine to Florida with his girlfriend. Given his limited knowledge of boatbuilding and limited resources, his first launch failed because of a serious leak, and the boat sank. Nevertheless, driven by his passion, he rose above this problem by treating it as a learning experience. He made the changes to launch again the next year. As Doane noted, passion and vision created the passage to happiness, not the money! He says, "After all, it is easy enough for those who have both resources and expertise to make their dreams come true. The most beautiful dreamers—the ones who live life to the fullest—are those who sail only on a wing and a prayer" (p. 28).

Happiness and Belonging

Insofar as happiness through self-actualization is reaching and attaining higher values through others, we cannot attain such happiness in isolation. We must do so through establishing connections to others or through belonging to social networks that support our values and aspirations to contribute. Bearing in mind that retirement will increase your social isolation from the corporate life that you led, consider these questions:

- To what extent did your social life evolve around your corporate being, the lunches, dinners, picnics, and circle of colleagues and their families? This will slow up if not end as the glue of the common corporate being is ruptured in retirement.
- To what extent is your social life based on noncorporate relationships? If this is low, you will need a replacement strategy in retirement.

Remember from Maslow's Hierarchy of Needs that it will be impossible to move into self-actualization, our highest need, without our social needs being met. *Self-actualizing individuals need a social system to do so.* This won't happen in isolation. Given the increase in social isolation involved in retiring from the social life of the corporate being, a social strategy of belonging to relevant groups is an essential building block of the self-actualizing person. Continuing to focus on the competitive pursuits of wealth creation of the corporate being is not a good basis to create new social connections, which must be based on sharing and on noncompetitive collaborative and cooperative pursuits. In this sense, if you want to create a life plan to actualize your dreams, you will need the appropriate social connections, friends, and partners to do so. Happiness is related to belonging, for it gives us the social outlet to share, help others, and give back to the community. You will not attain your highest level of satisfaction in self-actualization without belonging to relevant community organizations, having friends or colleagues who share your values and have similar pursuits, and having a social outlet to implement your life plan.

Health

The striving for money is still the drive for the fulfillment of a lower-level need. Like the hunter seeking to stockpile meat to ward off possible future scarcity, the single-minded pursuit of money is based on the fear of not having enough to survive. As long as we stay in this zone of the fear of the corporate being, our striving evolves into a competing for wealth. This competition for wealth is the false self-attempting to define self-worth through money and fails. It is important to free ourselves of this fear as we shed our corporate being, because fear is internalized stress that can build up over the years to cause disease and shorten our retirement years.

On the other hand, the activities of individual self-actualization are creative, arising from our freedom, our thoughts and the discovery of our unique potential. As opposed to being based on fear, self-actualizing behaviors are based on love. By letting go of the scarcity mind-set of the primitive hunter, we can attain or "consume" the ultimate luxury: our love of our own potential and higher purpose to create meaning for ourselves and others. This makes all the difference in the world for our happiness insofar as we reach out and connect with others and create new value for them. We are not only happy but by definition have less stress than the competitive corporate being. Competing for wealth leads to less happiness and higher stress insofar as it is an unlimited pursuit. This learned behavior is not our real selves and carries the stress of being a continuation of our false self or corporate being. Getting over this corporate being hangover before retirement helps us find ourselves later. There is no reason to allow your corporate economic self to dominate your life. It is valuable to let it go. There is no need to continue the rat race after you have retired—get out of it as early as possible.

Norman Cousins (1980) shows how negative emotions lead to sickness. "Cancer, in particular, has been connected to intensive states of grief or anger or fear" (p. 86). He in fact cured himself from an almost life-threatening infection by taking himself off drugs, taking himself out of the stressful environment of the hospital, and watching funny movies that helped rejuvenate his immune system. This experience led to his belief and theory being developed and supported by many physicians that not only does stress lead to disease, but that joy and happiness can actually cure disease by bolstering your natural immune system's ability to fight disease. Given the joy of creativity, this supports the view that creativity can extend life. Expressing your talent in your own authentic way is creativity. This elevates you holistically by channeling your talents and feelings into positive experiences, which replace stress with the joy of being your authentic self. Creativity is the passion of tapping into your highest self and adding new value beyond yourself through love in music, art, design, problem solving, or a new service to others that creates something unique that did not exist before. This is the real currency of happiness and health!

The hidden secret of attaining such a creative state of authenticity is to dissolve and rise above the narrow complexity of the corporate being. Replace it with the simplicity of being yourself by following and developing your creative passion. This is no time to get lost in the bias for complexity of the corporate being. Just remember the pure simplicity and beauty of the purpose of Mother Teresa, so authentically grounded that she had no problem expressing openly in her letters doubts of the existence of the deity (Van Biema, 2007). She was not worried in the least about potentially losing a legacy, a possible sainthood, by trying to hide such doubts from the corporate hierarchy of the Catholic Church. She had never allowed herself to be taken over by a corporate being of trying to fit into the hierarchy. It was by becoming her authentic self that she had freed herself of such corporate values of the hierarchy of power. The point here is that while many others have reached the self-actualizing firm belief in the deity through authentic soul-searching prayer, it is admirable that Mother Teresa never abandoned the authenticity of her deepest experiences of doubt in the face of the overwhelming hierarchy of the Catholic Church. In doing so, she overcame the collective beliefs of her organization's corporate being. Inversely, T. S. Elliot's play, *Murder in the Cathedral,* captures this same dilemma of authenticity: Thomas Beckett refused to compromise his authentic belief in the authority of the Catholic Church over that of King Henry II of England, given its spiritual supremacy. Beckett was martyred for his authentic beliefs. Neither Mother Teresa nor Thomas Beckett succumbed to their own fears of the collective authority as they had risen to personal power and tranquility given the authenticity of their deepest thoughts. Listening to their deepest inner conscience, rising beyond self-interest and refusing to conform to the collective thinking, allowed for their authentic originality; they neither did the right thing for the wrong reason nor the wrong thing for the right reason.

Chapter 10: The Meaning of Life

Man can endure any "how" if he has a "why."
—Frederick Nietzsche

I shall grow old, but never lose life's zest,
Because the road's last turn will be the best.
—Henry Van Dyke

The greatest use of life is to spent it for
something that outlasts life.
—William James

Few men think of death, until they are in its jaws.
—Henry Fielding

Retirement has an abundant potential by thinking of it as only a change of role, despite the fact that the word implies a passive withdrawal or a retreat to a quiet place. It needs to be thought of not as a defensive retreat from life but as a new, boundless opportunity to passionately freely charge ahead toward your newly created purpose. Retirement, call it what you like, is the last full stage of our life. It is important to go beyond the concept and face the reality of eventual death particularly if we have not already done so. This reality brings everything important to your life into focus. The meaning of *carpe diem* gains a new poignancy as our purpose becomes more urgent. Thinking this way helps to overcome the fear to better embrace our final stage. The clear awareness and reminder of our limited time on earth can become an inspiration to do something that makes a difference or is meaningful. It is our essence to be finite, otherwise life would be totally different. Imagine a life that never ends. It would become as boring as anything that never changed. Life is finite because in essence it embraces the metamorphosis of complete change and transformation. The corporate being may be endless, but we are human with a beginning and an end. It becomes more an issue of how we can live to the fullest knowing our finitude.

In her famous study and the resulting book *On Death and Dying*, Elisabeth Kübler-Ross interviewed numerous terminally ill patients. One of her key findings was that in the final stages before death, accepting death was much easier and more possible without external intervention and struggle when the individual had experienced meaning in his or her life's work. These individuals who find meaning in their lives have a sense of fulfillment when they look back on their years of work. Those who cannot feel such contentment or internal meaning in their lifework are less fortunate, and often struggle in fear and despair in the face of death. When approaching death, the most important thing in our minds is the meaning of our life.

This very personal center provides a foundation to psychologically deal with anything including death. *This sacred center is our freedom to personally create and choose our own meaning despite the competing standard substitutes of diverse collectives.* The corporate being does not help executives prepare this in a "built to last" culture internalized by them. Arthur Miller's play unveiled in *The Death of a Salesman*, the hyperbole of a persona corporate being dying when being fired.

All professionals, managers, or executives had a corporate self or being from having seriously embraced the collective corporate culture of work. The question now is: Have we been able to grow beyond this in our retirement from that corporate role? Have we been able to put our own meaning on our work and intimately connected self-identity beyond that of our corporate role? Have we personally differentiated ourselves beyond the collective corporate mission and the consumer values of the corporate being of the particular corporation or companies in our careers? It is not the role of the corporation to provide your life with meaning, but inadvertently we often allow our careers to vicariously fill that need like a vacuum. Seemly innocuous, this insidiously creates the corporate being whose self becomes addicted to work, its tasks, and its social relationships for your own self-identity. Allowing the collective to become our self-identity alienates you from your real potential to fully fulfill your unique talents. Each of us must create our own personal, unique destiny no matter how simple. We all know we have potential to be something beyond our corporate or professional roles, but denying this reality by repressing the question of achieving our full potential or the freedom to create our own meaning does ourselves a great disservice. We chose to not try to actualize ourselves as we passively allow the career and company collective role definitions and meaning to become our own uniqueness. Nothing can be more fundamentally human than our own freedom to choose ourselves, and so we must somehow become emotionally disentangled from the corporate being. This doesn't mean leaving the company in every case, but it does mean becoming your own person in spite of the hierarchy and limitations of your job or role. No matter how you learn to adapt and resolve such an identity crisis with your corporate being, the sooner the better, because one day you will walk out of the office to retire and you cannot take this borrowed corporate identity with you. Ultimately, it is your own responsibility to find your own purpose and meaning for your work regardless of that of the corporate mission. Retirement is not the ideal time to deal with this issue, but still it is better late than never.

Creating or finding your own unique course and identity separate from that of the corporation is very difficult for the executive because it is the executive's role as a leader to walk the talk and be the role model for other employees the way to corporate success by following the corporate mission and values. Socializing employees into the corporate establishment by being the culture and its meaning is part of every leadership role, yet ultimately the executive must grow to differ and create his or her separate identity and values different from those of the company. This stage of the executive's coming of age and becoming his or her own person may mean leaving the company before retirement age. This is healthy, for the executive's soul and integrity are far more sacred than remaining a corporate clone. The issue of facing the free choice of your self-identity does not go away, and if you put it off until retirement, you will still have to face it.

The later you face this ultimate need, the harder it will be, given the years of allowing your corporate being to harden as a convenient substitute. In retirement, it is more difficult because this was not supposed to happen—remember, the corporate myth of retiring as a corporate being was supposed to be blissful. As the Kübler-Ross study showed, it was those who had not found personal meaning in their lifework who suffered the most in the face of death. The point is that substituting the collective corporate being for your personal meaning is shallow and empty. It is possible to find personal meaning while in your corporate role through your own values of service to others, but this is your own personal transcendence of the corporate being while on the job. You will be able to carry this beyond your role into retirement through personal projects and activities outside the corporation. Understanding your own personal values as unique but reconciling them with the corporate values will allow you to transcend the schism between the corporate being and your personal values, and to project meaning into retirement. However, this reconciliation and bridging of the personal and corporate values is rare for the executive according to Scott Peck (1978), who had many successful executives for patients. The example that comes to mind was not an executive but a factory worker who spoke poor English but had body language of joy with her ear-to-ear smile. Having raised her family and joined the workforce as a pharmaceutical factory cleaner, she adopted the co-workers as her new family. She worked very hard as if she was cleaning her own home, regularly brought an abundance of homemade cookies and pastries and if her job was completed for the moment always offered to help anyone. Her selfless caring devotion for others was infectious and she always seemed to raise the morale and productivity. Her meaning of life was clearly devoted to helping and caring for her family and work team … not on her job description. She was loved by her co-workers, not so much because she helped them but for the fact that she was an authentic person who had chosen her meaning and lived by it. She was luckier and happier than most executives in this regard.

One of the compelling aspects of the corporate being is that it is built to last, as Collins and Porras (1994) point out. This idea creates a personal sense of never stopping and going on forever as a being onto itself, unlike human beings. As a consequence, there is a reluctance to get off the great corporate train, which just keeps rolling on. It is addictive to think we are infinite and powerful. This feeling seduces us to avoid the reality of our own death. The corporate being is a colossus of ideas and structures built to grow continuously without limitations. Certainly not yours or anyone's retirement will stop it. As a member of this corporate train, we develop a fear of retiring from the enterprise that will never die. This is really our own fear of death insofar as we have failed to build in our finitude and individual separation from the corporate being to the extent that we deny our own freedom and individual choice. As we internalize the power vested in our corporate roles as our own, the corporate being has momentarily seduced us and addicted us to immortality, so why bother thinking of retirement!

Nevertheless, this subconscious fear of retirement is the growing fear of accepting our real mortal selves and fear of not dealing with the growing stress of adopting this borrowed false self without recognizing our freedom to be our own selves and our real need to create our own separate meaning. One executive described the experience of retiring from his job as "cutting off my right arm!" Although we leave behind the power of the role vicariously vested in us temporarily, we need to discover that our real power lies in our own freedom to choose our own meaning and purpose.

This neurosis of trying to be a false self is embedded in fear and stress, often in the subconscious. This denial of your real self and the failure to live your real life by failing your potential and authentic being is not only more stressful but can be devastating for your health. De Vries (1981) worked on the intangible aspects of healing and showed how important the mental approach to ailments and disease can be in improving the healing process. Taking responsibility for your own healing process is positively co-related to a faster rate of recovery. Having a personal meaning for living is also a positive co-related component and becomes the underlying reason for taking the responsibility for healing itself. De Vries conducted pioneering

experiments *on the healing power of meaning in his patients' lives.*
He worked with a group of patients suffering from diverse ailments
who had been referred by family doctors because they were not
responding well to treatment. He asked them to participate in six
different thirty-minute discussion groups. The patients and research
team discussed these kinds of basic questions:

- What do you really want to live for?
- What does your intuition tell you about your condition?
- What do you think you need to do to get well?
- How could you do this to get well?

De Vries's goal for the experiment was analyze the results of
facilitating patients to think about their physical ailments from the
perspective of the meaning in life. What the experiment found was that
all patients progressed by changing their attitudes toward themselves
as well as toward their ailments. By the end of the experiment, all
patients experienced a change in their actual physical complaints,
which became less severe. In some cases the physical complaints
disappeared!

What this shows is that taking personal responsibility for personal
issues and problems by itself ameliorates medical conditions to
some extent. Becoming aware and motivated by your own personal
meaning of life and reason to live, releases this new personal power
of taking responsibility. The traditional tendency of passing this
responsibility totally to the expert medical establishment is to a degree
a personal denial of your own freedom to take some responsibility,
which renders you passive and useless to improve your situation.
This relinquishing of responsibility to become passive is similar
to allowing the corporate being to take over your life. Allowing
the corporation the role of providing your meaning and mission
gives the corporate being complete power over your life and sets the
stage for a retirement of passivity. This is why it is a serious issue
in retirement if not before. The retiring executive has been used to
being very responsible but to the dictates of the role and corporate
culture, not responsible existentially for his or her own being. This

self-sacrifice occurs by avoiding conflict with the corporate being and surrendering his or her own freedom to be an authentic self in exchange for the rewards and success of the corporate role. However, once this external role is finished in retirement, if not sooner, it is vital for you, the executive, to assert the freedom to be your real self by discovering your authentic self and your reason to live the rest of your life. Discovering this reason is essentially the self-discovery of your personal passion for a cause outside of oneself. As a follower, you may have failed to grasp your full potential to be free of this collectivism and chose to be or become responsible for your health in retirement. This failure of the retiring corporate being likely causes increased stress and a higher morbidity rate, if not a shorter life!

Remember the performance experiments mentioned earlier where the same stress level for two separate groups was reduced in impact in one group simply because that one group felt in control, thinking that the stressor could be removed simply by throwing a switch—even though they never used the switch. Similarly, taking responsibility for an ailment or for being healthy can reduce the stress that can lead to illness. Passing the buck to the corporation and its paternalistic culture, which supplies answers to mission and meaning, is similar to passing the full responsibility for your well-being to the medical establishment. Doing so implies human beings are essentially passive and dependent on a collective power. A passive retirement is a stressful one if we fail to take charge and are highly dependent in our minds on external factors for fulfilling our most important needs. Conversely, we must be responsible for our inner needs. Allowing the collective corporate being to do so is more stressful and can be damaging to your health if you relinquish control and the power to help yourself.

Viktor Frankl, in his *Psychotherapy and Existentialism* (1967), describes logotherapy as the therapeutic or healing value in bringing the unconscious inner reason or meaning into a person's consciousness. He describes the tragic triad of human existence as pain, guilt, and death.

In applying this to our subject, these three all resonate for the retiring executive:

- *Pain* is the suffering based on the loss of your self-identity and the realization that the corporate mission and culture now fail in retirement as you are terminated in retirement from your leadership role.
- *Guilt* sets in because you realize that you have been rented in your leadership role and you cannot take it with you as the company marches on without looking toward retirees. Guilt also occurs because you realize that one believed the corporate myth of retiring into a golden age of fulfillment, enjoyment, and the pleasure of the consumption of the rewards of having been an executive. You may also feel guilt for giving up your freedom to become your full creative potential.
- Finally, you experience *death* as you experience the end of your role. Being simply replaced after retirement combined with the loss of your self-identity is a premonition of your own actual death.

Frankl shows that without a conscious meaning, human existence is bound for a vacuum of meaning leading to boredom, mass conformism, and a lack of care or sensitivity for others as well as oneself. Reviving health involves finding meaning and sensitivity for first yourself and then others. Frankl also says this lack of meaning is for the executive "a spiritual crisis of retirement" or a "permanent unemployment neurosis" (pp.124–125), a depression that affects people who become aware of the lack of content in their lives. The executive has replaced this lack of personal content through the "will to power" or "will to money'" (p.125), which is the addiction to the never-ending corporate being allowing one to escape the "inner void" and run away into work (p.125). This addiction to power to replace personal meaning breaks down and fails the retiring executive when the executive must relinquish power. Frankl calls this tragedy "the Executive Disease" (p.125).

Personal meaning is our ultimate power, for it unleashes our passion to create value far beyond what is possible as a rented corporate being. It is gaining touch with your life force or passion that can save your life! It can put you back into a sense of control lost in retirement, but this takes a positive, determined attitude to find yourself beyond your corporate being.

Suffering for Meaning

If finding our authentic self and meaning was so easy, everyone would have done it or do it routinely given the huge benefits for life. It appears that meaning is not easy to find because it is illusive. We tend to think that it must be very deep and so complex that we need a roomful of psychiatrists or spiritualists to help us find ourselves. We also have a need to fit in, and so we have a tendency to conform. However, joining organizations to fulfill our social needs must be separate from our search and self-discovery of personal and spiritual meaning.

The key is to develop self-awareness, reject the boredom and emptiness of the collective replacements for authenticity, and begin to take responsibility to overcome it. It is the experience of the pain of the psychological limits of your corporate being which is your friend as your subconscious sends you the message of boredom and futility to keep doing what you are doing. Pain is the body's signal of the need to heal and become whole. Being plateaued in your career when you know you can do and be more is like a death sentence. Accepting money and its consumer rewards as the replacement for fulfilling your higher needs to express your authentic spirit and talent is like the tragic Greek literary figure of Sisyphus who was condemned to a meaningless life having to roll a rock up a hill only to have it roll down again and again. Pain or boredom is our subconscious signal not to accept the meaninglessness of the collective being and to overcome it through our own original struggle to be authentic to reach our own unique brand, purpose, full potential and express our own talent. Only by experiencing the pain of the existing psychological level we have satisfied can we struggle to a higher level, in this case create a personally meaningful and authentic life outside of the collective conformity of our specific corporate being. Denying the pain only locks us into the boredom and limits of the corporate being whose highest joy and meaning will be like Sisyphus the repetitive highs and lows of consumption as the meaning of life. Repressing the pain and trying to embrace the collective as the ultimate, increases stress by denying your body's signal of pain as a signal to heal oneself and find your original self. This pain of the limit of the collectivity is often covered up through the overconsumption and dependency on drugs and alcohol. This is the executive neurosis of the collective self. This book aims to overcome this and create for you an individual growth transformation to your potential, original talent, and authenticity. This healing and reduction of stress will increase your health and well-being.

Maslow's (1954) Hierarchy of Needs shows us that we are motivated to move to a higher level of the need hierarchy when we basically satisfy the level we are in. Each level fails to completely satisfy. Ultimately, after we can afford to buy everything we need, we still feel a vacuum of meaning. The drive to find our personal meaning and purpose is the need to reach self-actualization based on the limits of security, consumption, job success, and more to satisfy us. Suffering this void of incompleteness helps us to face the last frontier for happiness and joy, our *need for self-actualization*. This is our highest need as we find our authentic self through using our talents and passion to create value for ourselves and others. We will suffer this gap of feeling incomplete, until we meet our full potential.

At the level of self-actualization, finding your meaning to live for the rest of your life is spiritual not material; it is based on talent and passion not skill. Finding a meaning of life arises from suffering the emptiness of its absence. As long as this awareness is substituted for by the neurotic executive's addictions to power and consumption, the suffering will be delayed until your experience the loss of your corporate being and its shock or hyper-stress in retirement. Suffering for meaning may sound trite, but it is the basis for the beginning of your spirituality as you connect and find meaning for your life as a free individual, connecting all of your life and unique potential together as value and meaning for others, as opposed to power over others.

The tragedy of the graveyard is not so much the end of life but the tragedy of the huge, undeveloped potential, creativity, and talent left behind. Wasted executive talent and leadership could have been of great value to others, not to mention oneself and could have creatively changed the world for the better. Failing to develop our potential to be our full authentic beings is life's greatest tragedy. Executives have the potential to be great beyond the constraints of the corporate being. However, they must separate themselves from the addictions of the corporate being by mobilizing the ultimate power of finding meaning and a personal mission. Moving on from a corporate being to the self-actualizing power of meaning may not pay as much materialistically, but it pays much greater in terms of spiritual meaning, personal health, and length and quality of life. By introspectively listening to your inner calling and intuition, you can begin to create this personal meaning. Overcoming the personal alienation from your inner, authentic being through discovering your freedom to be constructively creative will keep you out of the graveyard a lot longer.

The Freedom to Be Authentic

Only you can decide what your highest potential self should be. This is the highest level of freedom. Here, freedom escapes the lower levels of need. The need for safety involves freedom to escape danger but this offers few opportunities to extend the self. The freedom to gain economic security is constrained within the collectivity of the cultural rules for success. The need for ego and esteem also involves the freedom to choose the best fashions, styles, cars, and houses, which allows you to make the right statement of your success and status. Yet these are only surface external expressions and not internally authentic. This ego level of freedom is determined by the latest whims and trends and so is still determined by the collectivity in this case the consumer society at large. The only full freedom that optimizes your power and full sense of individual freedom is the freedom of choosing your authentic self and actualizing this being. This is the full sense of freedom, but is the hardest level of freedom to attain precisely because it is our ultimate statement of our identity. As such, it must involve responsibility to others of actualizing our highest values and potentiality.

The freedom to express your ego as value is transcended by the highest freedom of finding your ultimate self through providing value for others. The freedom to find yourself in truth, art, or meaningful service provides a value link to others. This value link to others can only be created by your authentic self as you move beyond the lower levels of being rented to choosing your own definition of value for others on your own terms. Authenticity is the result of reaching self-actualization. Paradoxically, this is the most difficult level of freedom for the very reason that it allows you to escape the ego and reach the level of connecting your talent and passion to others. This connection of value for others also provides the ultimate value to ourselves, for it creates the authentic self, our highest sense of responsibility to ourselves and to others. Freedom as creative responsibility is our highest possible level of self-actualization. This can only be achieved if we target our talents toward freely expressing them as value for not just ourselves but for others.

Creativity versus Workaholism

Workaholics work harder and harder but not smarter. Corporate structures, processes, methods, and cultures reward hard work. Tightly defined job structures limit the scope of each role integrated within a system of roles and accountabilities. If you see a better way, a new creative idea, a new reporting system, a new sales pitch or customer application, new suppliers, new software, you will cause problems in the minds of other executives whose roles are interdependent on yours. You will be overstepping your bounds and moving into their area of jurisdiction. This means that you will have to go to the top, and given the basic interdependency between all roles, changes will require a total buy-in based on the advantages for other areas not just your own. This assumes that you understand these other areas better than other executives, including the CEO. This can cause conflict, and it can easily lead to you not being rewarded for being creative: you may soon be seen as being disruptive and not fitting into the culture and how things are done around here. Each executive area has a successful track record and does not want to admit its limits, particularly to another executive.

Creativity and free thinking are usually discouraged through executive turf-ism and competitiveness. Executives learn quickly to compete and to become noticed not by being creative but by working harder than anyone else. As each executive wants to be differentiated through hard work, the culture easily rewards workaholism as the way to prove an executive's worth. Sticking to the knitting of your role and working hard prevents conflict. Being a change agent through your creativity can never be contained in just your own area, and may mean you are exceeding your authority and making changes beyond your own area. This is usually punished. Trying to always get the buy-in to implement your creative ideas may not be appreciated by other executives, who may turn on you if they see a glitch in your own specific area. The collectivity of multi-integrated roles means change is a slow process and must be driven from the top. Corporate processes are static and usually too paralyzed to foster significant executive creativity. Better to just work hard and keep your nose to the grindstone. Don't get into other executives' work even though all roles are interdependent. Simply offer analysis that contributes to a paralysis by analysis culture. Corporate politics kill good ideas every day. Everyone continues to work harder and harder and gets rewarded for being a workaholic.

CEOs usually are a product of their company's past culture and find transforming that company difficult. This is the biggest reason why smaller, more creative entrepreneurial upstarts unencumbered with a past bureaucracy and obsolete "winning formulas" eventually overtake the larger companies. The huge complexity of practices of larger companies causes inertia. The executive politics based on power in each specialized area prevents easy change or innovation.

Executive creativity is very restricted. For me personally, this restriction has been the main driver for leaving executive roles and returning to being an external consultant or change agent, in this case a writer. Change is easier from the outside because you escape the politics of inertia. The truly creative executives often leave the corporate quagmire to use their ideas in an entrepreneurial start-up. Many great start-ups came from executives who simply could not implement their ideas inside their existing company. This inability of corporations to maintain control of their processes and roles without a collective groupthink culture prevents creativity. This is not any executive's fault but more to the result of the structure and processes that cause such inertia more than the skill of any executive.

For the workaholic executive who stays in an environment where he or she cannot be creative is individually damaging. Personal growth and fulfillment of your own thoughts and dreams through your own thinking and creativity becomes retarded in the process of becoming a corporate being. As your creativity to help the company grow and improve becomes stifled, so is your desire to apply such free thinking to your own personal life. Denying your creativity is self-denial since creativity is the basis for personal renewal and for finding your own purpose and meaning through growth and authenticity. The collectivity of the corporate purpose and values internalized as a corporate being by the executive will fail the executive later in the primal need to creatively find and discover an authentic unique purpose and life after the corporation. Denying creativity for the life as a workaholic shrivels up the basis for re-inventing ourselves in retirement as a fulfilled and happy individual. Workaholism cuts the executive off from having the time to develop the personal activities, hobbies, and personal connections with others that can be the basis later for the executive to re-emerge as a fulfilled, happy, family-oriented community leader or volunteer or entrepreneur. The workaholic works from fear of failure in the corporate box. The workaholic is addicted to work as the basis for all things good. This addiction is self-deception and cuts off the free time and leisure needed by the more creative person. The extreme work sacrifices cut workaholics off from who they are as unique, free beings and allow them to become neurotic in their self-deception. They can no longer listen to themselves given their addiction to work. They cannot listen to their imagination. They will never hear their inner calling. They work out of necessity given their fear of failure. This atrophying of the creative process and cutting oneself off from leisure and what makes one unique is unhealthy and can cut life short. The creative person continually changes and reaches for innovation to find a better way. The creative mind is healthier than the workaholic mind because time is taken for personal feelings, intuitions, imagination, following one's hunches, and personal experimentation projects. Taking the freedom to nurture one's creativity becomes the foundation of a productive life based on one's own passion outside of the corporate role.

What ideas have you dismissed because they were discouraged by the corporate culture? How often have you compromised your innovative ideas to fit in to your peers' ideas? How often has the boss said that idea may not fit into the new head office initiative? What ideas did you feel a passion for but could never get any traction inside of the corporation? What ideas did you feel were the real you, ideas that you could base a start-up on? What ideas fit into your real calling in life but do not fit the corporation? How has the rejection of your ideas affected your motivation to do your job and your commitment to the company? Have you compromised your beliefs by backing away from your creative ideas for job security? How does not following your creative thinking and your dreams make you feel about yourself? Do you ever feel like you are rotting on the vine, inside of your corporate box or corporate being? Could you use your ideas to start a new company by yourself or with others? What's the worst case scenario if you quit and follow your own semiretirement project? What's the worst case scenario if you stay as a corporate being and deny your dreams? How can you ever be fulfilled and happy if you don't listen and respond to your inner calling, your special purpose and meaning in life?

Freedom and Creativity

Discovering your freedom beyond your corporate self is vital to embracing creativity. The corporate being is a restrictive system of processes and structures that does not reward thinking outside the box. You are paid to be in the corporate box of professional "best" practices, the job description, and set procedures. Becoming creative requires a new mind-set where anything is possible. Given that it is your life, it is time to throw off the collective constraints and your own self-restricting notions of your life. It is time to brainstorm options with no limits. The numerous life options in your career or retirement must be explored and considered creatively to bring your talent into alignment with realistic possibilities. This means beginning to separate and differentiate yourself from your corporate being. This may lower your commitment to the corporate role, but usually by this stage the executive is on autopilot and can plan a breakout on his or her own terms.

- What is unique and special about you? You know no one has ever existed who is like you. Define your difference, develop it, and live it.
- What are your talents and values? You probably never got to fully articulate these as a corporate being.
- What are your hidden aspirations? As a corporate being, you have had to hide your other life projects, hobbies, and passions!

All these areas are key considerations in planning your new freedom and breakout from the corporate being that have put you into a role box or job description. Liberating oneself from the limitations of the corporate box can be exhilarating and youthful as your passion surfaces around your new creative options. Planning personal action alternatives to reach your self-actualization must be done based on your uniqueness. This is why it must be a creative process as you create a new, personal, unique role with a purpose for pre-retirement or for later. It is only through this personal creative process can you find yourself in what you care passionately about outside of your corporate being. Tapping into a new special purpose and role allows you to base your life creatively on your passion and love. The corporate being was based on fear of scarcity and security. Your new role is creatively based on your personal freedom as you re-create yourself with a new purpose given your talents and passion. This is your true calling! It allows you to be your authentic self and to burn up debilitating stress through the energy and excitement of creativity.

As long as we allow ourselves to be in the box of the corporate being for security reasons, our creativity will be stifled by the self-imposed constraints of our own internalized "mental bureaucracy." In effect, we have sacrificed our higher-level needs for self-actualization, for greater and greater security, belonging, and self-esteem. As the corporate being restricts and limits the development of creativity through rules, it leaves the retiring executive ill prepared for the need for higher creativity as an adaptive and inventive personal process in retirement. Being satisfied with the status quo of the power and status of the corporate self may not be so bad except for the fact you cannot take these with you outside of the corporate role into retirement. The bottom line is this is not your real you anyway, so why not grow beyond it? If you don't, you will languish in the stress of the loss of your corporate being. Without a meaningful replacement and a surpassing of your corporate being, the vacuum will create the hyper-stress that will probably shorten your life.

Creativity and Health

As we move up the hierarchy of needs, money becomes less and less helpful to us. Overcoming the stress of getting rid of the addictions of power and dependency of the corporate being will lower the stress as we find our authentic selves. Doing what we are talented at and love can extend our lives. *Self-actualization is a health strategy after retiring from the corporation and is more important than wealth strategies.* This is contrary to the corporate myth of retirement, which instills the absolute need for greater wealth in order to have a better retirement equated with better consumerism. This retirement philosophy of the corporate being acts to control the executive to remain in the role as long as possible. However, the adverse affect of this is that the executive emerges into retirement ill prepared for the creativity needed to survive and thrive in the structureless world of retirement. This creates the hyper-stress of retirement as the executive waits for collective external structures and solutions which never come. Waiting is anticipatory stress, an inactive slow death, like getting dressed up each day for a big night out but never going out.

Self-initiated original action is now imperative. Creating your own solutions and new roles with a personal meaning will prove to be vital for your health and survival in retirement. Although conformity is a survival skill for the corporate being, in retirement it can kill you because there is nothing meaningful to conform to. Creativity is the survival skill in retirement. Think of retirement not as the inactive golden age of the corporate myth but as prime time, your time, your place, your final act! No one can tell you what to do but you. An active, purposeful retirement is driven by the creativity of the individual. As action is energy and passion, so it perpetuates itself through the joy of discovery of what new exciting projects turn up through serendipity.

In *The Art of Aging* (2007), Nuland describes how a group in an old age home became liberated and more autonomous as they discovered their creative talents in a regular art workshop. "Their encounters with creativity have brought about not only a liberation of something powerful and new within them, but a transformation in their aging" (p. 280). He goes on to identify creativity as the fountain of youth for old age. Instead of following a passive collective role of the retiree, creativity can help to extend your life by creating a new purpose and meaning to live. Further, this new creativity can blossom new sources of happiness, joy, and a basis for new focused self-actualizing activities and a productive final chapter to your life. Creativity is the wellspring of life that helps to differentiate yourself as a worthwhile person making a meaningful contribution. The amazing thing is that the creativity of self-actualization can increase your longevity and extend your life as passion burns up stress while you pursue new, focused, creative projects with a meaningful purpose. Such activities fit into your talent orbit as they pass the passion test of being fun.

While Norman Cousins (1980) was recovering from a life-threatening illness, he started to think about the connection between creativity and longevity. He went to visit Albert Schweitzer and Pablo Casals, who were both active in their eighties. What Cousins learned had a profound effect on him. He learned that a highly developed purpose, creativity, hope, faith, and will to live are the most powerful basis for life. In his visit with the great musician Pablo Casals, he was amazed to see Casals shuffle about early in the morning, barely able to walk or move with his arthritis and stiffness. However after breakfast, Casals sat down at his piano and soon transformed the room with not just beautiful music but with emotion and joy of his passion. The more he played, the more Casals became a young man with no signs of arthritis. After this, when he got up from the piano bench, he had lost his shuffle and went for his usual walk along the beach. Casals's purpose of expressing himself creatively and with passion acted not just like an anti-inflammatory drug but had magical effects on him. Cousins could see before his eyes an old man, constrained by his rigid body, become flexible and youthful through the transformational qualities of creativity and purpose.

It is the intensity of your passion devoted to the purpose you love that can provide you with the self-made "drug," the fountain of youth that can keep you healthy much longer than the stereotyped retirement of passive consumerism. *Creativity is not just making something; it is re-making yourself!* It has a positive side effect as it absorbs your whole being into the project. It has a transformational quality of health. Total absorption into the purpose, beauty, and the good of your purpose puts your being into the spiritual zone of creative joy. This state of nirvana, or flow of the universe, has the opposite impact of stress: it builds strength and unity of your being; it does not destroy it. It is possible that certain hobbies or entrepreneurial projects can be elevated to do this for you if you have enough commitment and focus. The key is that the project be creatively unique and come from the wellsprings of your own talent and passion, with a purpose or value taking you beyond yourself.

Creativity and Spirituality

Ultimately, we can live better and longer by creating the meaning and purpose for our life and actualizing it through action. To resolve the alienation of our being with the extraneous corporate mission, we can only transcend it through our creativity by dealing with our own existence. No one else can do this for us. Allowing the corporation or any organization to do so will prevent our self-actualization by keeping us as essentially passive and collective beings from a personal meaning perspective. As we rise beyond the collectivity of the corporate being and suffer boredom or ennui with the consumerist solution to the meaning of life, we look for spirituality as a creative quest or search for meaning. It is the pain of the experience of the boredom of consumerism and being the corporate being which is our mind sending us the message of the limits of the success of the corporate being and the need to rise to a higher level. The pain of boredom is our spirit trying to awaken us to become whole within our individual beings as the original being, spirit, and talent we were born to be. Creativity and spirituality are intimate partners insofar as there is no boilerplate prescription for how to be a spiritual person. It is a creative process of finding purpose and meaning for your life in your way through your human spirit. Learning to be creative is struggling to better understand yourself, your life as well as your Creator. This is an endless learning process that has its value in the journey to truth, love, art, and the joy of connectivity of the originality of your talent and passion to life in a meaningful way. Ultimately, it is your human spirit that inspires you and gives you meaning and the passion to make a difference in your life. This spirit adds value beyond yourself as you come to realize that self-actualization is paradoxically more about truth and value to others.

Ultimately, we all want to be remembered by others for making a difference to them, touching their lives and creating a valuable difference in their lives. In this sense, self-actualization is really going beyond yourself creatively and having the personal leadership ability to create value beyond the self. No life can be richer than one that has achieved self-actualization. *Money cannot buy it.* You can only get there by finding your own way through your creativity, values, personal meaning, and higher purpose. This is the ultimate spiritual journey—with no standardized cookie-cutter collective solutions.

In the last stage of our lives, we have a whole new opportunity to embark on a new, fresh, stimulating odyssey. This is our prime time to discover ourselves and our full creative potential to actualize our talents in ways that create new value for others. This creative process of meaning and purpose is not only going to extend your life but will add joy and happiness not only to yourself but to others. Why not use your last stage to explore and find the great unknown wilderness, yourself? Finding your creative spirit and living your own way is the best way to live a longer and more meaningful life and be remembered as someone who made a valuable difference. What could be more important?

Chapter 11: Transformational Life Planning

Made weak by time and fate, but strong in will,
To strive, to seek, to find and not to yield.

—Alfred Tennyson

We all die, but that doesn't mean we have to have dead lives and struggle to get a life. Looking at death not as the ultimate thief of life but as a friendly reminder of how limited our time is helps positively to motivate us to make a positive difference. If this is your only time on stage, your brief moment to exist in the billions of years of human existence, then why not discover whatever personal meaning you can that differentiates you as an individual and makes your life worthwhile, however relatively brief. To truly live to your fullest potential, you need to be free. You need to find what it is in yourself that taps your passion and energizes your life. What do you choose to live for, and what values or mission are you willing to die for? Are you willing to die for your corporate being's mission? Few if any executives look back on their careers and wished that they had spent more time at the office. Few would be willing to die for the corporation, but paradoxically many do from workaholism. *If you are not willing to die for the values of your corporate being, what would it be for?* The courage to define your life on your own terms and values brings your innermost being to life by rising beyond the secure existential boredom of collective conformity. What are your most cherished struggles and experiences that have made you unique? What values did you develop from these experiences that made you so different? It is in your risk to differentiate yourself that you discover and actualize your own uniqueness. Life at its fullest will involve getting out of the security cocoon of conformity, stepping up with courage, and taking the risk to be your potential and to fulfill your dreams. You only have one life. How do you want

243

to be remembered? Why not make it special! Only you can do it in your own way.

Happiness and Self-Actualization

How can you be satisfied and happy if you never reach your potential as a human being? As an executive, look in the mirror in the morning before going to work and ask if your life and mission are really defined by your corporate being, or must you personally create this by differentiating yourself from your job? As an executive and as a leader in the corporation, you are no doubt talented or you would never have gotten where you are. However, how could you accept that the job box that you are in can ever be the foundation for expressing your full potential? You are much bigger and talented than any corporate role. How can you accept anything but the very best value for your life? The corporation may be able to offer more money but not more value than you can create for your own life. The best life for you will be unique and as different as your potential is. Your authentic values and being will never be found in the corporate collectivity. Fulfilling the destiny of your sacred life is up to you to create through *actualizing* the artistic, intellectual, or spiritual extensions of your many talents. Doing this will take time, imagination, and creativity, but most importantly, it will take action. What will it take for you to blossom into your full potential?

EXERCISE

The temptation will be to simply read through the following and mull over a few personal reactions and possible answers. I want you to get the most value possible out of the process of transforming your life to self-actualize your retirement. Consequently, to optimize the value, I recommend that you do the following as a paper-and-pencil exercise. As the below spaces may be insufficient, you may prefer to use blank paper. No doubt you have already thought through some of these issues for your life. This exercise is meant to refine your thoughts. Writing out your answers will be more powerful for you and will help pin down more definitively your ideas and commitment to certain priorities. This is vital as you need to distill your roving thoughts and create a clear and simple life plan. Until you have such a cogent life plan, you need to share the development of it with significant others in your life who will be affected by such a plan. Ideally, you can develop and share your life plan with your life partner. As this cannot be done as a quick exercise, I recommend starting off doing it as a draft but redoing it in a month or so, until you have a simple life plan and have reduced the many complexities in your life to the few actionable priorities. This aims to allow you to focus and use your talent, tap your passion, and create new value for others within your life mission.

TRANSFORMATIONAL LIFE PLANNING

1. PREPARATION

The following questions and spaces for writing out your responses aim to facilitate this transformation to gain awareness of your own unique needs by asking:

What level of the Hierarchy of Needs are you currently meeting?

....

....

....

....

....

....

....

....

....

....

....

Why?......

....

....

....

....

....

....

....

....

....

....

....

Do you identify specific needs that are not being fully met? Why not? What are the factors that have limited your needs being fully met?

....

....

....

....

....

....

....

....

....

....

....

....

....

....

What stresses are you currently under? Identify the specific stressors in order of priority.

…………...…………………………………………………………………..…

…………...…………………………………………………………………..…

…………...…………………………………………………………………..…

…………………..…………………………………………………………………

…………………..…………………………………………………………………

…………………..…………………………………………………………………

…………………..…………………………………………………………………

…………………..…………………………………………………………………

…………………..…………………………………………………………………

…………………..…………………………………………………………………

…………...………………………………………………………………………

…………………………………………………………………………………

What is your highest level of need? Is this need increasing or lessening? Is it a new need or from the past?

…………...…………………………………………………………………..…

…………...…………………………………………………………………..…

…………...…………………………………………………………………..…

…………...…………………………………………………………………..…

…………………..…………………………………………………………………

…………………..…………………………………………………………………

…………………………………………………………………………………

…………………………………………………………………………………

…………………………………………………………………………………

…………………………………………………………………………………

…………………………………………………………………………………

What are the results of your three circles exercise of skills, talents, and passion, in chapter 7? What were those overlapping areas between your skills, talents, and passion circles? What are the skills and talents that you have a passion for? Write a statement defining this.

....
....
....
....
....
....
....
....
....
....
....

What new education, training, and development would enhance your talents in the area of your passion?

....
....
....
....
....
....
....
....
....
....
....

What are your publicly accepted talents? What are your secret or hidden undiscovered talents, not identified above, waiting to be more developed and actualized?

....
....
....
....
....
....
....
....
....
....
....

What are your inner or secret desires you wish to accomplish? These are your dreams that you have never told anyone.

....
....
....
....
....
....
....
....
....
....
....
....

What are the Top 10 of your Top 100 Things You Want to Do before
You Die List?

1...
....

2...
....

3...
....

4...
....

5...
....

6...
....

7...
....

8...
....

9...
....

10..
....

What are the three most important results that you wish to create before you die?

1..

....

2..

....

3..

....

What percent of your time do you spend per day to actualize your unique potential talents? What are you now doing to use your talents?

....

....

....

....

....

....

....

....

....

....

....

....

....

....

....

What further information and data or feedback do you need on your special talents and how and where to apply them?

....
....
....
....
....
....
....
....
....
....
....

What issues still need to be resolved? Name other friends or significant others with whom you can reality test and discuss your ideas to gain new insight and support.

....
....
....
....
....
....
....
....
....
....
....
....

Changes and Commitments

What specific changes are you able and willing to make in order to make the above happen?

....

....

....

....

....

....

....

....

....

....

....

....

....

What specifically do you need to do to actualize your potential?

....

....

....

....

....

....

....

....

....

....

List major personal changes necessary for you to reach your full potential.

....

....

....

....

....

....

....

....

....

....

....

....

What will happen to your life if you do nothing? How do you feel about that?

....

....

....

....

....

....

....

....

....

....

....

....

2. MISSION AND LIFE PURPOSE

What are your most important life-struggle and personally derived sacred values that came from these personal experiences? State your personal description of these values and why they are sacred to you.

....

....

....

....

....

....

....

....

Given all of the above personal information, define your personal mission or life purpose. Focus on your talents of passion and your personal values that inspire you. This should not feel like a massive burden like solving world poverty but in terms of, what is realistic in your retirement? Ensure it is creative. Make sure it feels right. Above all, it must pass the test of being satisfying and allowing you to have fun!

....

....

....

....

....

....

....

....

....

How do you want others to remember you? How will your life purpose and mission affect others and leave the memory that you want?

....
....
....
....
....
....
....
....
....
....
....
....

What will be your legacy for your family and other causes?

....
....
....
....
....
....
....
....
....
....
....
....

What difference will your life have made for your significant others, community, nation, or the world?

....

....

....

....

....

....

....

....

....

....

....

....

Life Purpose and Mission Statement:

....

....

....

....

....

....

....

....

....

....

....

....

3. ORGANIZATION OF YOUR LIFE PLAN

Organization of your life plan is best done around the three life modes: *Being, Doing,* and *Having.* Since retirement is the time to self-actualize around your highest principles, consider attaining an artistic, intellectual, or spiritual level of enacting your mission, values and talents. This means starting with *Being, Doing,* and *Having* must be supportive to be consistent and supportive of your self-actualization.

Now that you are retired, it is time for you and your highest *Being* to become the center of this organization of your life.

Being: Picture and describe yourself as the self-actualized person of your values and dreams given your life purpose and mission.

....

....

....

....

....

....

....

With whom and where can you and will you attain this dream?

....

....

....

....

....

....

....

State the artistic, intellectual, and spiritual dimensions of your self-actualization.

....
....
....
....
....
....
....
....
....
....
....
....

How does this differ from your corporate being?

....
....
....
....
....
....
....
....
....
....
....
....

Doing: Define the actions and projects that will get you to the top of your mountain to attain your life purpose, mission, and your highest being.

....

....

....

....

....

....

....

....

....

....

....

Define the results or difference that you will make as a self-actualized being.

....

....

....

....

....

....

....

....

....

....

....

Prioritize these actions. Identify specifically your "first steps," for example, personal development and learning that will help you to better apply your talents to the area of your life purpose and mission.

....
....
....
....
....
....
....
....
....
....
....

Having: Define what things, money, and assets you need to realize your dreams.

....
....
....
....
....
....
....
....
....
....
....

Doug Treen

Given your above life purpose and defined plans, develop a retirement or financial plan or rework your existing retirement/financial plan to better fit your new life plan.

....
....
....
....
....
....
....
....
....
....
....
....

What new things, including equipment, books, technology, vehicle, house, will you need, and where and how will you need them?

....
....
....
....
....
....
....
....
....
....
....

To do Transformational Life Planning, keep it as simple as possible. Any dynamic life plan requires personal change and transformation away from your corporate being. You can always revise your plan over time. However, you will never get started in this transformation if the life plan is too complex and cumbersome. The following examples try to show how this can be done simply as a good basis for starting and taking control. These examples show the final results of a lot of thinking. They also show the importance of distilling any life plan down to simple action and change of priorities. Remember, having too many priorities is similar to having no priorities and is a sign that no critical decisions have been made, and no transformations are going to happen. A good Transformational Life Planning has worked through the normal complexities to the simplicity of an action plan.

LIFE PLANNING: Case 1 (retiring advertising executive)

This individual was a talented and creative advertising executive but wanted to apply his skills to his personal passion for adventure and nature. He wanted to grow artistically become more original, given his talent, and not have to continually compromise his ideas to please the clients. He also had grown bored of commuting, travel, and the grind of corporate life. Further, he longed for and dreamt of a life of freedom and adventure.

Being:

- Values: creativity, beauty, nature, adventure, family
- Life Purpose Statement: to combine my passion for photography, sailing, and adventure with my wife to discover and bring undiscovered beauty to others through photographic journalism.

Doing:

- Further Learning: take underwater photography course, get scuba diving license, improve sailing navigation skills, take a course on journalism, and research exotic destinations.

- Mission Statement: sail around the world with my spouse searching for unique undiscovered places to get rare pictures of aquamarine and coastal nature beauty for the creation of an illustrated journal or a corporate gift book, ad materials, and calendars.

Having:

- Buy new photographic equipment; buy a new, seaworthy sailboat but sell the second vehicle and the house; place my portfolio into globally diversified electronic traded dividend funds connected to my bank so he could get access to the cash anywhere in the world.

Reality Testing:

- In testing his plan, he found that his spouse did not want to sail around the world, and so he modified his plan to do numerous trips with his spouse to exotic destinations and bareboat sail charters.

LIFE PLANNING: Case 2 (retiring chief financial officer)

This individual was a former CFO of a pharmaceutical company. He was very people oriented and a talented coach of managers of financial matters. He was always sought after at budgeting times and helped other executives see where they fit into the financial puzzle. His passion was coaching others on financial matters.

Being:

- Values: financial soundness, small business entrepreneurship, family, community
- Life Purpose Statement: coach my son in his small business as well as assist the youth to be more business oriented and successful; provide eldercare for aging parents.

Doing:

- Further Learning: investigate the needs of the community youth, learn how to set up a local Junior Achievement Program, learn about elder-care programs.
- Mission Statement: assist son in his fledging retail start-up and help it grow with knowledge and contacts; assist local youth in setting up a few successful small businesses that provide college money for disadvantaged kids, provide his parents with an eldercare program support.

Having:

- Buy a larger house, a bungalow with a live-in apartment for his parents near a hospital, and other needed services.

Reality Testing:

- In testing his plan, he found that his parents did not really want to move at this time because they felt they could handle things, and so he revised his plan and set up elder-care in-house services for his parents several times a week, allowing his father to give up driving because of his failing eyesight.
- He found his son did not really want his coaching regarding the new start-up bicycle/ski equipment retail business, but the son said he could use the cash; so he promised a capital injection on the condition he could audit and manage the books and saw that the business had potential.
- He found that the local high school welcomed his initiative of setting up a Junior Achievement program.

LIFE PLANNING: Case 3 (retiring CEO of a large gas utility)

This individual rose up the ranks as a chemical engineer with wonderful people skills and outstanding communication skills. As a single mother, she left her post well before retirement age to spend more time with her children whom she felt had grown closer to the nanny than to herself given her constant travel, board meetings, and management responsibilities. Her kids had become the most important thing in her life along with her deep religious beliefs.

Being:

- Values: family, church, and helping those in the community in need.
- Purpose Statement: to serve my family, church, and bring my community together as a caring and compassionate leader.

Doing:

- Further Learning: study to become a church minister.
- Mission Statement: raise my children to be responsible, caring, and successful, be there with my children when they are home and in activities, get more involved with the kids' school and activities. Fulfill my dream of becoming like my father a church minister.

Having:

- Keep the large home near the children's school.
- Continue with the nanny.
- Sell my recent 7 series BMW company car and buy a more practical hybrid minivan; start to use public transportation to attend the university courses.

Reality Testing:

- In testing her ideas, she found an inconsistency between being there for the children and pursuing her bachelor of divinity degree at the university, given the commute and so she settled on becoming a lay minister with the longer-term goal of getting her BD after the children were also in university and their lifestyles would better fit hers.

Comments on Cases

It is important to see the similarities in why all of these cases reflect self-actualization. First, they are not based primarily on making more money (Having) nor on hobbies (Doing) but on the higher value of attaining artistic value (Case 1), intellectual or financial learning for others (Case 2) and spiritual value (Case 3). They all transcend the narcissism of pure hobbies but use the talents and passions of each former executive aiming to achieve greater community, family, and personal value for others.

These goals of self-actualization do not exclude making money, nor do they preclude the fun of hobbies. Rather, such actualizing people combine making money doing hobbies creatively with their values and purpose of adding value for others. Everyone is unique and so the trick is to find the sweet spot between one's talents, passion, and to determine how use your God-given talent to create value for others. By doing so, you will paradoxically create the highest possible value for yourself, that of reaching your full potential as a human being through self-actualization. In the end, you will want to know that you have made a difference, and that your life did have value. Using your talents and passions to make a value-added difference for others is all you can ask of yourself in life. This is the basis for becoming one's authentic self and for being rewarded and fulfilled with real happiness!

You are great!

Everyone is great but we will never attain it if we collectively copy each other to get by. This is safe but is the basis for mediocrity. Only by rising above the fear of being different can you discover the uniqueness of your talent as an individual. Greatness does not reside in the collectivity of groupthink or mental conformity but in the self-established security and desire to ignite your freedom to risk being yourself, the original. By taking your special strength and rising above the average as an individual in the dimension of your discovered talent, you can be great. Collective conformity of

Doug Treen

the corporate culture creates boring administrative mediocrity and the hubris of past success. The larger "excellent" companies through inward-looking complacency and hubris leaves them vulnerable to smaller more creative individuals and entrepreneurial upstarts to surpass them. Only individuals can find greatness by looking within to discover the potential, once they find their unique difference and special God-given talent and calling. Following the collective, leads you only to the dead end of the standardized job description and its personal emotional sacrifices of groupthink and professional and corporate conformism.

Becoming great and differentiating yourself by working harder and harder within the collective conformity of the job box fails your potential greatness because a workaholic works harder and not smarter. The workaholic fails to refresh the creative juices and ends up simply digging the hole faster and faster, deeper and deeper and then finds it harder to get out and to change direction when it is too late. Doing so denies the creativity needed to think outside the box and discover your unique special talent. The collective corporate rewards and praises are not your proof of authenticity and greatness because retirement simply takes them away. Your greatness and authenticity are more uniquely tied to your heart, mind, and inner self and are inseparable from you as an individual. Your greatness is not your collective practices and professional skills but the inner connection of your heart and mind through your passion and talent. Actualizing your greatness will come through discovering the purpose and life mission that propels your passion and uses your unique talent to make an active transformational difference to others. You must be willing to differentiate yourself from the collective but this comes at a price and could even cost you your job. Yet what one loses by rising above the collective rabble of conformity opens the door to new higher spiritual and creative rewards of your inner authentic self and your unique talent. Doing so can make your retirement emotionally richer and extend your life as you reduce the stress of conformity to actualize your personal power and passion through and your special talent.

The Rest Is Up to You (I Know You Will Be There!)

This is it! You have proven that you are talented as an executive, but what about you alone, standing tall as an individual free of the collective confines of your corporate being? If you don't fight for the chance to find your special talent, purpose, and authentic self, no one else will do this for you. This requires contemplation and action. Up until now, your needs can be or have been met through a large, collective effort of following an accepted corporate passage or career path. Now, to reach the top of the mountain through self-actualization, only you can do so by tapping into your freedom to be creative and personal meaning to act on your talents, which are unlike any other that exist. You must fight for the only chance you have to be yourself. Surprisingly, from a spiritual and emotional point of view, it is actually harder and more painful not to do so. Being robbed of the chance for reaching our potential is tragic. The unique journey and exploration toward self-actualization is the easier path once you come into touch with who you really are, your values, meaning, purpose, and special talents, to bring these elements into reality. If not before, retirement is the last opportunity to fulfill your sacred destiny, your last exciting odyssey to creating value for others with your special talents. Ultimately, this will be your sweetest satisfaction! How do you want to be remembered? What difference will your short life make to the millions of years of civilization? What will be your obituary? Who will stand up and speak it with tears in their eyes? You have the opportunity to be a hero or heroine to someone, to your community or your country or even to the world! Take the chance. What do you have to lose? Death is inevitable anyway, but your life can shine a light on others … and yourself!

> We shall not cease from exploration
> And the end of all our exploring
> Will be to arrive where we started
> And know the place for the first time.
> —T. S. Eliot

Bibliography

Books

Blanchard, Ken, and Michael O'Connor. *Managing by Values*. San Francisco: Barrett-Koehler, 1997.

Burton, Mary Lindley, and Richard A. Wedemeyer. *In Transition*. New York: HarperCollins, 1991.

Byrne, Rhonda. *The Secret*. New York: Atria Books, 2006.

Carlson, Richard. *What About The Big Stuff?* New York: Hyperion, 2002.

Collins, James, C., and Jerry I. Porras. *Built To Last*. New York: HarperCollins, 1994.

Cousins, Norman. *Anatomy of an Illness*. New York: Bantam Books, 1980.

De Angelis, Barbara. *Passion*. New York: Delacourte Press, 1998.

De Bono, Edward. *Simplicity*. London: Penguin Books, 1998.

De Vries, Marco J. *The Redemption of the Intangible in Medicine*. London: Psychosynthesis Monographs, 1981.

Dyer, Wayne. *Your Sacred Self: Making the Decision to Be Free*. New York: Harper Collins, 1991.

Flach, Frederic. *The Secret Strength of Angels*. New York: Hatherleigh Press, 1998.

Frankl, Viktor. *Psychotherapy and Existentialism*. New York: Simon & Schuster, 1967.

Freedman, Marc. *Prime Time: How Baby Boomers Will Revolutionize Retirement and Transform America*. New York: PublicAffairs Books, 1999.

Gray, John. *How to Get What You Want and Want What You Have.* New York: HarperCollins, 1999.

Hippocrates. "Hippocratic Writings." trans. Francis Adams. *The Great Books.* Chicago: University of Chicago, 1952.

Jung, Karl. *The Portable Jung*, ed. Joseph Campbell, trans. R. F. G. Hull. New York: Penguin, 1976.

Katzenstein, Larry. *Secrets of St. John's Wort.* New York: Penguin, 1998.

Kets de Vries, Manfred, and Danny Miller. *The Neurotic Organization.* San Francisco: Jossey-Bass, 1984.

Kubler-Ross, Elizabeth. *On Death and Dying.* New York: Scribner, 2003.

Laing, R. D. *The Divided Self.* London: Penguin Books, 1972.

Le Blanc, Donna. *The Passion.* Deerfield Beach, FL: Health Communications, 2006.

Maslow, Abraham, H., *Motivation and Personality.* New York: Harper & Row, 1954.

Mate, Gabor. *When the Body Says No: The Cost of Hidden Stress.* Toronto: Alfred A. Knopf, 2003.

McGraw, Phillip C. *Self-Matters: Creating Your Life from Inside Out.* New York: Simon & Schuster, 2001.

Nedd, Kenford. *Power over Stress.* Toronto: QP Press, 2004.

Nuland, Sherwin B. *The Art of Aging.* New York: Random House, 2007.

O'Neil, John R. *The Paradox of Success.* New York: Penguin Group, 1993.

Peck, M. Scott. *Further along the Road Less Traveled.* New York: Simon & Schuster, 1993.

Peck, M. Scott. *The Road Less Traveled.* New York: Simon & Schuster, 1978.

Peters, Tom, and Robert Waterman. *In Search of Excellence.* New York: Warner Books, 1982.

Sartre, Jean-Paul. *Being and Nothingness,* trans. Hazel E. Barnes. New York: Washington Square Press, 1968.

Schaef, Anne Wilson. *When Society Becomes an Addict.* San Francisco: Harper & Row, 1987.

Schaef, Anne Wilson, and Diane Fassel. *The Addictive Organization.* San Francisco: Harper & Row, 1988.

Sears, Barry. *The Anti-Aging Zone.* New York: Harper Collins, 1999.

Sheehy, Gail. *Passages: Predictable Crises of Adult Life.* New York: E.P. Dutton, 1977.

Souza, Brian. *Become Who You Were Born to Be.* New York: Random House, 2005.

Whyte, Jr., William H. *The Organization Man.* New York: Simon & Schuster, 1956.

Articles

Barnett, Bronwyn. February 21, 2003. "Genetics may help solve mysteries of human evolution, anthropologist says." *Stanford Report.*

Berman, David. June 26, 2008. "Quiz: What's bigger, Harley or GM?" *Market Blog.*

Conference Board Report. February 2005 and February 2007. "Job Satisfaction Survey."

Cook, Derek. April 30, 1994. "Retirement may be death sentence for some." *The Mercury.*

DeMente, Boye Lafayette. May 2002. *Asian Business Codewords.* Asia Pacific Management Forum.

Doane, Charles, J. March 2008. "Beautiful Dreamers." *Sail.*

Dychtwald, Ken. February 24, 2006. "The Changing Face of Retirement." *The Motley Fool.*

Fox, Maggie. March 3, 2008. "Money buys happiness—if you spend it on someone else." Reuters.

Fry, Patricia. 2000. "Retirement, Baby Boomer Style." Matilija Press.

Greenwald, John. December 7, 1998. "Thomas Watson, Jr." *Time.*

Herzberg, Frederick I. 1968. "One More Time, How Do You Motivate Employees?" *Harvard Business Review.*

Kerstetter, Jim. September 12, 2005. *C/Net News.com.*

Kehn, Diane, J. 1995. "Predictors of Elderly Happiness." *Gerontology,* Rutgers University.

Kinch, John. January 1963. "Experiments in Factors Related to Self-Concept Change." *American Journal of Social Psychology,* vol. 68.

Leonetti, Micheal E. 2000. "Lifestyle changes: Myths & misconceptions about life in retirement." American Association of Individual Investors (AAII).

Lin, S. March 2002. "Optimum strategies for creativity and longevity." National Council of Chinese Institute of Engineers, New York Chapter.

Merrill Lynch. February 22, 2005. "The New Retirement Survey." *Harris Interactive.*

Nelson, L. Debra, and James Quick, 1985. "Professional women: Are distress & disease inevitable?" *Academic of Management Review,* University of Texas at Arlington.

"Retire 'Retirement' Say 87% of Canadians 45 and over." December 7, 2005. BMO Financial Group, Ipsos Reid.

Royal Bank of Canada. September 13, 2007. "Money or Health?" Financial Retirement and Affluent Client Strategy Group, www.rbc.com/your future.

Tom's of Maine. www.tomsofmaine.com.

Van Biema, David. August 23, 2007. "Mother Teresa's Crisis of Faith." *Time.*

Wikipedia. August 2008. "Nathan's Hot Dog Eating Contest." http://en.wikipedia.org/wiki/Nathan's_Hot_Dog_Eating_ Contest.

About the Author

Doug Treen, PhD, M.B.A, has been an executive in pharmaceutical and financial corporations for twenty years, a management consultant, and a M.B.A. lecturer of organizational behavior. He studied psychology, social science and philosophy for his PhD. He has published numerous business articles on organizational effectiveness. He lives with his family near Toronto.

Printed in the United States
140918LV00002B/4/P